HANDBOOK OF INTERNATIONAL PSYCHOLOGY ETHICS

The *Handbook of International Psychology Ethics* discusses the most central, guiding principles of practice for mental health professionals around the world. For researchers, practicing mental health professionals, and students alike, the book provides a window into the values and belief systems of cultures worldwide. Chapters cover ethics codes from psychological associations and societies on five continents, translating each code into English and discussing vital questions around how the code is put into practice, what it means to association members and society at large, as well as how the code was developed within its unique historical, political, and cultural context.

Karen L. Parsonson, PhD, is the director of the graduate forensic psychology program and assistant professor of psychology at the University of Houston Victoria. Her research encompasses ethics, forensics, and cross-cultural studies. Formerly a practicing clinical and forensic psychologist for over 25 years, she was also an expert witness for many years. As a clinical hypnotherapist, she was president of the Canadian Federation of Clinical Hypnosis-Alberta Division, teaching clinical hypnosis to healthcare professionals for many years. She has published numerous self-help books, novels, and scholarly articles.

HANDBOOK OF INTERNATIONAL PSYCHOLOGY ETHICS

Codes and Commentary from Around the World

Edited by Karen L. Parsonson

Routledge
Taylor & Francis Group

NEW YORK AND LONDON

First published 2021
by Routledge
52 Vanderbilt Avenue, New York, NY 10017

and by Routledge
2 Park Square, Milton Park, Abingdon, Oxon OX14 4RN

Routledge is an imprint of the Taylor & Francis Group, an informa business

Library of Congress Cataloging-in-Publication Data
A catalog record for this title has been requested

ISBN: 978-0-367-37446-4 (hbk)
ISBN: 978-1-032-01515-6 (pbk)
ISBN: 978-0-367-81425-0 (ebk)

Typeset in Bembo
by Taylor & Francis Books

This book is dedicated to my loving husband Adison, who has believed in me from the beginning and our adorable fur-baby Lola, whose unconditional love sustains us both.

CONTENTS

FIGURES

PREFACE

This has been an immense undertaking, as it began with emails to 101 Psychology organizations around the world. In the process, some were unable to contribute due to time constraints or inability to access the information. However, what is presented is a tribute to international collaboration and collegiality. Every continent on the globe has been represented in this compendium of international Psychology ethics codes, as written by those who contributed to their development. The kindness of my contributors has been immense and for that, I have heartfelt appreciation. Their dedication is exemplified by the English translation from their original language. Additionally, they provided their chapters in their own native language so that their compatriots can read what they have presented. In the process, I have met some wonderful colleagues and friends, who have taken their valuable time to share with the world their insights and the labor of love they put into developing their ethics codes. Perhaps, this initial representative overview of ethics codes across the globe will prompt other countries to be willing to contribute the same work for their countries, as well. What follows is the first of its kind, in the words of those who have dedicated themselves to ensuring ethical practice in each of their own countries.

LIST OF PSYCHOLOGICAL ASSOCIATIONS AND LINKS TO THEM

Australia: Australian Psychological Society (www.psychology.org.au/)
Chile: College of Psychologists of Chile (http://colegiopsicologos.cl/)
Colombia: Colombian College of Psychologists (COLPSIC) (www.colpsic.org.co)
EFPA: European Federation of Psychologists' Associations (www.efpa.eu/)
Guatemala: College of Psychologists of Guatemala (www.colegiodepsicologos. org.gt/)
Hungary: Hungarian Psychological Association (www.mpt.hu)
Indonesia: Indonesian Psychological Association (HIMPSI): https://himpsi.or.id/)
IUPsyS: International Union of Psychological Science (www.iupsys.net/)
New Zealand: New Zealand Psychological Society (www.psychology.org.nz/)
Nigeria: Nigerian Psychological Association (www.npa.com.ng)
Singapore: Singapore Psychological Society (https://singaporepsychologicalsoci ety.org/)
Slovenia: Slovenian Psychologists' Association (www.dps.si/o-drustvu/)
UK: British Psychological Society (www.bps.org.uk/)
Venezuela: Federation of Psychologists of Venezuela (www.fpv.org.ve/)
Zambia: Psychology Association of Zambia (https://paz.co.zm/)

CONTRIBUTORS

Gboyega Emmanuel Abikoye is a Clinical Psychologist and Associate Professor at the University of Uyo, Nigeria, where he was the immediate past Head of Department of Psychology and Vice Dean of the Faculty of Social Sciences. With research interests in addictive behavior, health-related quality of life, psychopathology and psychological underpinning of social issues, Dr. Abikoye has more than 90 scientific publications to his credit. He is a member of the Board of Trustees and the General Secretary of the Nigerian Society of Substance Use Prevention and Treatment Professionals (ISSUP Nigeria Chapter). He is a member (Fellow) of both the Nigerian Psychological Association (NPA) and Nigerian Association of Clinical Psychologists (NACP). He is the Editor-in-Chief of Nigerian Journal of Clinical Psychology and Regional Editor (West Africa) of African Journal of Drug and Alcohol Studies.

Maria G. Adiyanti is a practicing Developmental and Child Clinical Psychologist, and teaches at Universitas Gadjah Mada. She holds the position of Chair III of HIMPSI (Indonesian Psychological Association) in charge of coordinating the development of the psychological profession and the code of ethics.

Alfred Allan practiced as a lawyer before he became a full-time academic and commenced his studies in psychology, qualifying as a clinical and later forensic psychologist. He has taught law, psychology and professional ethics in Law, Medical and Psychology Schools in South Africa and Australia. He was a member of the inaugural Psychologists Board of Australia and is the chair of the Standing Committee on Ethics of the International Association for Applied Psychology (IAAP) and a Fellow of the Australian Psychological Society (APS). He has served on the boards of national professional organisations and is a past president of the Psychology and Law Division of the IAAP, Australian and New Zealand Association of Psychiatry, Psychology and Law and a past chair of the APS College of Forensic Psychologists, the Ethics Committee of the APS, the Ethics Committee of the Psychology Association of South Africa; and of the

Working Group that reviewed the APS' Code of Ethics. He is an associate editor of Psychiatry, Psychology and Law and a member of the editorial boards of Philosophy, Ethics, and Humanities in Medicine and Ethics and Behavior and has served on various state government committees, such as the Dangerous Sexual Offender Review Committee. He frequently presents continuing professional development workshops and publishes widely in psychology, legal and medical journals.

Rubén Ardila is a Colombian Psychologist. He received a Bachelor's Degree in Psychology from the National University of Colombia and later a Doctorate in Experimental Psychology from Nebraska University, Lincoln, United States. His main fields of work and research have been experimental psychology, history of psychology and social issues. In 2003 Ardila received the degree of "Doctor honoris causa", granted by the University Ricardo Palma (Peru). Ruben Ardila was granted the National Science Award- Life and Work in 2004. This is the main Award granted in Colombia to a scientist for a lifetime devoted to science. In 2007, Ardila received the APA Award for Distinguished Contributions to the International Advancement of Psychology. In 2014, Ardila received the degree of "Doctor honoris causa", granted by the University Inca Garcilaso de la Vega (Peru). In 2016, he received the degree of "Doctor honoris causa", granted by the National University of Rosario (Argentina). He has published 34 books in total, several of them translated into other languages. With more than 300 scientific papers and book chapters, the topics of these are experimental psychology, behavior analysis, professional issues, social problems, conceptual problems, history of psychology, psychology in Colombia and Latin América, international psychology and others. One of his most recent research publications is on the social perception of science and the psychology of scientists: Science and the Scientists: A Psychological Perspective.

Juan Carlos Canga is an Organizational Development Specialist from the Andres Bello Catholic University (UCAB). Degree in Psychology from the Central University of Venezuela (UCV). Full professor in the Department of Industrial Psychology of the UCV, Professor at the UCAB School of Psychology. President of the Federation of Psychologists of Venezuela (FPV). Coordinator for Venezuela of the Project of Reasoning and Ethical Judgment of Professional of Psychology in Iberoamerica. Organizational Consultant in the area of Change Management and human resources processes. Facilitator of workshops on the Impact of New Technologies in psychology and especially in human resources processes. Extensive experience in data-based human resources management (BigData), process design in digital environments and development of self-service portals in human resources. Leader of different projects in Organizational Climate, Job Satisfaction, Recruitment and Selection of Personnel, Career Development, both in the public and private sectors. Moderator of the Virtual Community of Venezuelan Psychologists (Psique-I), with more than 3,000 members. He has organized and participated in training events and congresses, nationally and internationally, and has been a tutor for undergraduate and graduate work. Participations and presentation of research works in various Congresses of Psychology in: Colombia, Brazil, Chile, Guatemala, Mexico and Argentina.

Sergio Lucero Conus is a Clinical Psychologist and Accredited Clinical Supervisor, Family and Couples Therapist, Psychodramatist and Dramatherapist. President of the College of Psychologists of Chile AG. 1993–1995. President of the Professional Ethics Commission of the College of Psychologists from 1996 to 2008 and from 2011 to 2018. Psychologist of the Committee for Peace in Chile and the Health Team of the Vicaría de la Solidaridad (1974–1992), ecumenical institutions and respectively of the Catholic Church, supporting victims and their families during the Pinochet dictatorship. Teaching at different universities in the country in Criminology, Social Pathology, Professional Ethics, Family and Society. Currently teaching at the School of Psychodrama and Dramatherapy of Santiago (Edras Chile). He was a political prisoner of the dictatorship (October 1973 to February 1974) in the Chacabuco concentration camp, where he exercised therapeutic group work with fellow inmates and created the basis for the methodological model "Psychodrama Without Words". He is a speaker and workshop leader in Ibero-American and European psychodrama congresses. He is co-editor and author of chapters "Dramaterapia y Psicodrama. An encounter between Theater and Therapy" (University of Chile, 2013) and "TeatroSalud. Medicine- Theater-Therapy" (Universidad de Chile, 2018). He is a member of the College of Psychologists of Chile, the Chilean Society of Clinical Psychology, and the Spanish Association of Psychodrama.

Michael Onyeka Ezenwa is Professor of Clinical Psychology, Department of Psychology, Nnamdi Azikiwe University. He has chaired many Senate Committees for his university, was twice-elected onto the Management Committee of the School of Postgraduate Studies, and currently serves as Associate Dean. A Fellow of Nigerian Psychological Association and Nigerian Association of Clinical Psychologists, he has held numerous posts in these organizations. He is founding National President of Gestalt Education Network International Alumni Association, Nigeria Chapter, member National Executive Council of ISSUP Nigeria and Head, South East Zone of ISSUP Nigeria, national vice-chairman of International Consortium of Universities on Drug Demand Reduction, Nigeria chapter as well as UNIZIK Research Ethics Committee. In 2017, Professor Ezenwa became the 10th substantive President of the Nigerian Psychological Association, which continues to today. Professor Ezenwa completed training in Gestalt Therapy from The Gestalt Education Network International in Frankfurt, also one of few Nigerians who received formal training in Eric Berns' Transactional Analysis in Johannesburg. More recently, his work has focused on areas of hypertension, trauma and bereavement management, drug demand reduction, stress and PTSD. He has diverse work experience from many organisations in multiple capacities. These include global, international, continent-wide and national organizations, as well as Presidential Committees. He has published widely nationally and internationally, many articles in Scopus-indexed journals, with some works widely cited. He edited a foundational book on Gestalt Therapy in Nigeria, entitled Opening up Gestalt Therapy in Africa. In addition, he is a founding member of Employee Assistance Professionals Association Nigeria.

1

John Fitzgerald leads the team at WorkSafe focused on Mentally Healthy Work. He is a NZ Registered Psychologist within the Clinical Scope of Practice, who has worked in adult mental health; alcohol/drug services; and child & family psychological health. He has particular research interests in suicide prevention and non-suicidal self-injury, and professional ethics and practice. Prior to joining WorkSafe, John was a Senior Lecturer in Clinical Psychology at Massey University (Wellington). He is a Fellow and Immediate Past-President of the New Zealand Psychological Society, a member of the Society's Institute of Clinical Psychology and of the NZ College of Clinical Psychologists, and a member of the Psychology Panel of the Health Practitioners Disciplinary Tribunal.

Judit Szimethné Galaczi graduated as a psychologist from Kossuth Lajos University in Debrecen in 1984, and then as a pedagogical psychologist at Eötvös Lóránd University in Budapest, Hungary. She has been working as a psychologist for almost 40 years, first in the field of work psychology, then as an educational counselor, later as a school psychologist, and in the last decade as a kindergarten psychologist. She is a member of the board of the Hungarian Association Protection of Psychologists' Interests and a member of the board of the Kindergarten and School Psychology Section of the Hungarian Psychological Association. As chairman of the Ethics Committee jointly run by these two organizations, she has been organizing and directing its work for three years.

Claire Jackson has been the Archivist and Manager of the British Psychological Society History of Psychology Centre since 2017. Her background is in the history of science and with a particular interest in the development of specialist professions, she has previously worked with collections at the Wellcome Library, Science Museum, Natural History Museum, Royal College of Surgeons of England, Royal Society of Medicine and the Royal College of General Practitioners amongst others.

Zoltán Jakab has his MA in psychology from Eötvös Loránd Univeristy, Budapest, 1990, and his PhD in cognitive science from Carleton Univerity, Ottawa, 2001 (supervisor: Andrew Brook). Between 2001–2003 he was a postdoctoral fellow at the Department of Philosophy, Rutgers University. Currently he is an associate professor at the Faculty of Special Needs Education, Eötvös Loránd University, Budapest. His areas of research are philosophy of mind, and cognitive development. He is a member of the Ethics Committee of the Hungarian Psychological Association representing special needs education.

Lohsnah Jeevanandam is a Clinical Psychologist who trained at the University of Queensland, Australia. Lohsnah is currently a Senior Lecturer at the National University of Singapore, where she is also the Director of the Clinical Psychology Programme. She is a Senior Consultant Clinical Psychologist with the Cognitive Health Consultancy International clinic, as well as, an expert trainer for a range of topics for mainstream and special needs educators. Lohsnah has a strong interest in Ethics and has taught on this topic at James Cook University

(Singapore), Singapore Social Sciences University, and currently, at the National University of Singapore. Lohsnah was the Chairperson of the second revision of the Singapore Psychological Society'Code of Ethics and led a working team of Psychologists from both the private and public sectors. When not working, Lohsnah enjoys movie nights with her two lovely daughters, exercising, and catching up with friends.

Jacqueline P. Jere-Folotiya is an Educational and Developmental Psychologist. She is a Trauma Focused Cognitive Behavioural Therapy (TF-CBT) and Common Elements Treatment Approach (CETA) therapist for children and adolescents. Jacqueline works as a lecturer and researcher in the Department of Psychology at the University of Zambia. She is the Coordinator for the Centre for the Promotion of Literacy is Sub-Saharan Africa (CAPOLSA) located in the Department of Psychology at the University of Zambia. She conducted research in education and early childhood development with various organisations. Jacqueline is the President of the Psychology Association of Zambia. She serves as an Executive member of the International Society for the Study of Behavioural Development (ISSBD). Jacqueline has published research in various local and international journals. Her research interests include early childhood development, specially Early Childhood Education (ECE), early grade literacy acquisition, teacher training and assessments in early childhood.

Ana María Jurado graduated as a Psychologist from the Rafael Landívar University with a Masters in Clinical and Medical Psychology from the Francisco Marroquín University, both in Guatemala City. For more than 40 years she has worked as a clinical psychologist. At the same time she has developed extensive work as a university teacher, as well as in the union field. She was the founder and first president of the Guatemalan Psychology Association. She was part of the founding of the College of Psychologists of Guatemala and president of the first Court of Honor of the college and drew up the first Code of Ethics in the country.

Richard Kwiatkowski is a full Professor of Organizational Psychology at Cranfield, the UK's only wholly postgraduate University. He is a Chartered (BPS) and Registered (HCPC) Occupational Psychologist and Counselling Psychologist, former Chair of the British Psychological Society's Division of Occupational Psychology, BPS Council, and Board of Directors. He is a Member of the Division of Occupational Psychology, Founder Member of the Division of Counselling Psychology, Founder member of Special Group in Coaching Psychology. His PhD was on the contribution of ethics to applied psychology, and he has served on numerous academic and professional ethics committees and boards for over 25 years; as Former Chair of the British Psychological Society's Ethics Committee, is proud to have been involved in helping to draw up the modern code. His research centres around the application of psychology to individuals and organisations including change, stress, and latterly on applying psychology to politics (a longitudinal study running for over 20 years). He has published and presented over a hundred papers and contributed to several books. He is a Chartered Scientist and Senior Fellow of the Higher Education Academy. In 2011 the prestigious award of Academician of the Academy of Social Sciences (now Fellowship) was conferred for significant contribution to Social Science in the UK. He has been quoted extensively in the Media. He acts as a consultant to many companies, partnerships and consultancies across the world. He is married to a psychologist and has three children, and two cats, and is active in his local community.

Geoff Lindsay has extensive experience as a practitioner educational psychologist (EP) and as a researcher. His Psychology degree was from the University of Durham (1969) and he qualified as an EP at the University of Birmingham (MEd (Ed. Psych), 1973) where he also undertook his PhD part time while working as an EP (1979). Geoff was an EP for Sheffield LA for (1972–95), including 13 years part-time tutor to the University of Sheffield educational psychology professional training programme (1978–91); and as Principal Educational Psychologist and head of the service (1991–95). Geoff was appointed as inaugural Professor of Educational Psychology and Special Educational Needs at the University of Warwick in 1995, where he has also been Director of CEDAR (Centre for Educational Development, Appraisal and Research) since 1999. Geoff's main research areas are special educational needs, particularly speech, language and communication needs, parenting support, early intervention, the evaluation of government educational initiatives, and professional ethics, primarily of psychologists. He has undertaken more than 100 research projects and programmes, over 80 as director, and has published over 170 peer reviewed papers as well as a large number of research reports, chapters and books, including as lead author of Ethics for European Psychologists and co-editor of The Oxford Handbook of International Psychological Ethics. Geoff is a past President of the British Psychological Society (BPS) and a Fellow and Honorary Life Member of the BPS, a Fellow of the Academy of Social Sciences, and Fellow of the Royal Society of Arts.

J. Anitha Menon is Professor of Health Psychology in the Department of Psychology, University of Zambia and Chairperson for University of Zambia Committee on HIV/AIDS. She is also Founding President of the Psychology Association of Zambia. Prof. Menon holds PhD in Psychiatry/Health Psychology from University of Nottingham, UK. For more than 24 years, she has been involved in research and service-related projects of public interest, with major research interest on the issue of HIV and overall well-being of adolescents, Neuropsychological Challenges of HIV, Sexual Harassment and Communication Skills of Health Practitioners. She has numerous other research interests, as well. Prof. Menon spearheaded the formulation of University of Zambia HIV and AIDS policy and as Chairperson of University of Zambia HIV and AIDS response, coordinates all HIV related service and research at the University through the HIV and AIDS Response Programme. She teaches and supervises undergraduate, Masters and PhD student research while being involved in various national and international research projects, including team leader for several including DFID funded Development for Higher Education (DelPHE) partnership and NORAD funded Norad Master's program (NOMA). Through NOMA, she has successfully introduced a multidisciplinary Master's program in Clinical Neuropsychology and research on neuropsychological effects of HIV in Zambia. She is on the editorial team for numerous journals, serves as reviewer for various national and international scientific journals, and has more than 100 peer-reviewed publications to her credit. She has won numerous national and global/international awards for her teaching, leadership, innovation, and professional achievement.

Dabie Nabuzoka is Associate Professor of Psychology at the University of Zambia (UNZA), and currently chairperson of the Ethics Committee of the Psychology Association of Zambia. He has taught on ethical issues in psychological research and practice at both undergraduate and postgraduate levels at UNZA and previously as Principal Lecturer in Psychology at Leeds Metropolitan University (UK) and Senior Lecturer at Sheffield Hallam University (UK). He has also been a member and Chartered Psychologist of the British Psychological Society (BPS). Professor Nabuzoka is a developmental psychologist with particular interest in research on developmental disabilities and psychopathology, and the development of assessment tools for screening and informing efforts at amelioration of developmental difficulties in children, especially in the Zambian context. Work in these areas both in the UK and Zambia has highlighted the importance of adherence to ethical considerations in psychology research and practice. Professor Nabuzoka is author of Children with learning disabilities: Social functioning and adjustment (2000, BPS Blackwell) and editor (with Janet Empson) of Culture and psychological development (2010, Palgrave MacMillan) and Atypical child development in context (2004, Palgrave MacMillan).

Ibolya Oláh graduated as a psychologist from Eötvös Loránd University, Budapest, with a Masters in Clinical and Developmental Psychology. She is trained professionally as a child- and adolescent clinical psychologist and as a psychotherapist. For more than 20 years she has worked as a psychologist in a hospital and an educational councelling center. At the same time she worked as a practical course tutor in Károli Gáspár University. She is an active member and instructor of Hungarian Assosiation of Individual Psychology. She is the founder and instructor of World Test Training at Polcz Allaine Foundation. She is a member of the Ethics committee of Hungarian Psychological Association.

Vita Postuvan is an Associate Professor of Psychology and the Deputy Head of the Slovene Centre for Suicide Research (UP IAM). Her main professional focus is framed around the research, prevention and postvention of suicidal behaviour, from the perspective of public-health interventions as well as the support to the individuals in need. Vita is an active member of several international and national associations in the fields of suicidology, psychology and ethics, such as the Board of Ethics of Slovene Psychologists' Association and Board of Ethics of EFPA. Besides her activities in home country Slovenia she has worked professionally in Austria, Japan, China, and India.

Yusti Probowati is a professor in forensic psychology at the University of Surabaya, Chair II of HIMPSI (Indonesian Psychological Association) in charge of developing HIMPSI members' competence, also member of the Psychology Practice Bill drafting team.

Paulo Daniel Acero Rodríguez is a Psychologist at the National University of Colombia, Specialist in Conflict Resolution from the Pontificia Universidad Javeriana, Master of Integration of People with Disabilities from the Pontificia Universidad de Salamanca, Certified Thanatologist from the Higher Institute of Pastoral Theology of Puerto Rico, training in Trauma and Hebrew resilience at the University of Jerusalem and doctoral student at the National University of Cordoba in Argentina. He has been a teacher at the Universities Manuela Beltran, San Buenaventura, El Bosque and Javeriana and visiting professor at the University of Manizales. He has authored and co-authored 11 books on grief, trauma and resilience and various articles on these same topics. For nine years he was a magistrate of the deontological and bioethical Courts of Psychology and president for two periods of the National deontological and bioethical Courts of Psychology. He is currently Executive Director of the deontological and bioethical Courts of Psychology.

Adrian Toh is the current Chairperson of the Singapore Register of Psychologists (SRP), who oversees the registration, professional development and ethical practice of psychologists. He was involved in the recent revision of the code of ethics for the Singapore Psychological Society (SPS) and contributed to the research-driven Ethical Decision-Making Model to guide psychologists to arrive at a decision that is "more right". This research was also presented at the ASEAN Regional Union of Psychological Societies (ARUPS) Congress in 2018. Adrian is a Registered Clinical Psychologist who had worked in the public hospital for the last decade and currently provides therapy for adolescents and adults in a private clinic setting.

Éva Kovácsné Vajger graduated as a psychologist at Eötvös Loránd University, Budapest. She works as a work and organizational psychologist (graduated at Budapest University of Technology and Economics, where she is a practical course tutor now). She is a member of the joint Ethics Committee of Hungarian Psychological Association and Hungarian Association Protection of Psychologists' Interests, representing the Defense and Law Enforcement Division and the Work and organizational Psychology Section of Hungarian Psychological Association.

Andrew E. Zamani is Professor of Clinical Psychology, former Dean of Faculty of Social Sciences, and current Director of Institute of Governance & Development Studies, Nasarawa State University, Keffi. He holds a Doctorate from the University of Jos, Nigeria, and has varied work experiences – schoolteacher and school counselor; Behavioral Science Lecturer; Honorary Consultant Psychologist with Jos University Teaching Hospital. He taught at Department of Psychiatry, University of Jos, then transferred to University of Abuja Teaching Hospital, Gwagwalada, founding the first mental health service program in Abuja. There, he was Head of Clinical

Psychological Services, Coordinated the Hospital's HIV/AIDS Services, serving as member of both Medical Advisory and Medical Research Ethics Committees. He has served as consultant to many national and international organizations. In 2009, he was appointed to multiple ECOWAS technical working groups. He is an Israeli government's MASHAV Scholar, specializing in Psychosocial Care of AIDS Orphans, a Forgarty Scholar, and Behavioral Science Mentor for Social Scientists Delivering Care in Nigerian Health Settings. He convened the Association of Practicing Psychologists of Nigeria in 2015 as a voice for Psychology in Nigerian public service. He is Editor-in-Chief and/or serves on Editorial Boards of numerous Nigerian and continent-wide journals. Prof. Zamani has provided much community service to multiple social development organizations. He is co-Founder and Board of Directors member of WaterBirds International – an Israeli-based Trauma Intervention Training Organization – was Immediate past-President of Nigerian Psychological Association and Executive Council Member of Pan-African Psychology Union. He has many and varied research interests.

1

UNDERSTANDING PSYCHOLOGY'S ETHICS CODES FROM AN INTERNATIONAL PERSPECTIVE

The Importance of Non-Ethnocentric Appreciation and Comparisons

Karen L. Parsonson

Introduction

To begin with, I am indebted to the many Psychology professionals around the world who have contributed to this work. Their belief in my vision, to present their ethics codes in their own words, is the essence of not only collegiality, but idiographic study. What they have provided is the ultimate in every cross-cultural psychologist's dream: their knowledge and experience, in their own words.

In keeping with the theme of this book, we will begin by explaining the purpose and importance of ethics codes for the practice of psychology. For those of us who have or are practicing, it is a moot point, but bears explication. It is the basis of ethical practice, which is a cornerstone of the profession. This is followed by a brief history of Psychology ethics codes across the world in order to provide a frame of reference. Next, we will explore how Psychology ethics codes are culturally based, an assertion that has become well-accepted among researchers and theorists, alike. Further to this, we will examine earlier research comparing and contrasting international Psychology ethics codes, followed by non-ethnocentric research that compares the codes taking an idiographic approach with no value judgments. Finally, we will present the intent and accomplishments of this book, presenting a representative sample of ethics codes from each continent around the world as described by those who developed them. The participation of these individuals and the work it has entailed is indescribable. They have contributed immensely to the knowledge and understanding of international ethics codes far beyond what has been available ever before.

Further to the aim of non-ethnocentric comparison, this book represents the first attempt to not only address the cultural contribution to the development and writing of ethics codes, but it is explained by the actual professionals who have contributed to the development and writing of their country's ethics codes or their subsequent revisions. Each country's representative not only addresses the contribution of culture to their ethics code, but also explains the history and development of their respective code, as well as what it means to them as mental health professionals and their fellow citizens.

All continents are represented, along with access/links to their ethics codes that are both translated into English (if necessary) by themselves (not simply individuals who happen to know their language), as well as presented in their native language if it is not English. What follows is the developers' stories of their own countries' ethics codes (or revisions), in their own words. The book will also discuss the EFPA's Meta-Code, the template for all European countries' ethics codes, as well as the Universal Declaration of Ethical Principles for Psychologists and culminates in a qualitative, non-ethnocentric discussion and comparison of the ethics codes as presented.

Of particular note, a number of countries have anecdotally reported that this process has helped them immensely in understanding their own history of their psychological societies, the original development of their codes, as well as re-connected them to important individuals in their countries' history of the practice of Psychology. That, in and of itself, is noteworthy, as it ensures the recognition and contribution of generations past and the continuity of consistent professional growth.

The Purpose and Importance of Ethics Codes to the Ethical Practice of Psychology

The first recognizable ethics code is the Hippocratic Oath (between the 5th and 3rd centuries BCE). It applies to medical ethics but is still in use in various forms for physicians today. Ethics codes are prevalent in just about every profession in existence today. They are of paramount importance to ethical practice within the field of Psychology. Their aim is to protect clients, research subjects, clinical practitioners, and the public in general.

Without getting too much into the history and theory of ethics (which dates back thousands of years and is an area of study unto itself independent of psychology), one question begs answering. Should following ethics codes be simply what one "ought to do", or should it be what a "virtuous person" does? This takes us back to Aristotelian ethics (which is far outside the purview of this book), but should it be something professionals want to do or have to do? This is an important point to consider, not only in the teaching of ethics to Psychology graduate students but in how ethics codes are both framed and applied in practice.

To put it simply, deontological ethics focuses on whether the action is right or wrong, based on a set of rules or moral obligation. Conversely, virtues-based ethics focus on the consequences of actions, with a virtuous person choosing to do what is right, not what they "ought to do". Anderson and Handelsman (2010, 2013) elegantly transpose this issue into the discussion of virtue ethics as applied to the mental health professions. They define ethical virtues as encompassing the "their own personal and professional qualities or traits that guide their choices" (p. 5), which are a part of professional identity. Further, they suggested that these "internal aspects" are a part of the decisions clinicians make every day. Even more specifically, to Kitchener and Anderson (2011) virtue ethics (or "moral character") "is more important than conformity to rules because a virtuous person is more likely to understand the principles and rules on which he or she acts" (p. 58).

Returning more specifically to ethics codes in Psychology, Pettifor (2004) clarified that the objective of Psychology ethics codes was to focus on promoting ideal professional behavior using aspirational principles that encourage reflection and ethical decision-making within a moral framework, and regulation of professional behavior practicing monitoring and disciplinary action against those who violate established standards of conduct. This definition includes both an aspirational (non-enforceable but guidance-based) component and standards of practice (enforceable and subject to disciplinary action).

Further, Oakland et al. (2012) clarified four specific purposes of Psychology ethics codes. These included:

1   to educate both professionals and the public about behaviors to expect from psychologists;
2   to promote the public trust;
3   to exemplify legislative, judicial, and administrative policy as it applies to actual practice; and
4   to provide for professionals who do not work in institutions with ethics codes the framework within which to advocate for higher standards.

Additionally, they explained that ethics codes express virtues of moral excellence, principles that are aspirational but advocate aspirational broad rules of conduct, as well as standards that specify behaviors that are enforceable by law.

In terms of social science/psychological research, Wassenaar and Mamotte (2012) traced back the ethical guidelines to protect the welfare of research subjects following the "research" that occurred after World War II with atrocities suffered at the hands of Nazi scientists. Following the Nuremberg Code of Ethics in Medical Research (1947), the authors noted the critical importance of informed consent, which was then followed by the Declaration of Helsinki by the World Medical Association (1964), requiring an ethics review process by research ethics committees. The Belmont Report followed in 1979, written be the National Commission for the Protection of Human Subjects of Biomedical and Behavioral Research. This report provided an ethical framework to help with resolving ethical dilemmas when it came to research with human subjects. The intent was to emphasize "the basic ethical principles that should underlie the conduct of biomedical and behavioral research involving human subjects and developing guidelines to assure that such research is conducted in accordance with those principles". Towards this end, three basic principles were presented. These included respect for persons, beneficence, and justice via consent (taking into consideration risk/benefit assessment and fair selection of subjects). In a follow-up to this, in 2010 the APA developed a Code of Ethical Conduct for researchers that emphasized:

1   that the ends of research do not justify the means; and
2   that research ethics committees were required to ensure subjects' dignity and welfare, to prevent harm, and to defend subjects' rights.

More recently, Rangi and Stoffel (2015) explained that like any discipline, Psychology shares a framework of its own ethical standards that are based specifically on the foundational values of human dignity, caring about people's well-being, integrity in relationships, and responsibility. The authors noted that these values matched exceptionally well with the four principles of the Universal Declaration of Ethical Principles for Psychologists (to be discussed in greater length later). From a process perspective, they suggested that values or beliefs shared by members of a culture would be expressed as principles. For example, the value of human dignity would be expressed as Respect for persons and their rights. More specifically with respect to Psychology, the authors proposed that ethical issues most highly relevant would be informed and free consent (since both clients and research subjects are vulnerable populations), privacy, the degree of harm (as in minimal risk, for either client or research subject), deception, and debriefing.

A Very Brief History of Psychology Ethics Codes

We clearly see that both the purpose and objectives of Psychology ethics codes are critically important to the ethical practice of Psychology, whether as a clinician or researcher. They provide a set of values and principles, as well as guidelines, rules, direction, courses of action to address ethical dilemmas, and explicit parameters that delineate what is ethical/acceptable behavior and what is not for professionals in the field of Psychology. Without them, judgment about conduct considered "professional" or acceptable is entrusted to the practitioner, which is highly subjective.

The American Psychological Association has frequently been credited with producing the first Psychology ethics code (1953), yet Australia had already published its first ethics code in 1949. Granted, the Australian Overseas Branch of the British Psychological Society (the regulatory body for Australian psychologists at the time) credits having used the Minnesota Society of Applied Psychology's ethics code from 1947 as a template, but such is the Western-centric focus of Psychology in general. Nevertheless, the APA's Committee on Ethical Standards for Psychologists was established in 1947. A provisional draft of ethical standards came out in 1953. The Canadian Psychological Association adopted the APA's ethical standards as set out in 1953 (later to publish its own code in 1986), but following publication of the APA's ethics code, France and Norway went on to develop their own ethics codes. The British Psychological Society presented its first ethics code in 1954. From the sample discussed in this book, Colombia developed its first ethics code in 1965, Hungary in 1975, and Chile in 1976.

In Europe, the European Federation of Psychological Associations (EFPA) developed the Meta-Code (1995), with a revision in 2005. Its purpose was to serve as a framework from which European countries could develop their own ethics codes. Four aspirational principles were agreed upon: Respect for Person's Rights and Dignity, Professional Competence, Responsibility, and Integrity.

Meanwhile in South America, six countries (Argentina, Brazil, Chile, Paraguay, Uruguay, and Venezuela), who are members of the economic and political bloc known as the Mercosur, developed an ethical protocol similar in intent to the Meta-Code in 1997. They agreed upon five ethical principles in their template: Respect for People's Rights and Dignity, Professional Competence, Professional & Scientific Commitment, Integrity, and Social Responsibility. This was developed out of the Psychologists' Committee of Mercosur and Associated Countries (1997). It is important also to note that two of these countries (Chile and Venezuela) are represented in this book.

In another example of an international effort to ensure the pre-eminence of ethics in the practice of Psychology, the Universal Declaration of Ethical Principles for Psychologists (UD) was adopted by the International Union of Psychological Science (IUPsyS) and the International Association of Applied Psychology (IAAP) in 2008. As Parsonson and Alquicira (2018) noted in their analysis of international Psychology ethics codes, IUPsyS (with a membership of 85 countries) and IAAP (with a membership of 60 countries) actively enjoined countries worldwide to provide consultation on the UD's development with focus groups on every continent.

A number of these ethics codes have frequently been cited as references/templates for the development of ethics codes for international Psychological Associations, as we shall see later on. These include the APA's, the Canadian Psychological Association's first ethics code in 1986, the European Federation of Psychological Association's Meta-Code of 1995 and the International Union of Psychological Science's Universal Declaration of Ethical Principles for Psychologists in 2008.

Psychology Ethics Codes are Culturally-based/Culture-centered

Increasingly, over time, it has been asserted that ethics codes (whether those in psychology or other professions) mirror the beliefs and values of a country, its culture and society. For instance, Stevens (2012) asserted that ethics in psychology relate to social changes in the larger society. More specifically, he described psychology as being constructed by the social fabric of a society, with economic and political events and forces helping to shape countries' ethics codes. Further, he argued that ethics codes not only mirror changing societal values over time, but also that the welfare of psychology as a profession relates to the economic and political welfare of a country.

More specifically, Leach and Gauthier (2011) argued that ethics codes are culture-centered as they reflect a society's values. Ethics codes they describe as based on shared human values across cultures but at the interface between cultures and values, based on shared human values across cultures. Similarly, Oakland et al. (2012) emphasized that ethics codes reflect a country's culture, with culture inclusive of its unique history, customs, and practices.

Taking it a step further, Pettifor and Ferrero (2012) asserted that "culturally-sensitive rules cannot be resolved by codified rules" (p. 28). More specifically, they noted the importance of ethics codes not promoting any discriminatory practices that fit only with the values and beliefs of the majority culture, such that they demonstrate respect for all. In other words, even within a country, its multicultural nature can impact upon the applicability of its ethics code to individuals outside the majority culture for which it was written.

In a similar vein, applying ethics codes to research, Hyder et al. (2004) asked researchers in developing countries whether the application of institutional review board regulations from the US were sensitive to local cultures. Over 80% of respondents indicated that they found them not only insensitive to local cultures but most likely either inadequate or misunderstood. This suggests that a potential bias may occur when applied to a research perspective.

As a relevant example of how cultural factors impact on the development of a country's ethics codes, Canada adopted its first Code of Ethics in 1986, in response to changes made in the APA's Code of Ethics. According to Sinclair (2020), the CPA had originally "adopted the 1959 ethics code of the APA for a three-year trial, followed by adoption (without restrictions) of the APA code's first two revisions (APA, 1963, 1977)" (p. 249). Sinclair noted that the CPA began to develop its own ethics code in the late 1970's in response to a number of issues. These included observations that the APA's code had been created within an American cultural, legal and social context, and other countries had already developed their own ethics codes. It was felt that there was a need for a national code of ethics, as the APA's had begun to reflect a more culturally distinct and legally specific tone as compared to Canada (Parsonson & Alquicira, 2019; Sinclair, 2020). By comparison to the APA's code, Canada's ethics code expressed itself as a social contract with society, less in legalistic/enforcement terms, focused more on ethical reasoning and decision-making, and organized its standards encompassing ethical principles. The resultant first Canadian Code of 1986 represented both a uniquely different fundamental perspective and intent.

Similarly, in developing the EFPA's Meta-Code, Lindsay (2011) noted that the Scandinavian countries had established a common code, and Southern European countries had developed a "Carta Etica", which was eventually appended to the resultant Meta-Code. One concern that was noted in developing the Meta-Code was that there are potential "problems in generalizability across different countries," as well as the concern of "borrowing" one from another country/continent (as in that of the APA). Further examination noted the variation within Europe, itself. Another initiative came about as a result of the development of the Meta-Code, which was *Ethics for European Psychologists* (Lindsay et al. 2008), which presented ethical dilemmas and how to address them. More recently, (Lindsay, in this volume) notes that from the very beginning of development of the Meta-Code, the culture, history, socioeconomic, and language differences were in evidence between national associations in their comparison and examination of European countries' ethics codes.

It is evident that cultural factors play a role in the development of countries' ethics codes and in the resultant codes, themselves. As such, it is important to understand where these factors fit into the overall picture as countries look to develop their own ethics codes. It would also be interesting to know the reasoning behind integrating these unique cultural factors into a country's ethics code, as well as their particular relevance to the practice of psychology.

Comparisons and Contrasts between International Ethics Codes in the Literature

In the interest of examining international Psychology ethics codes for comparison and contrast, Leach and Harbin (1997) examined the ethics codes of 24 countries, comparing them with the APA's (1992) Code of Ethics. More specifically, they found that ten of the standards were common in 75% of the codes, with issues on disclosure of information found in 100% of the codes and maintaining confidentiality occurring in 95% of them. With regard to the APA's Code of Ethics, on average the 19 countries covered 70.4% of the APA principles. With respect to standards, their finding was that on average 34.3% of the standards were represented in the sample. The authors went on to explain that both universal and culture-dependent principles and standards are in operation.

Again comparing international ethics codes to the APA's, Leach, Glosoff and Overmeir (2001) re-examined the data from the Leach and Harbin study. More specifically, they focused on inconsistencies but were able to find eight overall categories in which they fit. The authors concluded that despite there being more features in common than differences between codes, unique standards reflected countries' distinctive sociopolitical climates and histories.

In reviewing psychologists' perceptions of ethically troubling incidents in nine Western countries, Pettifor and Sawchuk (2006) used Pope and Vetter's (1992) methodology to access a representative sample of APA members to aid the APA in relevant revisions to its ethics code at the time. A similar strategy was used by the British Psychological Society, the Canadian Psychological Association and other European countries to help them develop better-targeted and more useful ethics codes, among other objectives. Nine separate studies were done, one for each country. One finding highly in common between countries was that confidentiality issues were common in most ethical dilemmas and dual relationships were the second most cited concern. However, the authors noted a number of relevant limitations, including that there were problems using the Pope and Vetter categories for analysis and there was no representation in the sample of non-Western or aboriginal cultures, so that the generalizability of the results is questionable.

Examining 35 countries' ethics codes with respect to test use and development, Leach and Oakland (2007) compared testing standards with those of the APA's (2002) Ethical Principles of Psychologists and Code of Conduct. The authors found that one third of the ethics codes examined did not address test use. However, in countries with ethics codes in place, all had at least one test standard consistent with the APA's. The guidelines most commonly found were the requirement to explain test results, to use tests properly, and to limit test use to only qualified individuals. Interestingly, they noted that a discussion of test construction and any restriction from use of obsolete tests was uncommon. Of similar interest, whereas the APA guidelines were not explicit with regard to reproduction of test protocols or restricted purchasing of tests, it was discussed in other codes.

Leach (2009) specifically examined the duty to protect in international ethics codes for 34 ethics codes from 38 countries. He found that 70% of the ethics codes examined referenced such concerns (as in confidentiality and disclosure), with all codes including general disclosure statements. While some countries addressed the issue more explicitly, others did so more implicitly. Additionally, he found that some countries had more principles than standards (guidelines that were enforceable). An important conclusion was that both ethical and legal decisions are culture-specific, and that ethics codes are culture-centered, reflecting cultural values. The author also noted that many of the ethics codes used the APA code and other Western codes as a model, adopting many of their ethical guidelines.

Examining ethical standards from a cross-cultural perspective, Weifel and Khamush (2012) compared 13 countries with respect to their specific standards, credentialing, and accountability. The authors found large differences not only between countries' psychologists per capita, but between countries on the same continent, as well. There were substantial differences between the requirements for credentialing/licensing, as well as whether governments legally recognized the profession. Whereas some countries had developed their own ethics codes, others had developed their own using the EFPA's Meta-Code, the Mercosur, or the Universal Declaration of Ethical Principles for Psychologists. Still others simply used that of the APA or CPA. The authors noted the remarkable variability in the practice of psychology, how it was regulated, licensed, and the educational levels required to practice in their sample.

With regard to international licensing standards, Kuo and Leach (2017) specifically defined ethics codes as expressing the professional expectations of a field. Three raters examined 47 ethics codes from 51 countries, finding 17 competency standards in more than five of the countries. In their sample, 80% of the ethics codes demonstrated agreement on three standards: providing services with competency, awareness of personal issues, and obtaining and maintaining competency. Six standards were unique to certain countries' ethics codes, while 10 to 55% of standards were similar between codes. As the authors noted, a limitation of this study was that the ethics codes were found online either in English or translated into English by bilingual speakers. More specifically, the authors explained: "Translations typically may lead to some language nuances being lost or changed, and is a limitation of the study" (p. 5). Another important caveat they noted was that even if standards appeared similar, there could be different interpretations, implementation, and enforcement of them.

It is important to note that many of the international ethics codes compared in the research have tended to reflect European/Western culture. Those cultures have a tendency to focus on individualism rather than collectivism, which neglects the cultural values of collectivistic societies. Another relevant observation is that many studies use the APA's code of ethics for comparison purposes. Interestingly, even in North America, there is a different focus between the ethics codes of the American Psychological Association and the Canadian Psychological Association. The former concentrates more on enforceable rules, while the focus of the latter is more on ethical principles and providing steps for ethical decision-making.

Non-ethnocentric Comparison of Ethics Codes

As noted, much of the research comparing international ethics codes up to this point has done so by comparison to the APA's ethics code. Further to Parsonson and Alquicira's (2019) assertion that this is ethnocentric, in using one ethics code as a "gold standard", this practice ignores the unique richness of each code and the contribution of each country's culture to its development. Not only is this to the detriment of recognizing the achievement of each country in developing its own code, it denigrates any that deviate from the "gold standard". Kuo and Leach's (2017) reminder bears repeating here, as they warned that even if standards appeared similar, there could be different interpretations, implementation, and enforcement of them (which further reinforces the argument for the importance of a non-ethnocentric perspective).

To be more specific, 'ethnocentrism,' as defined by Merriam-Webster (www.merriam-webster.com/dictionary/ethnocentrism) is "the attitude that one's own group, ethnicity, or nationality is superior to others." That is exactly what happens when ethics codes are measured by comparison to the "standard". If we accept the well-established premise that ethics codes are culture-centered, then it follows that any comparisons made must be non-ethnocentric. In other words, different countries' ethics codes deserve appreciation, respect, and acceptance at face value, with no value judgments. Any attempts to establish superiority of one over another ignores and disparages the contribution and importance of cultural/historical/political contexts to each country's ethics code.

In comparison to the above-mentioned research approach, others have followed a more idiographic path to exploring international ethics codes. In so doing, their focus is on describing the unique aspects and perspectives of individual countries with no value judgments. Examples of this include Cooper's (2012) description and discussion of ethics with respect to South African psychology, Consoli, Ardile, and Ferraro's (2012) description of ethics codes and psychology in Latin and South America, and the discussion presented by Koocher and Hadjistavropoulos (2012) comparing Canadian and American licensing and ethics codes.

Other examples of idiographic research include Chan et al.'s (2012) description and discussion of psychological ethics in Chinese societies, Aaronsen and Althaus's (2012) examination of similarities and differences between European countries' psychological ethics, and Garton and Allan's (2012) examination of psychological ethics in Oceania. Similarly, Ferrero (2012) explored psychology and psychological ethics in Argentina, while Seymour and Nairn (2012) did the same for Aotearoa/New Zealand, as did Velchkovsky and Yuriev (2012) for Russia, and Korkut (2012) for Turkey.

The assertion is that "ethics codes cannot be evaluated against a standard, nor should value judgments be made. That, in and of itself is unethical" (Parsonson & Alquicira, 2019, p. 95). The authors further noted that international ethics codes cannot be understood "without the interpretation and historical background unique to each country that would best be explained by professionals within that country" (p. 95). The point is that then, there are no value judgments (ethnocentrism) or misinterpretation. This book meets that mandate and fulfills that goal.

An International Effort

In alphabetical order of continents and countries within them, it is important for me to acknowledge the dedication of the illustrious authors who have provided their knowledge and experience in the development of their countries' ethics codes.

For African countries, Drs. Gboyega Abikoye, Michael Ezenwa, and Andrew Zamani provided their insights on the Nigerian Psychological Society's Code of Ethics. Drs. Dabie Nabuzoka, Jacqueline Jere-Folotiya, and Anitha Menon contributed the chapter on the code of ethics for the Psychological Association of Zambia.

With respect to Asian countries, Drs. Maria Adiyanti and Yusti Probowati provided the chapter on the Indonesian ethics code. Drs. Lohsnah Jeevanandam and Adrian Toh contributed the chapter on Singapore's ethics code.

The continent of Australasia is represented by Dr. Alfred Allan for Australia's ethics code and Dr. John Fitzgerald for New Zealand's ethics code.

Four countries from Central and South America have contributed to this book. The chapter on the code of ethics for Chile is presented by Dr. Sergio Lucero Conus. Drs. Paulo Acero Rodriguez and Ruben Ardila contributed the chapter on Colombia's ethics code. Dr. Ana Maria Jurado provided the chapter on Guatemala's code of ethics. Dr. Juan Carlos Canga did the same for Venezuela's Code of Ethics.

With regard to European countries, three are represented here. The chapter on the Hungarian Psychological Association's code of ethics is provided by Drs. Judit Galaczi, Eva Vajger, and Ibloya Olah (with English translation by Dr. Zoltan Jakab), while the Slovene Psychologists' Association's Code of Ethics is presented by Dr. Vita Postuvan. Drs. Richard Kwiatkowski and Claire Jackson have presented the chapter on the British Psychological Society's codes of ethics.

Dr. Geoff Lindsay, the original Convenor of the European Federation of Psychological Association's committee on the Meta-Code, provides information on its history and development.

All of these authors have either been involved in the development of their countries' original ethics codes or the revisions to previous versions, so they have intimate knowledge of the processes and development of them. These authors have worked incredibly hard to trace their codes' origins, many calling in other original ethics committee board members from previous generations and iterations of their codes. To put this into perspective, this was a time when the world was being ravaged by the COVID-19 virus. Nevertheless, the contributors' tireless dedication to this endeavor has been immense.

References

Aaronsen, A., & Althaus, K. (2012). Psychological ethics in Europe: Convergence and divergence. In M. M. Leach, M. J. Stevens, G. Lindsay, A. Ferrero, & Y. Korkut (Eds.), *Oxford library of psychology. The Oxford handbook of international psychological ethics* (p. 337–357). Oxford University Press.

American Psychological Association (1963). Ethical standards of psychologists. *American Psychologist*, 18, 56–60.

American Psychological Association (1992). Ethical principles of psychologists and code of conduct. *American Psychologist*, 47, 1597–1611.

American Psychological Association (2002). Ethical principles of psychologists and code of conduct. *American Psychologist*, 57, 1060–1073.

Anderson, S. K. & Handelsman, M. M. (2013). A positive and proactive approach to the ethics of the first interview. *Journal of Contemporary Psychotherapy*, 43, 3–11.

Anderson, S. K., & Handelsman, M. M. (2010). *Ethics for psychotherapists & counselors: A proactive approach*. Wiley & Sons.

Canadian Code of Ethics for Psychologists, 4th Edition (2017). Canadian Psychological Association: Author.

Chan, C. C., Leung, A. S., Lee, P. W., Wang, L., & Zhang, K. (2012). Psychological ethics in Chinese countries. In M. M. Leach, M. J. Stevens, G. Lindsay, A. Ferrero, & Y. Korkut (Eds.), *Oxford library of psychology. The Oxford handbook of international psychological ethics* (pp. 328–336). Oxford University Press.

Consoli, A. J., Ardila, R. & Ferrero, A. (2012). Latin and South America. In M. M. Leach, M. J. Stevens, G. Lindsay, A. Ferrero, & Y. Korkut (Eds.), *Oxford library of psychology. The Oxford handbook of international psychological ethics* (pp. 308–320). Oxford University Press.

Cooper, S. (2012). Ethics and South African Psychology. In M. M. Leach, M. J. Stevens, G. Lindsay, A. Ferrero, & Y. Korkut (Eds.), *Oxford library of psychology. The Oxford handbook of international psychological ethics* (pp. 299–307). Oxford University Press.

European Federation of Psychological Associations (1995). *Meta-Code of ethics*. Author.

European Federation of Psychological Associations (2005). *Meta-Code of Ethics*. Retrieved fromwww.efpa.eu/ethics/ethical-codes

Ferrero, A. (2012). Argentina. In M. M. Leach, M. J. Stevens, G. Lindsay, A. Ferrero, & Y. Korkut (Eds.), *Oxford library of psychology. The Oxford handbook of international psychological ethics* (pp. 321–327). Oxford University Press.

Garton, A. F. & Allan, A. (2012). Psychological ethics in Oceana: Convergence and divergence. In M. M. Leach, M. J. Stevens, G. Lindsay, A. Ferrero, & Y. Korkut (Eds.), *Oxford library of psychology. The Oxford handbook of international psychological ethics* (pp. 358–374). Oxford University Press.

Hyder, A. A., Wali, S. A., Khan, A. N., Teoh, N. B., Kass, N. E., & Dawson, L. (2004). Ethical review of health research: A perspective from developing country researchers. *Journal of Medical Ethics*, 30, 68–72.

Kitchener, K. S. & Anderson, S. K. (2011). *Foundations of ethical practice, research, and teaching in psychology and counseling*, 2nd ed. Routledge/Taylor & Francis Group.

Koocher, G. P., & Hadjistavropoulos, T. (2012). North America: Canada and the United States. In M. M. Leach, M. J. Stevens, G. Lindsay, A. Ferrero, & Y. Korkut (Eds.), *Oxford library of psychology. The Oxford handbook of international psychological ethics* (pp. 321–327). Oxford University Press.

Korkut, Y. (2012). Turkey. In M. M. Leach, M. J. Stevens, G. Lindsay, A. Ferrero, & Y. Korkut (Eds.), *Oxford library of psychology. The Oxford handbook of international psychological ethics* (pp. 443–450). Oxford University Press.

Kuo, P. & Leach, M. M. (2017). A cross-sectional examination of international competency standards. *Ethics & Behavior*, 27(7), 562–581. doi:10.1080/10508422.2016.1193439.

Leach, M. M. (2009). International ethics codes and the duty to protect. In J. R. Werth, E. Weifel, & G. H. Benjamin (Eds.), *The duty to protect: Ethical, legal, and professional Considerations for mental health professionals* (pp. 41–58). American Psychological Association.

Leach, M. M. & Gauthier, J. (2011). Internationalizing the professional ethics curriculum. In F. T. L. Leong, W. E. Pickren, & M. M. Leach (Eds.), *International and cultural psychology: Internationalizing the psychology curriculum in the United States* (pp. 29–50). Springer.

Leach, M. M., Glosoff, H., & Overmeir, J. B. (2001). International ethics codes: A follow-up Study of previously unmatched standards and principles. In J. B. Overmeir & J. A. Overmeir (Eds.), *Psychology*. IUPsyS Global Resource.

Leach, M. M. & Harbin, J. J. (1997). Psychological ethics codes: A comparison of twenty- four countries. *International Journal of Psychology, 32*, 181–192.

Leach, M. M., & Oakland, T. (2007). Ethics standards impacting test development and use: A review of 31 ethics codes impacting practices in 35 countries. *International Journal of Testing, 7*, 71–88.

Lindsay, G. (2011). Transnational Ethical Guidance and the Development of the EFPA Meta-Code of Ethics. *European Psychologist, 16*(2), 121–131.

Lindsay, G., Koene, C., Ovreeide, H., & Lang, F. (Eds.). (2008). *Ethics for European psychologists*. Hogrefe.

Nuremberg Code of Ethics in Medical Research (1947). *Trials of war criminals before the Nuremberg military tribunals under Control Council Law No. 10: Vol. 2* (pp. 181–182). U.S. Government Printing Office.

Oakland, T., Leach, M. M., Bartram, D., Lindsay, G., Smedler, A., & Zhang, H. (2012). An international perspective on ethics codes for psychology: A focus on test development and use. In M. M. Leach, M. J. Stevens, G. Lindsay, A. Ferrero, & Y. Korkut (Eds.), *Oxford library of psychology. The Oxford handbook of international psychological ethics* (pp. 19–27). Oxford University Press.

Parsonson, K. L. & Alquicira, L. M. (2019). International psychology ethics codes: Where is the "culture" in acculturation? *Ethical Human Psychology and Psychiatry, 20*(2), 86–99.

Pettifor, J. L. (2004). Professional ethics across national boundaries. *European Psychologist, 9*(4), 264–272. https://doi.org/10.1027/1016-9040.9.4.264

Pettifor, J. L. & Ferrero, A. (2012). Ethical dilemmas, cultural differences, and the globalization of psychology. In M. M. Leach, M. J. Stevens, G. Lindsay, A. Ferrero, & Y. Korkut (Eds.), *Oxford library of psychology. The Oxford handbook of international psychological ethics* (pp. 28–41). Oxford University Press.

Pettifor, J. L. & Sawchuk, T. (2006). Psychologists' perceptions of ethically troubling incidents across international borders. *International Journal of Psychology, 41*, 216–225.

Pope, K. & Vetter, V. A. (1992). Ethical dilemmas encountered by members of the American Psychological Association: A national survey. *The American Psychologist, 47*(3), 397–411.

Psychologists Committee of Mercosur and Associated Countries (1997). Ethical principles. Framework for professional practice of psychology in the Mercosur and associated. Countries. In *Conselho Federal of Psychology* (Federal Board of Psychology), (pp. 11–14) . Author.

Rangi, S. & Stoffel, D. (2015). Ethics assessment on different fields: Psychology. UNESCO: Annex 2.d.1: Ethical Assessment of Research and Innovation: A comparative analysis of Practices and institutions in the EU and selected other countries. Retrieved from https://Sa toriproject.eu/media/D1.1_Ethical-assessment-of-RI_a-comparative-analysis/pdf

Seymour, F. and Nairn, R. (2012). Aotearoa/New Zealand. In M. M. Leach, M. J. Stevens, G. Lindsay, A. Ferrero, & Y. Korkut (Eds.), *Oxford library of psychology. The Oxford handbook of international psychological ethics* (pp. 405–423). Oxford University Press.

Sinclair, C. (2020). Developing and revising the Canadian Code of Ethics for Psychologists: key differences from the American Psychological Association code. *Ethics & Behavior, 30*(40), 249–263.

Stevens, M. J. (2012). Psychological ethics and macro-social change. In M. M. Leach, M. J. Stevens, G. Lindsay, A. Ferrero, & Y. Korkut (Eds.), *Oxford library of psychology. The Oxford handbook of international psychological ethics* (pp. 375–393). Oxford University Press.

Velchkovsky, B. B. & Yuriev, A. I. (2012). Russia. In M. M. Leach, M. J. Stevens, G. Lindsay, A. Ferrero, & Y. Korkut (Eds.), *Oxford library of psychology. The Oxford handbook of international psychological ethics* (pp. 424–442). Oxford University Press.

Wassenaar, D. & Mamotte, N. (2012). Ethical issues and ethics reviews in social science research. In M. M. Leach, M. J. Stevens, G. Lindsay, A. Ferrero, & Y. Korkut (Eds.), *Oxford library of psychology. The Oxford handbook of international psychological ethics* (pp. 268–282). Oxford University Press. doi:10.1093/oxfordhb/9780199739165.013.0019

Weifel, E. R. & Khamush, B. K. (2012). Ethical standards, credentialing, and accountability: An international perspective. In M. M. Leach, M. J. Stevens, G. Lindsay, A. Ferrero, & Y. Korkut (Eds.), *Oxford library of psychology. The Oxford handbook of international psychological ethics* (pp. 103–112). Oxford University Press. doi:10.1093/oxfordhb/9780199739165.013.0008

PART 1

African Countries: Nigeria and Zambia

2

DEVELOPMENT OF NIGERIA'S CODE OF ETHICS FOR PSYCHOLOGY

Gboyega E. Abikoye, Michael O. Ezenwa and Andrew E. Zamani

Background

The Nigerian Psychological Association (NPA) was formed in 1984 to further the development and professionalization of psychology in Nigeria. The NPA is registered with the Corporate Affairs Commission and has a duly-constituted Board of Trustees. The Association organizes annual conferences, workshops, leadership summits and other activities at regular intervals since its founding. These fora were used as platforms to explore professional and academic issues and networking imperatives among psychologists. The Association has also effectively served as the regulator of the training and practice of psychologists in Nigeria.

Over the years, psychologists in Nigeria have emphasized the need for NPA to make herself relevant by ensuring that the work of psychologists in academic and applied settings are consistent with the needs of the country and are in line with international best practices (Njoku, 2012). In order to achieve this, the NPA took cognizance of the necessity of the following:

- Development of research agenda such that its methodology and interventions would be grounded in science, with a view to promoting the science of psychology in Nigeria;
- The need to establish a licensing and or certification pathway for all psychologists, especially clinical and counselling psychologists who practice diagnosis, treatment planning/recommendations and psychotherapy;
- The need to periodically review the training of psychologists so that theory and practice would be integrated in the curriculum for both undergraduate and graduate education;

- The need to make continuing education a requirement for professional psychologists and those in the academic settings, toward the training of a new generation of psychologists, with the founding and accreditation of graduate programs in psychology across the country;
- Development of psychologists' register, as this may help to curb the excesses of pseudo-psychologists who brand themselves as psychologists in varied work settings; and,
- Development of a code of ethics with a view towards regularizing and standardizing the training and practice of psychologists in Nigeria. It could also be helpful to adopt existing ethics code of other established national psychological associations, such as American Psychological Association (APA) and British Psychological Society (BPS), modifying the code as needed to match the Nigerian context;

While the first four goals have been fairly achieved, to a very large extent, NPA was still battling with the last two until 2018 when the first "Ethical Principles of Psychologists and Code of Conduct" was published. It is noteworthy that the publication of the maiden code of ethics happened some 54 years (1964–2018) after the first academic department of psychology was established in Nigeria in the Department of Psychology of the University of Nigeria, Nsukka, under the guidance of Professor Carl Frost of Michigan University, United States of America. It is pertinent to mention that several attempts had been made prior to the publication of the maiden edition of "Ethical Principles of Psychologists and Code of Conduct" in 2018 without success. There have been some positive developments in the past few years, including increased awareness of the value of psychology in the country, the need to protect the profession of psychology and the consumers of psychological services, better organizational and leadership commitments in the NPA, and the unprecedented increased cohesion among members of the NPA. These have created a widespread sense of urgency on the need to have a document outlining the core ethical principles that should guide the training and practice of psychologists in Nigeria. The code of ethics for Nigerian psychologists, therefore, has a relatively short but active history.

One of the major reasons for the long delay in the development and publication of the code of ethics was the initial slow pace of organization of the profession. Within the last decade however, there has been a giant leap in the leadership and organization of the professional society, which has culminated in the approval and publication of the ethical code. At the same time, the Nigerian Psychological Association proposed a Bill for an Act to establish the Nigerian Council of Psychologists. This is based upon the realization that the absence of an enabling law to regulate psychology in Nigeria has meant that activities of *pseudo-psychologists* and charlatans could not be checkmated or curtailed. Fortunately, the Bill has been passed by the House of Representatives and the Senate of the Federal Republic of Nigeria, and has been transmitted to the President of the Federal Republic of Nigeria for Assent to become an act of the National Assembly. As at the time of this report, the President is yet to act on the bill.

Development of NPA's Code of Ethics

It is imperative to align NPA's code of ethics with an international framework of ethical principles to guide all aspects of training and practice of psychologists in Nigeria with a view to promoting global best practices and with regard to the scientific nature of the psychology profession. Consequently, in order to ensure robust training of psychologists and strict adherence to best practices, the NPA "Ethical Principles of Psychologists and Code of Conduct" (NPA, 2018), was modelled after the code of ethics of the American Psychological Association (APA). Apart from the great focus on protection of the consuming public and the profession that characterize APA's ethics code, other influences of the APA codes on the Nigerian code of ethics came about due to the fact that the first department of psychology in Nigeria was established by an American psychologist whose professional background extended to the Nigerian trained pioneer psychologists. Additionally, many psychologists in Nigeria trained and worked as psychologists in the United States of America before taking up teaching, practice and research positions in Nigeria. A good number of psychologists in Nigeria also received their training in other Western countries, especially Germany, Italy, United Kingdom, and Canada all of whose backgrounds in one way or the other shaped the NPA's ethical code. It is however important to emphasize that despite the contributions from other psychological associations and climes, the NPA deliberately ensured that the uniqueness of Nigeria in terms of her extant laws, culture and other epistemological realities were taken into account in arriving at the ethical code.

The need for development and publication of ethics code for psychology in Nigeria had been emphasized and several attempts in that direction had been made in the past, but the concrete process of developing the code commenced formally with the setting up of a Committee for the development of Code of Ethics of NPA during the 2017 Leadership Summit in Abuja, Nigeria. The Committee submitted her reports to the Special Executive Council Session of the NPA held in Awka, Anambra State, in 2018. After a clause-by-clause consideration, the draft ethics code was approved by the Executive Council of the NPA. Finally, the ethics code was presented to Congress during the 2018 National Convention for consideration and approval.

The Code of Ethics

Like the APA's Ethical Principles of Psychologists and Code of Conduct which consists of an Introduction, a Preamble, six General Principles (A–F), and specific Ethical Standards (Metcalf, 2014), the NPA's Ethical Principles of Psychologists and Code of Conduct (NPA, 2018) also consists of an Introduction, a Preamble, the five General Principles (A–E) and the Specific Ethical Standards.

The Introduction discusses the intent, organization, procedural considerations, and scope of application of the Ethics Code. The Preamble and General Principles are aspirational goals to guide psychologists toward the highest ideals of psychology. Although the Preamble and General Principles are not themselves enforceable rules, they are considered by psychologists in arriving at an ethical course of action and may also be considered by regulating bodies in interpreting the actions or inactions of psychologists. Most of the Ethical Standards are written broadly in order to apply to psychologists in varied roles, although the application of an Ethical Standard may vary depending on the context. These Standards are not exhaustive. The fact that a given conduct is not specifically addressed by the NPA's Ethics Code does not necessarily mean that it is either ethical or unethical.

The NPA Code of Ethics applies to psychologists' work-related activities, that is, activities that are part of the psychologists' scientific and professional functions or that are psychological in nature. It includes the clinical or counselling practice of psychology, research, teaching, supervision of trainees, development of assessment instruments, conducting assessments, educational counselling, organizational consulting, administration, and other activities including public statements.

Specifically, the NPA's "Ethical Principles of Psychologists and Code of Conduct" (NPA, 2018) has the following General Principles:

1 **Beneficence and Non-maleficence:** This principle requires that psychologists make effort to ensure that they benefit those with whom they work and ensure that they are not exposed to harm. In essence, the welfare of persons psychologists work with should be uppermost in their consideration.
2 **Fidelity and Responsibility:** This principle is set on the foundation that psychologists establish relationships of trust with those they work with. They should also be aware of their professional and scientific responsibilities to society and the target communities where they work. They should not engage in acts that are inimical to established laws or expose individuals and communities to hazards.
3 **Integrity**: Psychologists should at all times seek to promote and uphold accuracy, honesty and truthfulness in all ramifications of psychology. They should not engage in any form of fraud or dishonesty. They should keep their promises and ensure that they do not make commitments they cannot keep.
4 **Justice:** Psychologists are to deal fairly with all people. In doing this, they should allow all persons equal access and benefits from the contributions of psychology. Psychologists are careful that their personal tendencies do not get in the way of their professional conducts which may lead to unjust practices.
5 **Respect for people's rights and dignity:** Psychologists recognize and respect the fundamental rights of all people and, therefore, do not engage in practices that may violate these rights. In addition, cultural practices and role differences bordering on age, gender, ethnicity, religion, and sexual orientation are to be respected. Psychologists strive to eliminate biases based on these factors.

The NPA's specific Ethical Standards are presented as follows:

1 Resolving Ethical Issues

1.01 Misuse of Psychologists' Work
Psychologists take appropriate steps to correct or reduce misuse or mis-representation of their work when such cases are brought to their knowledge.
1.02 Conflict between Ethics and Law, Regulations or other Governing Legal Authority
In cases of conflict with the law, regulations or other legal bodies, psychologists make clear the nature of the conflict, and take their stand for the Ethics Code, and take steps to resolve the conflict in line with the General Principles and Ethical Standards of the Ethic Code. This standard should not be used to justify violation of rights.
1.03 Conflicts between Ethics and Organizational Demands
Psychologists are duty bound to affirm their commitment to the Ethical Principles of Psychologists and Code of Conduct in cases of conflict between the Code and the demands of the organization where psychologists work. Psychologists should resolve the conflict accordingly.
1.04 Informal Resolution of Ethical Violations
If psychologists have sufficient reason to believe that another psychologist has violated the Ethical Principles of Psychologists and Code of Conduct, they normally bring the matter to the attention of the person concerned, if informal approach will best address the matter without doing damage to other considerations.
1.05 Reporting Ethical Violation
Ethical violations which may not be appropriately addressed under informal resolutions are taken further action on by psychologists. This may be in the form of reporting to state or national bodies on professional ethics, or licensing bodies to take appropriate actions.
1.06 Cooperating with Ethics Committees
Psychologists cooperate with Ethics Committees of the Associations they belong to, which are investigating violations of the Code of Ethics. Failure to cooperate is in itself a violation of the Code of Ethics. However, a request for deferment of hearing of an ethical complaint does not imply non-compliance.
1.07 Improper Complaints
It is not proper for psychologists to file or encourage others to file ethics complaints which have no facts to back them up.
1.08 Unfair Discrimination against Complainants and Respondents
Psychologists do not discriminate against individuals based on the fact that they have been the subject of ethical complaint. Individuals are not denied their rights and privileges because complaints are lodged against them.

2 Competence

2.01 Boundaries of Competence

a Psychologists do not operate outside the boundaries of their competence. The roles they play such as rendering services, teaching and conducting research are all within the boundaries of their competence. All these roles should be based on their educational and professional experience.

b Psychologists may engage in profiling people in terms of age, gender, ethnic nationality, culture and religion where it is necessary for effective implementation of their services.

c Psychologists who intend to work in relatively new places, or handle unfamiliar cases or adopt new techniques and technologies will do well to update their knowledge on those new areas.

d In cases involving mental health services, where psychologists are asked to provide services, they should make effort to obtain the competence required to ensure that services are not denied.

e In areas that are still emerging and where standards are yet to be adopted, psychologists should take appropriate steps to protect people they work with from harm.

f Psychologists are expected to be reasonably familiar with legal provisions when they play forensic roles.

2.02 Providing Services in Emergencies

Psychologists without necessary training may provide services to individuals who lack mental health services in times of emergency to ensure that services are not denied. However, such services should end as soon as normalcy is restored.

2.03 Maintaining Competence

Psychologists seize every opportunity to develop and maintain their competence.

2.04 Bases for Scientific and Professional Judgements

The work of psychologists is based on established scientific and professional knowledge of the discipline.

2.05 Delegation of Work to Others

Psychologists may delegate work to Assistants provided the Assistants are not sufficiently close to the person who are being served to avoid exploitation and loss of objectivity. Again, such Assistants should be persons of proven competence based on their education or training.

2.06 Personal Problems and Conflicts

a Psychologists avoid engaging in activities they know their personal problems cannot allow them to accomplish competently.

b When psychologists know that their personal problems may impede the performance of their tasks, they seek assistance to determine what their level of commitment should be.

3 Human Relations

3.01 Unfair Discrimination

Psychologists do not discriminate against persons on the basis of age, gender, ethnicity or religion in their daily tasks.

3.02 Sexual Harassment

Psychologists abhor engagement in sexual harassment, which manifests as sexual solicitation, physical advances, verbal or nonverbal conduct that is sexual in nature in the course of their work. It is unwelcome, offensive and creates a hostile work environment.

3.03 Other Harassment

Psychologists, in carrying out their duties, do not deliberately engage in acts that may be viewed as harassment or demeaning to individuals as they relate to such sensitive factors as age, gender, culture and ethnicity.

3.04 Avoiding Harm

a   Psychologists take steps to avoid harm to their clients/patients or persons they work with, and by so doing minimize foreseeable harm.

b   Psychologists abhor all forms of torture and therefore do not participate or engage in it.

3.05 Multiple Relationships

a   Psychologists avoid entering into multiple relationships where the likelihood exists that the relationships could impair their objectivity. However, multiple relationships that would not impair objectivity are not unethical.

b   When it is observed that multiple relationships have arisen that may affect objectivity, psychologists take steps to resolve them in the interest of the persons involved in compliance with the Ethics Code.

c   Psychologists clarify their role expectations and the extent of confidentiality at the outset when they are required by law to serve in more than one in a judicial or administrative panel.

3.06 Conflict of Interest

Psychologists avoid working in situations where their personal or professional interests could stand in the way of objectivity and effectiveness or expose others they work with to harm.

3.07 Third Party Request for Service

Psychologists make clear at the beginning of a service what the nature of the relationship should be when engaged by a third party to render service to a person.

3.08 Exploitative Relationships

Psychologists do not set out to exploit persons over whom they have authority such as clients/patients, students and supervisees.

3.09 Cooperation with other Professionals
Psychologists cooperate with other professionals when it is professionally appropriate and it is so indicated for better service delivery.

3.10 Informed Consent

a When psychologists perform their roles such as conducting research, therapy, or consulting in person, or through electronic means, it is important that they obtain the informed consent of the person using language that the person clearly understand, unless conducting such activities without consent is mandated by law.

b When dealing with persons who are legally not in a position to give informed consent, psychologists provide an appropriate explanation, seek the person's consent, consider such person's interests and obtain permission from legally appropriate authority.

c When services are ordered by the court, psychologists inform the persons concerned about the nature of the services, whether they are court ordered and the limits of confidentiality.

d Psychologists document written or oral consent, permission and assent.

3.11 Psychological Services Delivered to or Through Organizations
Psychologists who deliver services to or through organizations usually give information beforehand to the clients about the nature and objectives of the services, the intended recipients, the target clients as well as the relationship the psychologists will have with each person or organization.

3.12 Interruption of Psychological Services
Psychologists make contingency plans for facilitating services in the event that psychological services are interrupted by factors like death, illness, relocation and retirement of the psychologist or that of the client. If the service is covered by contract, these circumstances will have to be taken care of in the contract.

4 Privacy and Confidentiality

4.01 Maintaining Confidentiality
Psychologists have an obligation and exercise caution to ensure confidentiality of information obtained through or stored in any medium as the confidentiality of such information may be regulated.

4.02 Discussing the Limits of Confidentiality

a Psychologists discuss with persons they work with limits of confidentiality and the uses of the information generated

b The discussion of confidentiality is set at the onset of the relationship and as new circumstances may dictate, unless this is not feasible.

c Psychologists have a duty to inform clients/patients of the risks to privacy and limits of confidentiality provided they offer services or products through electronic means.

4.03 Recording

Psychologists obtain permission of their clients or their legal representatives before recording their voices or images.

4.04 Minimizing Intrusion on Privacy

a   Psychologists include in their written or oral reports only information that is useful to the purpose of the communication.

b   Psychologists discuss confidential information obtained in their work only for appropriate purposes and with only persons concerned with such matters.

4.05 Disclosures

a   Psychologists may disclose confidential information with the consent of the client on behalf of the client.

b   Psychologists can only disclose confidential information without the consent of the person only as mandated by law or for a valid purpose such as to provide needed services, obtain professional consultations, protect the client and others concerned from harm and obtain payment for services where limited disclosure is necessary.

4.06 Consultations

Psychologists do not make known confidential information that may lead to the identification of a client or other persons they have confidential relationship with when discussing with colleagues. Information necessary to achieve purposes of consultation is what can only be disclosed.

4.07 Use of Confidential Information for Didactic or other Purposes

Psychologists do not make any form of public disclosures of confidential, personally identifiable information concerning their clients or other persons who receive their services except that they disguise the person or organization, or the client consented in writing, or is authorized by a legal authority.

5   Advertising and other Public Statements

5.01 Avoidance of False or Deceptive Statements

a   Psychologists do not deliberately make claims or statements that are false, deceptive or fraudulent in their research, practice or other activities related to their work, or those of other persons they work with.

b   Psychologists do not make false claims about their training, or competence, academic degrees, credentials, institutional affiliations, services, success of their services, fees, and publication of research findings.

c   Psychologists only claim degrees for their services when they are earned from accredited institutions or where they are the basis for granting of license by a licensing body.

25

5.02 Statement by Others

    a   Psychologists who engage others who create and place public statements take responsibility for such statements.

    b   Psychologists do not pay for publicity in news items.

    c   Every paid advertisement in connection with the work of a psychologist must be clearly recognized as such.

5.03 Description of Workshops and Non-degree-granting Educational Programmes

Psychologists accurately describe the target audience for which announcements, or advertisements describing workshops or seminars are made.

5.04 Media Presentations

Psychologists who provide advice or comments in the media should ensure that the comments are based on their professional knowledge or training and are in agreement with the Ethics Code and do not show that a professional relationship has been established with the recipient.

5.05 Testimonials

Psychologists do not solicit for testimonials from present clients/patients or other persons who are vulnerable to undue influence because of their particular circumstances.

5.06 In-Person Solicitation

Psychologists do not engage by themselves or through others in uninvited in-person solicitation of business from people who are vulnerable to undue influences because of their circumstances.

6   Record Keeping and Fees

6.01 Documentation of Professional and Scientific Work and Maintenance of Records

Psychologists create records of their work. They control, maintain, store, retain and dispose of such records to enhance provision of services by them or by other professionals later. They allow replication of research design and analyses and meet requirements by institutions. Psychologists ensure accurate billing and payments and ensure compliance with the law.

6.02 Maintenance, Dissemination, and Disposal of Confidential Records of Professional and Scientific Work

    a   Psychologists ensure confidentiality in creating, storing, accessing, transferring and disposing of records whether written or otherwise.

    b   Psychologists use coding or other systems to avoid including personal identifiers when information about clients is entered into databases which are accessible to unauthorized users.

    c   Psychologists make appropriate plans for transfer and protection of records to maintain confidentiality ahead of withdrawal of service.

6.03 Withholding Records for Nonpayment

Psychologists may not withhold clients' records under their control which are requested and needed for emergency services.

6.04 Fees and Financial Agreements

a   Psychologists and recipients of services reach agreement early enough, specifying compensation and billing arrangements.
b   Psychologists' fees practices are in line with the law.
c   Psychologists do not misrepresent their fees.
d   Financial limitations which may limit services, if anticipated, should be discussed with the recipients of services.
e   Psychologists should first inform the recipients of service of their intention to use collection agencies or legal measures in case of failure to pay for services rendered by the clients.

6.05 Barter with Clients / Patients

Psychologists may barter only if it is not clinically contraindicated and when the resulting arrangement is not exploitative.

6.06 Accuracy in Reports to Payers and Funding Sources

Psychologists must ensure that accurate reports of the nature of the service provided or research conducted, including fees and charges are made to the payers for services or sources of funding.

6.07 Referrals and Fees

The fees that psychologists pay and payments they receive from other, or fees divided with other professionals, other than in employer-employee relation-ship, is based on the services provided and not on the referral itself.

7   Education and Training

7.01 Design of Education and Training Programmes

Psychologists who are responsible for education and training programmes ensure that programmes are designed to provide appropriate knowledge and experiences, and to meet licensing and certification requirements, or other goals for which claims are made.

7.02 Description of Education and Training Programmes

Psychologists responsible for education and training programmes ensure that there is up-to-date description of the programme content, training goals, objectives, stipends, and benefits and other requirements to be met for satis-factory completion of the programme. This information must be available to all interested parties.

7.03 Accuracy in Teaching

a   Psychologists ensure that course syllabi are accurate in relation to the subject matter to be covered which forms the basis for evaluation.

They take step to update the curriculum when necessary and duly inform students of the development.

b   Psychologists present information accurately when engaged in teaching or training.

7.04 Student Disclosure of Personal Information
Psychologists never require students to disclose their personal information in the course or programme related activities.

7.05 Mandatory Individual or Group Therapy

a   Psychologists allow students to select individual or group therapy from practitioners not affiliated to the programme.

b   Staff members who form part of the evaluating team do not themselves provide the therapy.

7.06 Assessing Student and Supervisee Performance

a   Psychologists establish specific processes for providing feedback to students and supervisees in academic and supervisory relationships.

b   Psychologists use actual performance of students and supervisees on relevant and established programme requirements as the yardstick for evaluation.

7.07 Sexual Relationship with Students and Supervisees
Psychologists do not engage in sexual relationships with students and supervisees who they evaluate.

8   Research and Publication

8.01 Institutional Approval
Psychologists provide accurate information about their research proposals and receive approval before conducting the research when it is required that they get institutional approval. The research must be carried out in line with the approved protocol.

8.02 Informed Consent to Research
Psychologists obtain informed consent by informing participants about the purpose of the research, duration and procedures, and their right to refuse to participate or withdraw as the research gets underway.

8.03: Informed Consent for Recording Voices and Images in Research
Psychologists obtain the informed consent of participants before recording their voices or images.

8.04: Client / Patient, Student and Subordinate Research participants

Psychologists who conduct research with clients / patients, students or subordinates as participants ensure they are protected from any negative result of refusal to participate or withdraw.

8.05 Dispensing with informed Consent for Research

Psychologists may dispense with informed consent where the research would not create distress or harm as in the study of normal educational practice.

8.06 Offering Inducement for Research Participation

Psychologists avoid offering inappropriate inducements for research participation if the inducement will lead to coercion. When inducements are offered for participation in research, efforts are made to explain the nature of the service, the risks and limitations involved.

8.07 Deception in Research

Psychologists do not set out to use deception in research unless its use is justified. Deception should not be used when it will likely cause pain or distress to participants. Deception that is an integral feature of the design should be explained to participants.

8.08 Debriefing

Psychologists provide appropriate information to participants about the nature, results and conclusions of the research and correct misconceptions that participants may have.

8.09 Humane Care and Use of Animals in Research

Psychologists acquire, care for, use and dispose of animals in research in line with established laws. They take responsibility for the supervision of all procedures involving animals to ensure their comfort. Psychologists give instructions to all persons working under them and who use animals on the care and maintenance of those animals.

8.10 Reporting Research Results

Psychologists do not fabricate data. They avoid false or deceptive statements. If significant errors are discovered in their published data, they take steps to correct the errors.

8.11 Plagiarism

Psychologists do not present portions of other people's work or date as their own, even when cited occasionally.

8.12 Publication Credit

Psychologists take responsibility and credit only for work they did or those to which they make substantial contribution.

8.13 Duplicate Publication Data

Psychologists do not publish, as original data, those that have been published previously by other researchers. However, psychologists can publish previously published data if accompanied by proper acknowledgement.

8.14 Sharing Research Data for verification

Psychologists share data on which their findings are based with other researchers who wish to verify the claims and conduct further research.

8.15 Reviewers

Psychologists who review materials submitted for presentation, publication, grant and research proposal do so with utmost confidentiality and consideration of the rights of the people who submitted them.

9   Assessment

9.01 Bases for Assessment
Information and techniques sufficient to substantiate their findings form the bases of the opinion in the recommendations and reports of psychologists.
9.02 Use of Assessment
Psychologists administer, adapt, interpret, or use assessment techniques or instruments in a manner and for purposes that are appropriate for the research.
9.03: Informed Consent in Assessment
Psychologists obtain informed consent for assessment, evaluation or diagnostic services.
9.04: Release of Test Data
Psychologists may not release test data to protect a client / patient or others from harm, or misrepresentation of the data as the release of confidential information is regulated by law.
9.05 Test Construction
Psychologists develop tests and other assessment techniques using psychometric procedures and current scientific or professional knowledge for the test design, standardization and recommendation for use.
9.06 Interpreting Assessment Results
Psychologists take into account the purpose of the assessment and the test factors that may affect their judgements or reduce accuracy of their interpretation when interpreting results.
9.07 Assessment by Unqualified Persons
Psychologists avoid the promotion of assessment techniques designed by unqualified persons, except for training purposes with supervision.
9.08 Obsolete Tests and Outdated Results
Psychologists do not base their assessment or intervention decisions on recommendations on data or test results that are outdated or obsolete for the current purpose.
9.09 Test scoring and Interpretation
Psychologists accurately describe the purpose, norms, validity, reliability and applications of the procedures and any special qualifications applicable for their use when they offer assessment and interpretation services to other professionals.
9.10 Explaining Assessment Results
Psychologists explain results of scoring and interpretation to individuals or designated representatives unless the nature of the relationship precluded provision of an explanation of results.
9.11 Maintaining Test Security

Psychologists make effort to maintain the integrity and security of test materials and other assessment techniques in line with legal provisions and contractual agreements and in adherence to the Ethics Code.

10   Therapy

10.01 Informed Consent in Therapy

Psychologists inform clients/patients early enough in the therapeutic relationship about the nature and anticipated course of therapy, fees, involvement of third parties and provide clients the opportunity to ask questions when obtaining informed consent.

10.02 Therapy Involving Couples

Psychologists involved in the provision of services to many people who have a relationship (spouse, parents and children) take measures to clarify at the onset which of the individuals are clients/patients and the relationship the psychologists will have with each person.

10.03 Group therapy

Psychologists describe at the outset the roles and responsibilities of all parties and the limit of confidentiality when they provide services to several persons in a group setting.

10.04 Providing Therapy to Those Served by Others

Psychologists discuss treatment issues and the potential clients'/patients' welfare with the client / patient or other legally authorized person on behalf of the client/patient in order to minimize the risk of confusion and conflict, and consult with the other service providers when appropriate and when they are deciding whether to offer or provide services to those already being served elsewhere.

10.05 Sexual Intimacy with Current Therapy Clients/Patients

Psychologists avoid sexual intimacy with current therapy clients/patients.

10.06 Sexual Intimacy with relatives or Significant Others of Current Therapy Clients/Patients

Psychologists do not engage in sexual intimacy with individuals they know to be close relatives, guardians, or significant others of current clients/patients. Psychologists do not terminate therapy to circumvent this standard.

10.07 Therapy with Former Sexual Partners

Psychologists do not accept as therapy clients/patients persons with whom they have had sexual intimacy.

10.08 Sexual Intimacy with Former Clients / Patients

Psychologists do not engage in sexual intimacy with former clients / patients for at least two years after cessation or termination of therapy. Psychologist do not engage in sexual intimacy with former clients/patients even after a two year except in the most unusual circumstances

10.09 Interruption of Therapy

Psychologists provide for clients'/patients' care in the event that the contract they entered into ends

10.10 Termination of Therapy

Psychologists terminate therapy when it is clear that the client/patient no longer needs the service. Psychologists may terminate therapy if threatened by the client/patient or other persons related to the client/patient. Psychologists provide pre-termination therapy to ensure the welfare of the client/patient.

How Nigeria's Culture and History Influenced the Writing of Our Ethics Code

African cultures generally, and Nigerian culture in particular, are rooted in ethical considerations, many of which though unwritten, are generally shared and adhered to by a majority of the people. The African ethical framework focuses on the community good rather than the individual, the Ubuntu (literally translated to "I am because we are") spirit which is different from the Western ethics that lays emphasis on the autonomy, freedom, and moral inclination of the individual. While Western ethics conceives the individual as an intellectual being, emphasizing the faculty of reason as the basic tenet in moral conduct, African ethics conceives the individual as an ethical entity. According to Ewuoso (2016), while Western ethics appear to be driven by an attempt to sharply distinguish persons from the rest of the world, and then to identify the ways in which persons should be treated, the traditional African approach and ethical framework is different on both counts.

For instance, the ethics of "do good and cause no harm," is a generally acceptable code of behaviour in Nigeria. However, defining what constitutes harm is different in different cultures. An example of this would be female circumcision, which is perceived as harmful in most Western cultures but is generally perceived as largely beneficial by many indigenous Nigerian cultural traditions, especially in the belief that it reduces infidelity. Similarly, abortion is seen as harmful/malevolent in Nigeria and many African cultures, but not so in some other especially Western cultures.

Whereas one ethical framework in Nigeria may not be generalizable in absolute terms because of the pluralistic, heterogeneous nature of Nigeria (with 250 mutually-exclusive ethnic groups and more than 500 languages), Nigerians are considered to have ethical commonalities regarding the definition of what is appropriate and what is not. The NPA, in the process of developing the code of ethics for Nigerian psychologists, took the cultural peculiarities and commonalities of members into consideration. While adopting the APA Guidelines, special care was taken to domesticate most of the concepts, issues and considerations with a view to strengthening the validity and practical utility of the Guidelines. Most Nigerian psychologists, therefore, have different concerns and problems in the area of ethics that require a framework that is congruent with their cultural realities.

Nigeria is a developing and deeply religious country. Christianity and Islam are the two predominant religions in Nigeria and these permeate behaviours and human actions in the country, ranging from politics and economy to occupational and professional practices. Inadvertently, Nigeria's culture exerted (and still exerts) profound influence on psychology as a profession. Almost everybody considers him/herself to be a psychologist of some sort – the Pastor, the Imam, the motivational speaker, other religious consultants. This creates a very broad base for charlatanism. Until recently, and because the discipline of psychology in Nigeria was not well organized and was an "all comers" affair, which everybody delved into, the issue of code of conduct did not arise. The absence of a legal/ regulatory framework through an enabling act also means that activities of practitioners could not be regulated. Nevertheless, because Nigeria cannot be isolated from the rest of the world, the NPA's Ethical Principles of Psychologists and Code of Conduct represents a framework that is internally consistent based on basic moral sense with reference to epistemological worldview that also embraces a middle-ground to accommodate the moralistic, pluralistic, and heterogeneous society that Nigeria represents.

What our Ethics Code Means to our Members and Society at Large

The Nigerian ethical considerations derive from moral principles and values, which are the ethical responsibility of individuals and the community. Ethical codes, in the real sense, cannot function where there is no culture. Most culture is based on the principles of the "golden rule" – do unto others what you would like them do unto you. The NPA's Ethical Principles of Psychologists and Code of Conduct represents, to most members, a formalization of deeply held, morally entrenched and culturally prescribed ways of doing things. The code also represents professionalism, sanity, accountability and responsibility in the training and practice of psychologists in Nigeria. It prescribes a distinct professional identity for psychologists in Nigeria for independent recognition and patronage. The leadership of NPA commits members to adhere to the NPA Ethics Code and to the rules and procedures used to implement it. It also ensures protection of members, the consuming public and the profession of psychology.

To members of the NPA, there is an urgent need to professionalize psychology in Nigeria, and the publication of the code of ethics has been welcomed with great enthusiasm. To underlie the seriousness attached to the issue of professionalism and adherence to best global practices, the Association has inaugurated a Committee to monitor compliance and recommend sanctions for erring members. There is a consensus that the Committee should perform the regulatory functions while the Council for Psychologists (as contained in the Psychology bill) will be constituted as soon as presidential assent is secured.

The problem, however, is not with members of NPA but thousands of other *pseudo-psychologists* and other charlatans parading as psychologists and practicing in many Nigerian cities. Since these *pseudo-psychologists* are not members of the NPA. It is practically impossible to regulate their activities, especially because of the absence of an enabling legislation, as is the case currently. However, with the increased organizational activities, media presence, and engagements with relevant stakeholders by NPA at national and state levels, there is hope of more control and consumption of professional psychological services in the country.

The code of ethics is meaningful to psychologists in Nigeria (members of the NPA) but meaningless to other charlatans and *pseudo-psychologists* over which the NPA has no control. The Nigerian Council of Psychology Bill, when assented to by the President, would give the NPA the legal backing to ensure that only competent psychologists that are adhering strictly to the code are allowed to practise in Nigeria. The importance of the Act therefore cannot be overemphasized.

Conclusion

Psychology in Nigeria, often traceable to 1964 when the first academic department of psychology was established and 1984 when the NPA was formed, has a relatively short history. This notwithstanding, reasonable progress has been made, one of which was the development, publication and dissemination of ethics code for psychologists in Nigeria. The development of the NPA ethics code, though patterned after the APA ethics code, was done through an inclusive process involving key stakeholders, taking Nigeria's cultural peculiarities into consideration. Situating the ethics code in Nigeria's extant laws, culture and epistemological realities was borne out of the need to enhance relevance, acceptance and practical utility of the code in Nigeria. These considerations have led to wide acceptance of the ethics code by psychologists in Nigeria. Enforcement of the ethics codes and disciplinary issues have, however been problematic, due to absence of an enabling law regulating the profession and practice of psychology in Nigeria. We are optimistic that, with the passage of the Nigerian Council of Psychology Bill by Nigerian legislature in 2019 and the Presidential Assent being eagerly awaited, the issue of enforcement should be overcome soon. The prospects, therefore, appear very bright for the profession of psychology in Nigeria.

References

Ewuoso, O. C. (2016) Bioethics education in Nigeria and West Africa: Historical beginnings AND Impacts. *Global Bioethics*, 27 (4), 50–60. doi:10.1080/11287462.2016.1192448

Metcalf, J. (2014). *Ethics Code: History, Context, and Challenges.* Council for Big Data, Ethics, and Society. www.datasociety.net/

Nigerian Psychological Association (2018). *Ethical Principles of Psychologists and Code of Conduct.* Author.

Njoku, M. G. (2012). *Nigerian Psychological Association: The Way Forward.* A Paper Presented at the First Nigerian Psychological Association Southeast Regional Meeting/Professional Development Seminar (September, 2012).

3

CODE OF ETHICS FOR PSYCHOLOGY RESEARCH AND PRACTICE IN ZAMBIA

Dabie Nabuzoka, Jacqueline P. Jere-Folotiya and J. Anitha Menon

Introduction

This chapter discusses the development of the code of ethics for research in, and the practice of, psychology in Zambia. The chapter is divided into two main sections: conduct of psychological research and conduct in practicing psychology. Each main section first provides a historical national context. In the case of psychological research, consideration of ethical conduct is initially identified in the context of the subject area as a health-related field, and later developing its own ethical code of conduct for practitioners and researchers under the umbrella of the Psychology Association of Zambia (PAZ). The code of ethics is discussed as having initially being modelled after the British Psychological Society's code of conduct with some of the elements and standards being adapted to the special circumstances of Zambian society. The particular ways in which the ethics code was influenced by the country's history and culture are also briefly discussed, highlighting both structural and social factors as playing a significant part. Finally, the significance of the ethics code to psychologists and related professionals and researchers in the country is discussed, together with its practical implications and efficacy in contemporary Zambian society at large.

Conduct of Psychology Research

Historical Background

The National Health Research Authority

The development of the code of psychology ethics and conduct in Zambia can best be understood in the context of the regulatory framework for research and practice in health-related fields. Prior to the 2000s, Zambia lacked a legal frame-work for the conduct of health research, of which psychology was generally considered to be a related subject area. Several efforts towards filling this gap were made laying the foundation on which all future plans were built (Chanda-Kapata et al., 2012). In the late 2000s, the Ministry of Health constituted the National Health Research Advisory Committee (NHRAC) to brainstorm and plan for the management of health research in the country. The committee made recom-mendations for setting a Body that would coordinate and manage health research in the country. Committees and technical working groups were later formed including the National Health Research Advisory Committee Technical Working Group, and the National Health Research Ethics Committee. The recommenda-tions of the National Health Research Advisory Committee were that Zambia needed a health research body responsible for stewardship, financing, creating and sustaining resources, setting priorities and producing and using research results for knowledge translation to inform policy.

The years 2010 to 2012 were characterized by activities that resulted in the drafting of the National Health Research Bill, which proposed the creation of the Research Authority, a body that would be responsible for stewardship, financing, creating and sustaining resources, setting priorities and producing and using research for knowledge translation to inform policy. In March 2013, the National Health Research Bill was enacted and became the National Health Research Act No. 2 of 2013 (Government of the Republic of Zambia, 2013).

The National Health Research Authority Council (NHRAC) was established, as provided for in the National Health Research Act of 2013 and worked towards institutionalization of the National Health Authority. The Council appointed the National Health Research Ethics Board which it inducted in June 2017, and also provided for the establishment of health research ethics com-mittees and the regulation and management of research institutions, health researchers and health establishments involved in undertaking health research. The National Health Research Ethics Board was the first national regulatory body on research ethics in Zambia as the country. Prior to this the country, as in many other sub-Saharan African countries (Kruger, et al. 2014), lacked a national regulatory body to oversee the conduct of research in the country (Mwanyungwi, 2017).

The National Health Research Act No. 2 of 2013 defines "health research" as meaning an activity conducted which (among other functions) "contributes to knowledge of biological, clinical, psychological or social processes in human beings or animals" and "uses scientific methods to generate information to deal with health and disease." and "improves scientific methods for provision of health services." This conceptualization of health research includes a major proportion of the research generally covered in the field of psychology. In addition, and although there is no specific stipulation for a representative for psychology, the Act provides for the National Health Research Ethics Board to have representatives from a number of disciplines and sectors which include social sciences.

Procedure for Obtaining Authority to Conduct Research

All researchers are mandated to submit their research protocols to the National Health Research Authority upon receipt of approval from a Research Ethics Committee (REC) or an Institutional Review Board (IRB) as dictated by an Act of Parliament (No. 2 of 2013). Researchers who fail to submit their research protocol to the NHRA and begin to conduct research are subject to disciplinary action by the National Health Research Ethics Board. The process for obtaining the authority to conduct research includes the following requirements (NHRA, 2019):

- Submission of a request to conduct research when initiating a new study and after REC or IRB approval has been obtained.
- Submission of quarterly progress reports each quarter after receiving NHRA study approval.
- Submission of a Protocol Amendment whenever changes are made to a part of the research study, first to the relevant REC/IRB and then after receiving approval from the REC/IRB, the approval letter and the protocol amendment must be sent to the NHRA.
- Submission of a request to present findings or submit for publication before presenting or submitting findings for publication. First notifying the Authority, in writing, citing the research title and the ethical approval obtained from the Board.
- Submission of the protocol and a Material Transfer Agreement (MTA) form for those seeking to import biological samples.

Quality Management and Ethics

Research Ethics Committees in Zambia

Quality Management of research and ethics in Zambia has until recently mostly been undertaken at the University of Zambia (UNZA). Prior 2017 when the NHREB was established, for example, most of the health research outside of UNZA was being conducted without ethical approval. The university is the premier tertiary educational institution in Zambia. It is the oldest of the public universities established by the government to provide higher education in the country. Since its inception in 1966, UNZA has been carrying out research which has been internally and externally supported. Internally supported research is funded by resources generated within the University and these include government (GRZ) grants, revenue from business ventures, and donations. Externally supported research is funded by resources from commissioned research through MoU/agreements with local, regional and international bodies, MoU/Agreements with other universities, institutes, centers and units.

Historically, such support for research as has been the case with UNZA has had implications for quality management and adherence to ethical standards in the conduct of research. The university's objective has therefore been to provide a

Total Quality Management (TQM) system for all research activities under the umbrella of the Directorate of Research and Graduate Studies (DRGS); and build effective systems for compliance in issues related to the scientific and ethical management of research. To this effect, The University of Zambia Research Ethics Committees (UNZA-RECs) were set up. These Research Ethics Committees (RECs) for the University are charged with the responsibility of reviewing research proposals for research ethical compliance.

All research carried out by the University of Zambia staff is governed by the local ethical requirements. In the case of a collaborative research project involving one or more foreign institutions, ethical approval has to be sought both from UNZA where the research will be carried out and from the Institutional Review Boards (IRB) of the collaborating institutions. The main role of RECs is to review and approve research proposals and protocols dealing with human and animal participants for research ethical compliance. The Research Ethics Committees' mandate is not restricted to the University of Zambia researchers but also cover collaborative research with other institutions. To date (2020), University of Zambia has three Research Ethics Committees as follows:

a   Biomedical Research Ethics Committee;
b   Natural and Applied Sciences Research Ethics Committee; and
c   Humanities and Social Sciences Research Ethics Committee.

Psychological research may fall under any of the existing RECs at the university.
The specific functions of the Research Ethics Committees include the following:

a   Reviewing and approving all research proposals and protocols that deal with human and animal participants;
b   Enforcing high ethical standards on research done on human and animal participants;
c   Protecting the interests of researchers who are conducting research following the approved protocols/proposals;
d   Monitoring approved research projects to ensure ethical compliance;
e   Participating in the training and/or sensitization of staff and students in research ethics; and
f   Reporting to the relevant Research Board.

Ethical Requirements and Standards for Research

In regulating adherence to ethical requirements and standards, there is recognition that the integrity of any research depends not only on its scientific rigor but also on its ethical adequacy. Thus, there are basic principles and guidelines that are stipulated to underpin research on human participants in general and psychological research in particular. These form the basis for what RECs may or may not approve. There is a general recognition that ethical issues are many and varied, and may be quite complex. However, there is a requirement that all research involving human subjects or participants should be conducted in accordance with the three ethical principles of respect for persons, beneficence and justice. Since Zambia is part of the international research community, all research must strictly abide by the International Ethical Guidelines for research involving human participants. Therefore, emphasis must be placed on informed consent, equitable distribution of burdens and benefits, and safeguarding confidentiality. Thus, the requirements for conducting psychological research on, or with, human participants under the National Health Research Act is that it should not only be with ethical approval from the National Health Research Ethics Board or accredited health research ethics committee, but also that it should include such things as written consent of the person participating, after the person has been informed of the objectives of the research or experimentation and any potential risks or benefits on that person's health. In addition, the research should not violate social and cultural norms.

There is a requirement for research procedures to be explained in an information sheet written in simple language that is easily comprehensible by the potential research participant. Participant should be free from coercion of any kind and should not be pressured to participate in a research study. Participants in a research study have the right to give their informed consent before participating, and it is the researcher's responsibility to seek ongoing consent during the course of study. Where third parties – e.g., spouses, teachers, and health care professionals – are affected by the research, informed consent needs to be obtained. Honesty should be central to the relationship between the researcher, participant and institutional representatives. If deception is necessary, the reasons should be explained to participants after the study. Special consideration is required that some participants are unable to give informed consent and are therefore less able to protect themselves.

Thus, it is a requirement that no research on human participants should cause harm, and preferably, it should benefit participants. Potential risks to participants which might arise in the course of the research should be identified. Procedures must be justified, benefits clearly stated and researchers should sensitively and appropriately handle any cultural, religious, gender or other difference in research populations at all stages.

Consideration of risks versus benefits needs to be weighed by researchers. It is recognized that while in medical research physically invasive procedures are easily defined, what constitutes risk in social and psychological research may sometimes be less clear-cut. Thus, questionnaires, observations and interviews can all be potentially intrusive and provoke anxiety in participants, or worse, and therefore involve psychological risk. There is also a requirement that participants' confidentiality and anonymity should be maintained (except if subpoenaed by a court).

Finally, researchers have a duty to disseminate their research findings to all appropriate parties. However, in Zambia and as elsewhere in African countries such as South Africa (National Research Foundation of South Africa, 2019) and globally (www.singaporestatement.org), sound ethical principles should underpin such dissemination.

There is also a recognition that the use of animals is essential to teaching and research in many instances. While there is very little, if any, psychological research involving animals in Zambia, it is accepted that without the use of animals, adequate development of science and the instruction of students in many programs such as agriculture, biological sciences, and veterinary medicine would be impossible. However, those using animals in research are morally and legally obligated to care for them properly and treat them in a humane manner. There is a requirement that where necessary, animals should be used in research only as required to obtain new information, and achieve results, which will ultimately benefit society. The term "animals" in the research context includes embryos and as such must conform to relevant statutes.

There is also recognition that issues of misconduct by psychology researchers may arise. Where such issues arise, there is a requirement that they be brought to the attention of the appropriate Research Ethics Committee for the purpose of investigating allegations of misconduct committed during the conduct of research by any researcher. In general, requirements for the conduct of those involved in psychological research would be as outlined in the code of psychology ethics and conduct by the Psychology Association of Zambia (PAZ).

Conduct in Practicing Psychology

Development of the Code of Psychology Ethics and Conduct in Zambia

Historical and Cultural Considerations

Though psychology as a field of study has had a relatively longer history of existence in Zambia compared to most sub-Saharan African countries, it is only relatively recently that there has been an increase in its recognition as a specific field of practice in government institutions as well as in the numbers of those with postgraduate degrees. Recognition of this development led to the need for the formation of the Psychology Association of Zambia (PAZ). The expansion in the practice of psychology also gave rise to a need for a regulatory framework to oversee both the practice and research activities of psychologists in Zambia. The code of ethics was thus formulated in 2014.

The code of ethics for psychology practice and research in Zambia was largely modelled after that of the British Psychological Society (2008; 2009). This was to a large extent a result of most formal institutions reflecting the historical colonial legacy of British social institutions. However, there was also a recognition of structural, cultural and social differences between the British and Zambian context, which led to some revisions and modifications of some of the elements or standards of the code of ethics for the specific Zambian context. A few notable differences between the two codes: the Zambian code discusses more in depth "Access to records and record-keeping" as good and secure record keeping is usually a concern in Zambia. This is emphasized in detail to specifically address the confidential nature of most records maintained by psychologists and hence the need not only for good record keeping for future reference but also the need to store them securely. "Supervision" is also emphasized in detail in the Zambian code. As the field of Psychology is relatively young in Zambia, supervision is an important aspect in the profession of psychologists in Zambia.

The rationale for the contents of the code of ethics and conduct was based on considerations that while the principles that underpin it may largely reflect international concerns, psychology is still developing as a professional field and also in its status in Zambia. There are currently few psychologists with specialized postgraduate qualifications in any branch of psychology. There are also few positions in government, social services or industry specifically designated for psychologists outside of the academic field. In addition, and though the psychology department at the University of Zambia is one of the oldest in sub-Saharan Africa, it is still the only one training psychologists at postgraduate level in the country. Furthermore, recognition of psychology as an applied and formal field is still not widespread (though one cannot fail to notice widespread lay "knowledge of psychology" from the general public!). For example, seeing a psychologist is not the first thing that may be considered by most people experiencing psychological or mental health problems in Zambia. It was considered, however, that there is a growing formal recognition of the field as reflected in the demands for services of the Assessment Centre, and also for postgraduate study at the University of Zambia. Some of the origins of such recognition arise from work that has been conducted on developmental disabilities and psychopathology (Nabuzoka, 1998). Thus, the range of activities and scenarios reflected in the code of ethics and conduct may not necessarily at present be in the mainstream of what psychologists do, but all represent growth areas for the services of psychologists. The code of ethics and guidelines on conduct was therefore designed to focus on areas where psychologists and related professionals either are currently occupied or are envisaged to be involved. In this case, the inclusion of areas of potential expansion of activities means that the guidelines may require periodic review in light of experiences of practitioners and their monitoring by the PAZ, and to reflect those experiences and the changing environment accordingly.

The Psychology Association of Zambia adopted the code of ethics and conduct in 2014. This is being maintained with provision for regular updates, giving more emphasis on, and support to, the process of ethical decision-making. This seeks to set and uphold the highest standards of professionalism, and to promote ethical behavior, attitudes and judgments on the part of psychologists. This entails the following:

- being mindful of the need to protect the public;
- expressing clear ethical principles, values and standards;
- promoting such standards by education and consultation; and
- developing and putting in place methods to monitor the professional behavior and attitudes of psychologists.

The Code of Ethics and Conduct was designed to guide all members of the Psychology Association of Zambia. The conduct rules for members provide guidance on the behavior expected of members of the Association. The Code and guidelines on professional practice were informed by a range of similar existing codes for psychologists internationally such as, for example, The British Psychological Society (2008; 2009).

The code and guidelines apply to all psychologists and allied professionals who are members of PAZ. The focus is on the quality of decision-making that allows sufficient flexibility for various approaches and methods, but providing ethical standards applicable to all. Psychologists and allied professionals who are members of PAZ are expected to familiarize themselves with the legal framework, regulatory requirements and other guidance relevant to the particular context in which they work, including student members and other roles undertaken by psychologists such as those of colleague, consultant, counsellor, educator, employer, expert witness, evaluator, lecturer, manager, practitioner, researcher, supervisor or therapist.

The code and guidelines related to professional practice considers consumers of services provided by psychologists as "clients." In this context this refers to any person or persons with whom a psychologist interacts on a professional basis, including an individual (such as a patient, a student, or research participant), a couple, a family group, an educational institution, or a private or public organization, including a court. A psychologist may have several clients at a time including those receiving, commissioning and evaluating the professional activity.

The PAZ intended that the code and guidelines would be used to form a basis for consideration of ethical questions, with the principles outlined being taken into account in the process of making decisions, together with the needs of the client and the individual circumstances of each case.

Emphasis was placed on considering the application of technical competence and use of professional skills and judgement in making decisions as to what constitutes ethical practice. It was also considered important to foster and maintain good professional relationships with clients and others as a primary element of good practice, and that moral principles and the codes which spell out their applications would be guidelines for thinking about decisions individuals may need to make in specific cases.

It was recognized that factors involved are variable, such as the particular circumstances, the prevailing law, the cultural context, the likely consequences and the feelings coloring the judgement. Thus, the code of ethics and conduct was designed to be largely advisory as a framework in support of professional judgement, of which consideration would be made in terms of situations in which decisions are made, the outcomes and the processes involved.

There was also recognition that ethics is related to the control of power, and that while not all clients are powerless, many are disadvantaged by lack of knowledge and certainty compared to the psychologist whose judgement they require. The guidelines on professional practice and code of conduct therefore sought to encapsulate the wisdom of the Association to support its members in their professional activities both current and those envisaged for the future, and reassure the public that it is worthy of their trust and to clarify the expectations of all.

Guidelines on Professional Conduct

The guidelines on professional practice for PAZ members focus on issues related to contracting (establishing contacts with others as consumers of, or partners in delivering, psychological services); obtaining valid consent from clients; maintaining confidentiality of information obtained relating to clients; access to records and record keeping; supervision of trainees or for CPD; and working with other professionals. The guidelines on each of these are premised on asset of guiding principles (PAZ, 2014). The guidelines on contracting emphasize the need to provide relevant and accurate information about oneself including one's capabilities or qualifications, obtaining valid consent from those participating in the psychological activity, and on proving clear definitions of the terms of engagement.

The guidelines on obtaining valid consent relate to the client's right to choose whether to participate in the activity based on the best information available. They also include specific guidelines on the process of obtaining such consent, its timing, the steps that should followed, and the nature of information that should be provided. Factors that can influence valid consent are also identified, including issues of power and control, the emotional state of the client and of the psychologist, and the nature of therapeutic interventions involved. Other considerations include when a client may not be able to make decisions, dealing with children, and conducting research in the context of another psychological activity.

On confidentiality, the guidelines emphasize the need to not disclose information obtained from clients, but also outline the limits of such confidentiality and on the handling of confidential information. Specific guidelines are also provided regarding circumstances where disclosure of information may be necessary including in relation to risk assessment, case management, public interest, abuse of children, judicial proceedings, and disclosure to employers, insurance companies and others, and disclosure after a client's death.

The guidelines on access to records and record keeping focus on the need to follow local and statutory responsibilities on retention of records, specific purposes of making and keeping records and the form in which they should be kept. There are also guidelines on shared records, working notes, assessment materials, keeping records secure, and access to the records.

Supervision, including consideration of someone's work as a trainee or for purposes of reflection as in the context of CPD, is another activity the conduct of which has specific guidelines from PAZ. The guidelines include aspects of practice or work accessible to discussion in supervision, forms of supervision, the nature of the supervisory relationship, characteristics of supervision and consultative support; roles, responsibilities and competence of supervisors, confidentiality issues, and specific guidelines on supervision of trainees.

Guidelines on working with other professionals are premised on identified benefits of collaborating with other professionals and focus on working in multi-professional teams or multi-agency contexts while maintaining professional integrity as a psychologist. Aims and objectives are outlined for working in multi-professional and multi-agency contexts; and guidelines provided regarding situations where conflicts may arise.

Significance of the Code of Ethics for Zambian Psychologists

The significance of the ethics code of conduct to psychologists and researchers in the field of Psychology within the Zambian context cannot be over-emphasized. Until the Psychology Association of Zambia drafted the Ethics code of conduct for Psychologists in Zambia, there were no guidelines available for psychologists. This meant that there were no uniform rules for professional conduct and guidelines for how ethical dilemmas or conflicts are resolved in the profession. Practitioners and researchers in the field created their individual "codes of conduct."

Ethics are an important part of the field of psychology, particularly as it relates to therapy and research. In the provision of psychological services with patients and conducting psychological research, ethical and moral issues will arise. The code of ethics and conduct for Zambia psychologists was important because:

1   The code of ethics provided a standard set of expectations and procedures to which all psychologists working in Zambia are expected to adhere. This uniformity in standards was important for researchers and practitioners.

2   This standardization also meant that practitioners and researchers in the field of Psychology are held to the same standard in terms of expectations and accountability for their conduct.

3   The ethics code provided the Association to fully enforce the mandatory "do no harm" principle by providing guidelines of what this means within the Zambian context.

4   The code of ethics helped improve the perception of the field of Psychology as a professional field governed by rules, and regulations, guidelines and expected conduct of its members.

5   The code of ethics for psychologists in Zambia was important to help build confidence in the Psychology profession. This is very important given the fear that most people in Zambia have regarding confidentiality. Generally, there is a fear of disclosure on the part of the clients because they are concerned about confidentiality. The code of ethics helps to reaffirm the mandate that psychologists have to adhere to confidentiality and other principles. It assures clients that the code of ethics can protect them should there be a breach in confidentiality.

6   Given that psychologists work with individuals from varying socio-economic backgrounds, the ethics code of conduct was important to protect clients who may be disadvantaged due to lack of knowledge in terms of what to expect from the client-therapist relationship.

7   In the event of ethical dilemma or an issue related to professional conduct of a psychologist practitioner or researcher, the code of conduct clearly outlines guidelines on professional practice for members, which can be used to solve ethical dilemmas or provide guidance on what is acceptable conduct and what is not.

Within the Zambian context, the code of ethics and conduct marked a significant development for psychologists, researchers and practitioners alike. The common set of values accorded by the code of ethics served to unify Zambian psychologists as they strive to uphold the profession and serve the community with highest possible standard of conduct.

Conclusions

The code of ethics and conduct for psychologists and related professionals and researchers is important in a country like Zambia. There are some practical implications related to the image of the profession of psychology as well as the integrity of its members. The code also represents a framework that guides the activities of its members. However, considerations also need to be made of potential influences on its efficacy in contemporary Zambian society. While the principles that underpin the code of ethics and conduct largely reflect international concerns, psychology is still developing as a professional field and also in its status in Zambia. Thus, the range of activities and scenarios reflected in the code of ethics and conduct may not necessarily at present be in the mainstream of what psychologists do. The code has been developed, however, to meet the specific needs of Zambian culture. The guidelines focus on areas where psychologists and related professionals either are currently occupied or are envisaged to be involved. In this case, the inclusion of areas of potential expansion of activities means that the guidelines may need to be reviewed periodically to reflect the changing environment. One particular challenge being addressed by PAZ is a lack of a legal mandate for the Association to implement the guidelines in the event that some members do not adhere to them. The current regulatory framework for psychologists in Zambia is under the Health Professionals Council of Zambia for practicing psychologists, and the National Health Research Ethics Board for psychology research. In both these cases, the focus is largely on Clinical Psychology, which is but only one of a range of branches of the field of psychology as a whole. Efforts are thus underway to either increase representation of psychology in these two bodies or to institutionalize regulatory bodies that specifically focus on the wide range of psychology activities.

References

British Psychological Society (2009). *Code of Ethics and Conduct*. Leicester: The British Psychological Society.

British Psychological Society (2008). *Generic Professional Practice Guidelines*. Leicester: The British Psychological Society.

Chanda-Kapata, P., Campbell, S., and Zarowsky, C. (2012). Developing a national health research system: participatory approaches to legislative, institutional and networking dimensions in Zambia. *Health Research Policy and Systems*, 10(17). www.health-policy-systems.com/content/10/1/17

Directorate of Research and Graduate Studies (2009). *The University of Zambia Research Policy and Intellectual Property Rights*. DRGS University of Zambia.

Government of the Republic of Zambia (2013). *The National Health Research Act No.2 of 2013*.

Kruger, M., Ndebele, P. & Horn, L (Eds) (2014). *Research Ethics in Africa: A Resource for Research Ethics Committees.* Sun Press.

Mwanyungwi, H. (2017). Research regulatory environment in Zambia. www.cidrz.org/wp-content/uploads/2017/11/Research-Regulatory-Environment-in-Zambia.pdf

Nabuzoka, D. (1998). Contribution of psychology to services for disabled people in Zambia, *African Social Research,* 39(40): 51–73.

National Health Research Authority (NHRA) (2019). Authority to conduct research. www.nhra.org.zm/authority-to-conduct-research

National Research Foundation of South Africa (2019). Statement on ethical research and scholarly publishing practices. NRFSA. www.nrf.ac.za/sites/default/files/documents/STATEMENT%20ON%20ETHICAL.pdf

Psychology Association of Zambia (2014). *Code of Ethics and Conduct, Including Guidelines on Professional Practice for Members.* Lusaka: PAZ

Zulu, J. M., Sandøy, I. F., Moland, K. M., Musonda, P., Munsaka, E., and Blystad, A. (2019). The challenge of community engagement and informed consent in rural Zambia: an example from a pilot study. *BMC Medical Ethics,* 20(45). https://doi.org/10.1186/s12910-019-0382-x

PART 2

Asian Countries: Indonesia and Singapore

4

THE INDONESIAN CODE OF CONDUCT

Yusti Probowati and Maria G. Adiyanti

Introduction

The need for a code of ethics in Indonesia has grown since the first students of Psychology graduated in 1959 as indicated by a joint agreement between three Psychology faculties. The preparation of the code of ethics was felt not too easy so that it took a long time to arrive at the 2010 Indonesian Psychological Code of Ethics being used today. The 2010 code of ethics much refers to that of the APA (American Psychological Association). The code of ethics has five basic principles, including respect for human rights and dignity, integrity, professionalism, justice, and benefit. The Indonesian culture which includes the culture of helping and paternalism gives color to the preparation and application of the code of ethics in Indonesia, and so do the legal system and emerging issues in Indonesian society. The current psychological code of ethics binds the members of the HIMPSI (Indonesian Psychological Association) only. Currently, changes to the 2010 Psychology Code of Ethics are being drafted to generate the 2020 Indonesian Psychological Code of Ethics. At the same time, given the changing environment and community demands and the increasing number of practicing psychology graduates, a draft bill (*Rencana Undang-undang* or RUU) on psychological practice is also being drafted at the Indonesian House of Representatives (DPR RI). The bill regulates authorities and legal sanctions for those who are not authorized to better protect psychological practices. The 2020 code of ethics bill will accordingly refer to the Psychology Practice Act.

The History of Psychology in Indonesia

The awareness of the importance of Psychology in Indonesia grew around 1952 through the Professor Inaugural Speech of Prof. Slamet Iman Santosa. The movement began at Universitas Indonesia with activities related to psychological issues and it eventually established the Faculty of Psychology. Until 1979, only four universities in Indonesia had a Faculty of Psychology. They were Universitas Indonesia in Jakarta, Padjadjaran University in Bandung, Universitas Gadjah Mada in Yogyakarta, and Maranatha University in Bandung and there was no new Psychology Faculty establishment in the following years. It was only around 1993 that several Psychology Faculties were established again at various universities, including at Airlangga University, Medan Area University, Muhammadiyah Surakarta University, Surabaya University, etc. To date around 155 Psychology Faculties have been established throughout Indonesia.

All psychology education graduates in Indonesia are associated with the Indonesian psychological professional organization named *Himpunan Psikologi Indonesia* (HIMPSI) (Indonesian Psychological Association). HIMPSI was established on July 1, 1959, under the name ISPSI (*Ikatan Sarjana Psikologi*), 14 years after the Indonesian Independence Day (August 17, 1945). The first ISPSI Congress was held in 1979 in Yogyakarta. The 1998 Extraordinary Congress of ISPSI held in Jakarta decided to change the name from *Ikatan Sarjana Psikologi Indonesia* (ISPSIIndonesia) to *Himpunan Psikologi Indonesia* (HIMPSI). There are currently 34 regional HIMPSIs in Indonesia with 9,571 members (as of September 1 2020).

Psychology in Indonesia was initially part of medical science and only concerned with psychological testing. Psychological services have since developed rapidly and have become a necessity for people in various sectors including education, social, forensic, industry and organization, and sports. The psychological code of ethics was initiated in 1959 when psychology produced its first graduates. Since then, the ethics code it has continued to be evaluated, and any changes made to it must be legalized in the ISPSI or HIMPSI Congress.

The Need for and Development of the Indonesian Psychology Code of Ethics Over Time

When Indonesia had its first bachelor of psychology, the need for regulations for the graduates in providing psychological services was realized, with the following process. In 1959, when the first undergraduate student of Psychology graduated, the regulations regarding the practice of psychology were based on the agreement of three universities that had bachelor's degree programs in Psychology, namely Universitas Indonesia, Padjadjaran University, and Universitas Gadjah Mada. This was in effect until 1979.

In 1979, the 1st Association of Bachelor of Psychology (Ikatan Sarjana Psikologi shortened to ISPSI) Congress was held with one of its agendas being a discussion of the regulations of psychological practices. The regulations were revised and refined at every three-yearly ISPSI congress.

In 1991, a psychology code of ethics was drafted under the name *Kode Etik Sarjana Psikologi* (Code of Ethics of Psychological Graduates). This code of ethics was enacted at the ISPSI's 5th congress in Semarang on December 6, 1991. The term "Sarjana" (psychological graduate) in the code of ethics title refers to graduates of the Faculty of Psychology with an educational period of five to six years.

This code of ethics consists of seven chapters and 27 articles with preamble and closing chapters. The contents were very simple and arranged according to the needs of the time. The Code of Ethics was formally presented in writing in a book containing Statutes, Bylaws of ISPSI, and *Kode Etik Sarjana Psikologi*.

In its implementation, the code of ethics is reinforced and enforced by the Minister of Manpower Regulation Number PER-01/MEN/1993, concerning the licensing of psychological practice. The Article 7 of this Regulation states explicitly that violations to the psychological code of ethics will be subject to administrative sanctions and it is stated in the Article 8 that "psychological scholars who violate Article 2 Paragraph 1" (psychology graduates who practice psychology must have psychological practice license from the Minister of Manpower, the head the Regional Office of the Department of Manpower or the nearest location) are subject to criminal sanctions under Article 17 of Law No. 14 of 1969.

In 1998, at the HIMPSI Extraordinary Congress held on April 26, 1998, an updated code of ethics was passed under the name of *Kode Etik Psikologi* (Psychological Code of Ethics). The revised Psychological Code of Ethics contains a Preamble, seven chapters, 18 articles, and a closing article. In this code of ethics, differentiations are made between Psychological Scientists and Psychologists and between Psychological Practices and Psychological Services. This is in line with changes in the direction of higher education in Indonesia (Minister of Education Decree no. 18/D/0/1993), which includes academic education (to produce psychological scientists) and professional education (to produce psychologists), with the latter requiring a bachelor's and master's practice license.

In 2000, at the VIII HIMPSI congress on October 22, 2000 in Bandung, the revised Code of Ethics was legalized. In early 2000, the code of ethics, including the Preamble, 7 chapters, and 19 articles, and the Closing chapter was revised. The revision was made due to the increasing number of psychological graduates practicing psychology and at the same time increasing public awareness about the use of psychological services.

In 2004, at the IX HIMPSI Congress in Surabaya, a review and evaluation of the 2000 Code of Ethics were conducted and resulted in some revisions. However, due to administrative errors, the revisions could not be implemented in a structured script. Thus, what then applies was the 2000 code of ethics, which is accompanied by elucidations that cannot be separated from the code of ethics. This code of ethics (which is later referred to as the 2003 Code of Ethics) contained eight chapters and 19 articles accompanied by elucidations and is published in a small book that also contains HIMPSI's Statutes and Bylaws.

In 2007, the HIMPSI's 10th congress decided to revise the code of ethics, for which HIMPSI formed a code of ethics revision team. Some revisions were made because the 2003 Code of Ethics was no longer able to regulate the fast-increasing psychological practices and the growing demands of psychological services with emerging ethical issues. In the drafting process, the team held discussions and received suggestions from regional HIMPSIs with many members practicing psychology. The team worked for three years and came up with some important points of change. The revised results were presented at the subsequent HIMPSI Congress in 2010.

This 2010 revised code of ethics draft used the 2002 APA code of conduct as a reference and several other references. The team also included regional HIMPSI members in making reviews and revisions to the draft code of ethics to make it aligned with the psychological practice condition in Indonesia. This draft code of ethics was later referred to as *Kode Etik 2010* (2010 Code of Ethics).

In 2010, at the 11th HIMPSI Congress in Solo, one of the decisions was to ratify the 2010 Psychological Code of Ethics. This Psychological Code of Ethics contains a preamble, 16 chapters, 80 articles, and a closing chapter.

The 2003 Indonesian Psychological Code of Ethics	*The 2010 Indonesian Psychological Code of Ethics*
PREAMBLE	PREAMBLE
• Based on the 1945 Constitution and Pancasila as the national ideology.	• Based on the 1945 Constitution and Pancasila as the national ideology.
• Distinguishing Indonesian psychological scientists from psychologists while both must always strive for human welfare in every work they do.	• Distinguishing psychologists from psychological scientists while both always value and respect human dignity and uphold the preservation of human rights for the welfare of mankind.
• The demand for freedom of inquiry and communication in carrying out activities in the fields of research, teaching, consulting services/practices, and publications should be understood with full responsibility by psychological scientists and psychologists.	• The demand for freedom of investigating and communicating the results of activities in the fields of research, teaching, training, and psychological services including the consultation results and publications should be understood with full responsibility by psychologists and psychological scientists
• Competence and objectivity in applying professional abilities are bound to and highly considerate of service users, colleagues, and the community at large.	• Competence and objectivity in applying professional abilities in psycholoty are closely bound to and considerate of service users, colleagues, and the community at large
CHAPTER I **GENERAL GUIDELINES**	**CHAPTER I** **GENERAL GUIDELINES**
Article 1 Definition	Article 1 Definition
1 PSYCHOLOGICAL SCIENTIST 2 PSYCHOLOGIST 3 PSYCHOLOGICAL SERVICE 4 PSYCHOLOGICAL PRACTICE 5 PSYCHOLOGICAL SERVICE USER	1 PSYCHOLOGICAL CODE OF ETHICS 2 PSYCHOLOGY 3 PSYCHOLOGIST 4 PSYCHOLOGICAL SCIENTIST 5 PSYCHOLOGICAL SERVICE
Article 2 Responsibilities	Article 2 General Principles Principle A: Respect for Human Dignity Principle B: Integrity and Scientific Attitude Principle C: Professionalism Principle D: Justice

(*Continued*)

(Continued)

Article 71 General Guidelines
Article 72 Qualifications of Counselor and Psychotherapist
Article 73 Informed Consent in Counseling and Psychotherapy
Article 74 Psychological Counseling/Therapy Involving Spouse or Family Members
Article 75 Group Counseling and Group Therapy
Article 76 Providing Psychological Counseling/Psychotherapy to Those Who Have Previously Undergone Psychological Counseling/Psychotherapy
Article 77 Providing Psychological Counseling/Psychotherapy to Those Who Have Been Involved in Extramarital Sexual Intimacy
Article 78 Post-Counseling Debriefing
Article 79 Temporary Termination of Psychological Counseling/Psychotherapy
Article 80 Termination of Psychological Counseling/Psychotherapy

CHAPTER VII
CLOSING CHAPTER

Source: Pengantar psikologi klinis [The introduction to clinical psychology]. (Revised Ed.) by Prof. Dr. SUTARDJO A. WIRAMIHARDJA, Psi. (pp. 199 – 208).

CLOSING CHAPTER

References

American Psychological Association. (1994). *Ethical principles of psychologists and code of conduct.* Washington, DC: American Psychological Association.

Canter, M. B., Bennett, B. E., Jones, S. E., & Nagy, I. F. (1999). *Ethics for psychologists.* Washington, DC: American Psychological Association.

Delucia-Waack, L. J. (2006). *Leading psychoeducational groups for children and adolescence.* London: Sage Publication.

Himpunan Psikologi Indonesia. (2008). *Kode etik psikologi Indonesia* [The Indonesian psychological code of ethics].

Thomson, C., Linda, L. B., and Henderson, D. (2004). *Counseling children.* Belmont: Brooks Cole Thomson Learning

The Indonesian Psychological Code of Ethics Implementation Guidelines is attached to the Indonesian Psychological Code of Ethics

From November 2019 to the present (September, 2020), HIMPSI has been preparing a revision to the 2010 Indonesian Psychological Code of Ethics. The draft amendment to the 2010 Psychology Code of Ethics is planned to be completed and ratified as the Indonesian Psychological Code of Ethics in 2022 at the 2022

HIMPSI Congress in Medan. As additional information, HIMPSI has submitted a draft Psychology Practice Bill, the aim of which is to better protect psychologists and their service users. Consequently, the Indonesian Psychological Code of Ethics which will be ratified in 2022 will have to refer to the by then already enacted Psychological Practice Law.

The Indonesian Psychological Codes of Ethics Model the Codes of Ethics of Other Countries

The Indonesian Psychological Code of Ethics contains universal values related to human rights. Therefore, the contents of the Code of Ethics do not conflict with the Code of Ethics of Psychological Organizations in other countries. There are five basic principles of the code of ethics: Respect for human rights and dignity, Integrity, Professionalism, Justice, and Benefits.

The original Indonesian psychological code of ethics formulated by HIMPSI in 2003 with *Buku Pengantar Psikologi Klinis* [The Introduction to Clinical Psychology] by Prof. Dr. Sutardjo A. Wiramihardja, Psi. (pp. 199–208) cites the European code of ethics as a reference.

In contrast, the 2010 psychological code of ethics that aimed to revise the 2003 code refers to the APA code of ethics. The references included the APA's (1992) *Ethical principles of psychologists and code of conduct*, Canter et al.'s (1999) *Ethics for psychologists,* as well as the 2003 original Indonesian code of ethics, among others (Thompson et al., 2004).

For the most part, the 2010 Code of Ethics refers to that of the APA, but there are some differences between the APA Code of Ethics and the 2010 HIMPSI Code of Ethics as shown in the following table.

APA	*HIMPSI*
SETTLEMENT OF ISSUES Regulating how to resolve ethical issues through informal and formal channels.	**SETTLEMENT OF ETHICAL ISSUES** Regulating the authority duties of the HIMPSI assembly, types of violation, and the actions to be taken by HIMPSI members in case they are not satisfied with decisions, and regulating the actions to be taken by the authorities in case of violations.
HUMAN RELATIONSHIP Addressing discriminations, sexual harassment.	**HUMAN RELATIONSHIP** Addressing professionalism, exploitation
PRIVACY There are articles concerning consultation, procedures for data collection through audio and visual recording that must be agreed in advance with informed consent.	**CONFIDENTIALITY OF PSYCHO-LOGICAL EXAMINATION RECORDS AND RESULTS** Explaining data confidentiality in more detail including the data user position and responsibility

(Continued)

ADVERTISEMENT AND OTHER PUBLIC STATEMENT

There is an article that states that psychologists do not have the right to ask their clients to give testimony about the psychologist while they are still undergoing therapy with them.

Regulating solicitation for personal collaboration in business dealings between the psychologist and their client.

ADVERTISEMENT AND PUBLIC STATEMENT

There is a regulation that prohibits over self-advertising

PSYCHOLOGICAL SERVICE FEE

The psychological service fee is set by law. It is necessary to provide an early explanation of possible limited services due to financial constraints on the part of the client.

PSYCHOLOGICAL SERVICE FEE

Emphasizing the psychologists' competence and professionalism as the basis of their service fee; addressing pro-bono services that can be provided by psychologists.

EDUCATION AND TRAINING:

- Psychologists are responsible to ensure the appropriateness of program designs
- Participants must not be forced for any reason.
- Prohibition of duplicating publications.
- Addressing plagiarism.

EDUCATION AND/OR TRAINING:

- Designing programs based on theories and scientific evidence to make them understandable.
- Reporting results according to the set standards.
- There is an informed consent requirement in education and/or training
- Setting authority and responsibility limits to protect rights and well-being.

ASSESSMENT

- Assessments should be carried out according to individual language preference
- When a translator is used, the client's approval must be obtained

ASSESSMENT

- Explaining about administration and categorization of psychological tests which include categories A, B, C, and D.
- Mentioning the 2-year limit of test results validity.

INTERVENTION

Explaining the definition and forms

INTERVENTION

- Explaining the bases of interventions which include individual, group, community. and organizational interventions
- Explaining different intervention methods including psychoeducation, counseling, and therapy
- Explaining about debriefing and negative impacts prevention to clients
- Regulating temporary termination of counseling/psychotherapy and referrals

Not available	**FORENSIC PSYCHOLOGY**
	• Law and commitment to the Code of Ethics
	• Competence
	• Responsibilities, authorities, and rights
	• Statements given in the position of witness or expert witness
	• The multiple and professional roles of psychologists and psychological scientists.
	• Forensic psychology-related statements on the media
Addressing psychologists only	Addressing both psychologists and psychological scientists.

How our Country's National Culture and History Influenced the Formulation of the Psychological Code of Ethics in Indonesia

The Indonesian Psychological Code of Ethics is influenced by the noble values contained in Pancasila and the 1945 Constitution. At the same time, the Indonesian society, which is paternalistic in nature, also affects the organizational structure of HIMPSI which consists of *Majelis* (the Assembly) and *Manajemen* (the Management) in which the Assembly serves as a role model and has the authority to resolve ethical issues.

The helpful character of Indonesian people is also reflected in the psychological services. The code of ethics discussion concerning psychological services in Indonesia thus includes pro-bono services, providing services for free. However, cases of exploitation still happen quite frequently in Indonesia. This is reflected in Chapter III concerning Human Relations in which exploitation is explicitly mentioned in the Indonesian Code of Ethics to prevent exploitation cases from happening in psychological services.

Forensic Psychology (Chapter X) which does not exist in the APA code of ethics is deemed necessary to be explicitly regulated in the Indonesian psychological code of ethics considering that Indonesia has not had regulations regarding forensic psychology. The things that are regulated in the code of ethics include the role of forensic psychology for which psychologists/psychological scientists should not only have competency in forensic psychology but also be aware of the laws that apply in Indonesia, especially the criminal law. The articles related to forensic psychology cases are adjusted to the development of cases in Indonesia, for example, disputes between psychologists and disputes between psychologists and other experts.

The Meaning of the Psychological Code of Ethics for HIMPSI Members and Society

The HIMPSI code of ethics concerns HIMPSI members and it thus has impacts on the services provided to the community in that they become more ethical.

The psychological code of ethics is a written provision that guides psychologists' and psychology scientists' behaviors and conducts in carrying out their profession. Therefore, the Indonesian Psychological Code of Ethics serves as a self-regulation standard for psychologists and psychology scientists in providing services to the community. For example, psychologists must take their clients' rights into account in providing therapeutic services and psychological scientists must take their research participants' rights into account in doing their research.

The implementation of the Indonesian psychological code of ethics is a reinforcement of the authority of psychology in framing competency boundaries to emphasize its competence and show that the science and practice of psychology are different from other professions that intersect. This will also be clear in collaborations and discussions of issues from different perspectives. The code of ethics applies to all practicing psychologists and psychological scientists, especially those who are members of HIMPSI, in particular if the practicing psychologist or psychological scientists relate with service users/clients, either individual or group, research participants, and other professionals.

In the implementation of the code, especially for psychological practices, awareness of psychological services is expected from clients and the wider society so that in case of arising issues related to psychological ethics, they can report them to PP HIMPSI (HIMPSI National Board) **or** HIMPSI Wilayah (regional HIMPSIs). The report would be forwarded to the Assembly either at the regional or national level and then be discussed in the Assembly session. If more information was required, the defendant would most likely be invited to give confirmation. The defendant is also allowed to defend themselves. Whether or not the alleged violation against the code of ethics has happened and the types of violations are decided upon when the problem has been clarified. It is also possible that the defendant could be found not to have violated the Indonesian psychological code of ethics.

HIMPSI is currently submitting a Psychology Practice Bill to the House of representatives. This law regulates psychological practice in Indonesia, including the limits of authority in practicing psychology and the legal consequences for those who are not authorized. This law also regulates not only psychology personnel but also the society, especially those related to psychological practices. The HIMPSI's Psychological Code of Ethics will follow the Psychology Practice Law if and when it has been enacted by the House of Representatives of the Republic of Indonesia (DPR-RI).

Conclusion

The journey of developing and applying the Indonesian psychological code of ethics has taken a long pathway. At the same time when the first students of Psychology graduated, the awareness of the need for a psychological code of practice began to emerge, although it was limited to the agreement on the rules of practice between three universities that had produced psychological graduates. Since then, during approximately 65 years, the number of universities that offer psychological programs in Indonesia has been dramatically increasing, from only one university in 1959 to more than 150 universities in 2020, and so has the body of psychological graduates. The practice of psychology is expanding as well.

Given these conditions, HIMPSI (Indonesian Psychological Association) is aware of the importance of protecting both the practicing psychologists and the clients who come from various parts of Indonesia with different cultures, customs, and habits. HIMPSI (as the only professional organization of psychology in Indonesia) has revised the Indonesian psychological code of ethics several times based on an awareness of the peculiarities of Indonesia's condition, the diversity of cultures in Indonesia, the expanding psychological practice, and changes happening globally, making this code of conduct need to be updated from time to time. Besides, the psychological practice in Indonesia is guarded and monitored by HIMPSI. To strengthen the foundation of psychological practice in Indonesia, it is expected that the psychological practice bill will be passed in the near future.

References

American Psychological Association (1992). *Ethical principles of psychologists and code of conduct.* Washington, DC: American Psychological Association.

Canter, M. B., Bennett, B. E., Jones, S. E. & Nagy, T. F. (1999). *Ethics for psychologists.* Washington, DC: American Psychological Association,

Himpunan Psikologi Indonesia (1998). *Kode Etik Psikologi 1998* [The 1998 Code of Ethics].

Himpunan Psikologi Indonesia (2003). *Kode Etik Psikologi Indonesia* [The Indonesian Code of Ethics].

Himpunan Psikologi Indonesia (2010). *Kode Etik Psikologi 2010* [The 2010 Code of Ethics].

Ikatan Sarjana Psikologi Indonesia (ISPSI) (1991). *Kode Etik Sarjana Psikologi Indonesia* [The Indonesian Psychological Graduates' Code of Ethics].

Peraturan Menteri Tenaga Kerja Nomor: Per-01/MEN/1993 tentang Izin Prakik bagi Sarjana Psikologi [The Minister of Manpower Regulation No. Per-01/MEN/1993 on Practice License for Psychological Graduates].

Thomson, C.Linda, L. N., & Henderson, D. (2004). *Counseling children.* Belmont: BrooksCole Thomson Learning.

Keputusan Menteri Tenaga Kerja Nomor KEP-308/MEN/1993 tentang Petunjuk Pelaksanaan Izin Praktik bagi Sarjana Psikologi [The Minister of Manpower Regulation No. KEP-308/MEN/1993 on The Guidelines of Practice Licensing for Psychological Graduates]

Wiramihardja, S. A. (2006). *Pengantar psikologi klinis* [The introduction to clinical psychology] (Revised Ed.), pp. 199–208. Bandung: PT Refika Aditama.

5

THE SINGAPORE PSYCHOLOGICAL SOCIETY CODE OF ETHICS

The Beginning, the Current, and the Future

Lohsnah Jeevanandam and Adrian Toh

Introduction

Two cardinal characteristics make a profession: the first is a basic body of abstract knowledge that gives recognition of an exclusive competence to practice; the other is an ideal of service, which includes the code of ethics (Francis, 2009). The code of ethics and professional conduct guide towards high professional standards and set standards of behaviours for psychologists with respect to clients, colleagues and the public in general. Various psychological societies and associations have a governing code of ethics and so does the Singapore Psychological Society. Though somewhat distinct, there is substantial congruence between their ethical principles and respective standards, some of which includes confidentiality, competence and client's welfare. This chapter will shed light on the practice of psychology in Singapore, the unique development of the code of ethics, the challenges and advancements in setting high professional standards, and future directions.

Psychology in Singapore

Psychology, as an academic discipline and profession in Singapore, started to advance with the psychology programme offered to undergraduates at the National University of Singapore in 1986 (Tan, 2002). As a developing profession in the young nation, psychology has been growing progressively in the different specialisations to meet the increasing needs of the nation. With the increasing number of practising psychologists, there is also an increasing need for regulation of the profession to protect the consumers of psychological services. However, despite continuous attempts to lobby local authorities for assistance in regulating the psychology profession in the last two decades, the absence of a national regulatory system for the psychology profession remains. Consequently, the absence of it impedes and limits the enforcement of the ethical guidelines, with looming threats of unethical practices harming the consumers and the profession.

In the absence of a national regulatory system to practice psychology, the Singapore Register of Psychologists (SRP), a voluntary-regulatory system was proposed by Dr Thomas Lee Hock Seng and was established in 2001. The SRP primary aims are to protect the welfare of the consumers of psychological services, and to maintain and advance the professional standards of the psychological service providers. However, the SRP is a voluntary-regulatory system, and not all practising psychologists in Singapore are registered. As of September 2020, there were 504 psychologists registered with the SRP. This would mean that the ethical guidelines set forth by the Singapore Psychological Society (SPS) may not be adhered to by all practicing psychologists, and the guidelines can potentially fall short in protecting the public.

Code of Ethics: 1st Edition

The Society's first "Code of Professional Ethics" was published in the year 2000, 21 years after the society was founded. The document was built upon 19 specific principles, as described below:

1 Responsibility – the psychologist is committed to increasing the understanding of human behaviour and experience, places high value on objectivity and integrity, and maintains the highest standards in the services that are offered.

2 Competence – the maintenance of high standards of professional competence is a responsibility shared by all psychologists, in the interest of the public and of the profession as a whole.

3 Moral and Legal Standards – the psychologist in professional practice shows sensible regard for the social code and moral expectations of the host community. It should be recognized that the psychologist's violations of accepted moral and legal standards may involve associated clients, students, or colleagues in damaging personal conflicts, and impugn the psychologist's name and the reputation of the profession.

4 Mispresentation – the psychologist avoids mispresentation of professional qualifications, affiliations, and purposes, and those of the institutions, and organisations with which the psychologist is associated.

5 Public Statements – psychologists who supply information to the public either directly or indirectly are expected to show due regard for the limits

of present knowledge and exercise modesty and scientific caution in all such statements.

6   Confidentiality – safeguarding information about an individual that has been obtained by the psychologist in the course of teaching, practice, or investigation is a primary obligation of the psychologist. Such information is not communicated to others unless certain important conditions are met.

7   Client Welfare – the psychologist respects the integrity and protects the welfare of the person or group with whom work is undertaken.

8   Client's Relationship – the psychologist informs a prospective client of the important aspect of the potential relationship that might affect the client's decision to enter the relationship.

9   Impersonal Services – psychological services for the purpose of diagnosis, treatment, or personalized advice are provided only in the context of a professional relationship, and are not given by means of public lectures or demonstration, newspaper, or magazine articles, radio or television programmes, mail, or similar media.

10 Announcement of Services – a psychologist adheres to professional rather than commercial standards in making known the availability of professional services.

11 Interpersonal Relations – a psychologist acts with integrity with regard to colleagues in psychology and in other professions.

12 Remuneration – financial arrangements in professional practice are in accord with professional standards that safeguard the best interest of the client and the profession.

13 Test Security – psychological tests and other assessment devices, the value of which depends in part on the naivete of the subject, are not reproduced or described in popular publications in ways that might invalidate the techniques. Access to such devices is limited to persons with professional interests who will safeguard their use.

14 Test Interpretation – test scores, like test materials, are released only to persons who are qualified to interpret and use them properly.

15 Test Publication – psychological tests are offered for commercial publication only to publishers who present their tests in a professional way and distribute them only to qualified users.

16 Research Precautions – the psychologists assume obligations for the welfare of their research subjects, both animal and human.

17 Publication Credit – credit is assigned to those who have contributed to a publication, in proportion to their contributions, and only to these.

18 Responsibility towards Organisation – a psychologist respects the rights and reputation of the institute or organization with which there is an association.

19 Promotional Activities – the psychologist associated with the development or promotion of psychological devices, books, or products offered for commercial sale is responsible for ensuring that such devices, books, or products are presented in a professional and factual way.

Code of Ethics: 2nd Edition

Ethics is constantly evolving due to the changes and developments of the biology, human behaviours, culture, social rules, as well as psychological research and practice. Given that the first code had been in existence for more than a decade and that the landscape of the psychological profession had also advanced in that time, it became imperative that there was a need to revise the current code.

The Society appointed Dr Lohsnah Jeevanandam to lead the revision of the code of ethics, together with Mr Adrian Toh, Dr Anne-Marie Lew, Mr Kirby Chua and Dr Nina Powell, as members of the main committee. The first meeting was held in November 2015. The revised code took three years to be completed, and included two rounds of soliciting feedback from the SPS members. The revised code was formally launched at the SPS 40th Year anniversary on 30 March, 2019.

The Working Committee

The working committee had the privilege of working and consulting with representation from the government ministries, community organizations, healthcare and educational institutions, as well as the private practice on the revision of the code of ethics. The valuable inputs from these representations provided contextualized considerations to the revision. The representations included:

- Community Psychology Hub
- Clinical Imaging Research Centre/A*STAR
- Grace Counselling Centre
- Ministry of Defence
- Ministry of Education
- Ministry of Social and Family Development
- National Healthcare Group Polyclinics
- National University of Singapore
- Singapore University of Social Sciences

Additionally, the working committee had the privilege of working with Prof Catherine So-Kum Tang from the National University of Singapore and Mr Lim Tanguy from the Law Society Pro Bono Services who provided clinical research and legal perspectives, respectively.

Terms of Reference

The following codes were examined for frame of reference in developing the revised code:

- American Psychological Association: Ethical Principles of Psychologists and Code of Conduct, 2017.
- Australian Psychological Society: Code of Ethics, 2007.
- Birds and Animals Act, 2002.
- British Psychological Society: Code of Human Research Ethics, 2014; Code of Ethics and Conduct, 2018.
- Chinese Psychological Society Code of Ethics for Counselling and Clinical Practice, 2007
- Convention on the Rights of Persons with Disabilities, 2007.
- Hong Kong Psychological Society Code of Professional Conduct, 2012.
- Human Biomedical Research Act, 2015.
- Professional Practice Guidelines: Psycho-educational assessment & placement of students with special educational needs, 2018.
- Singapore Association for Counselling Code of Ethics, 2018.
- Singapore Personal Data Protection Act, 2012.
- Singapore Psychological Society Code of Ethics (Previous), 2000.
- The Ethics Guidelines for Human Biomedical Research, Bioethics Advisory Committee (BAC), 2015.

Aims of Revised Code

After extensive deliberation, the aims for the revised code were as follows:

1   Hold the psychology profession in Singapore to high levels of conduct and accountability.
    Rationale: The primary impetus for a code is to ensure that ethical practises are clearly spelt out, which can then translate into accordingly high-quality care and service.
2   Relevant for psychologists in the private and public sectors in Singapore.
    Rationale: The current code appeared to be more suited for psychologists in the public sector and hence it was vital that the revised code would be encompassing, and not distinguish psychologists based on their setting.
3   Representative of the various sub-disciplines within psychology.
    Rationale: The committee was driven to ensure that the revised code would be generic enough to be relevant to all sub-disciplines of psychology so that the identity of the psychologist becomes more unified.
4   As representative as possible of the ethical practises of organizations where psychologists practice in Singapore.
    Rationale: Given that many organizations have their own standards of protocol on ethical practise, it was essential that the code also augmented general recommendations so that it would be highly relevant.

5   Multiculturally sensitive

Rationale: Other than Singapore being a multiculturally diverse community, psychologists from other parts of the world also practise in Singapore. In addition, psychologists trained in Singapore also practise in other parts of the world. Together, these reasons gave new impetus to develop a code that would embrace diversity in its entirety and one that would be relevant to any psychologist from any part of the world.

General Principles

When narrowing down the significance of ethical psychology practice, the common themes that arose from the working committee discussion were Respect, Integrity and Beneficence, which are laid forth as the general principles

Respect

It is the responsibility of psychologists to accord respect onto everyone they professionally work with. This refers to being respectful of multicultural differences, such as, gender, race, religion, socioeconomic status, disability status, country of origin, language fluency, sexual orientation, marital or family situation, etc. It is considered discriminatory practice if psychologists deny a client service because of these diversities. Rather, psychologists are encouraged to recognise that while they are entitled to their own values and attitudes in their own personal lives, it is imperative to be as objective as possible when working with clients. Respect also refers to not imposing one's values onto the client.

Integrity

It is first important that psychologists are true to themselves. This refers to being reflective of how one feels and thinks about a certain client or process. Integrity also refers to being honest with all stakeholders that one works with. This genuineness is extremely critical for the establishment of trust between the psychologist and the client. It is also the responsibility of psychologists to practise within their areas of competence.

Beneficence

Psychologists always strive to do good for their clients. Sometimes the concept of 'good' is so broad that it may not always be clear whether certain decisions are inherently good. Psychologists need to be cognizant that decisions are made not on whether the client likes or dislikes their decisions, but rather whether the decisions have potential for positive impact for the client in the short and long-term.

Guidelines

The structure of the guidelines was considered from the various codes examined and the application of psychology in Singapore.

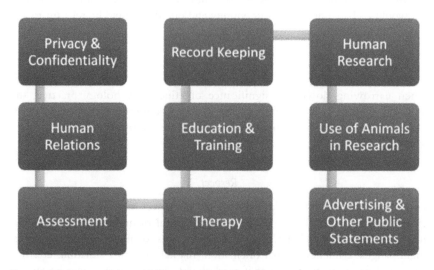

Figure 5.1 Structure of the guidelines examined: Singapore

Besides the updated ethical practices (e.g., on the use of deception in research), some of the unique additions to the revised code include having ethical consideration for use of social media and technology. This inclusion is timely as video communication for psychological services was widely used during the COVID-19 pandemic, in the year 2020. The video communication was especially helpful to overcome the limitation of the lockdown measures (such as limited face-to-face psychology services, trainings, etc.) and to ensure the safety of the psychologists and the clients (e.g., when working with COVID-19 positive clients). The ethical guidelines provided psychologists (especially those who are previously less familiar with the use of video communication) a reference to ethical consideration when carrying out video communication.

Ethical-Decision Making Model

In addition to the updated and contextualized code of ethics, the committee decided to improve ethical standards by including an ethical-decision making model in the code of ethics document.

We can all understand that decision-making to address an ethical dilemma is never an easy process. The dilemma is a conflict for which "no course of action seems satisfactory" and it "exists because there are good, but contradictory ethical reasons to take conflicting and incompatible course of actions" (Kitchener, 1984, p. 43). In resolving ethical dilemmas, there is no "right" decision, only a decision that is thoughtfully made and perhaps "more right" than alternatives (Hill, Glaser, & Harden, 1995).

Thus, when faced with an ethical dilemma, psychologists require more than the code of ethics for guidance to arrive at a decision that is "more right." A comprehensive decision-making process can facilitate a sound ethical decision when addressing an ethical dilemma. An ethical decision-making model examines the "internal processes" in an ethical dilemma, which include intentions, motivation, and ways of cognitively structuring the ethically sensitive situation (Welfel & Lipsitz, 1984).

Toh (2017) examined the factors that local practising psychologists consider in the ethical decision-making processes so as to formulate a model for application (Figure 5.2). The Ethical Decision-Making Model is embedded in the SPS Code of Ethics (July 2019). The reader may refer to the document to gain better understanding of its application.

Briefly, through qualitative interviews, the elicited participants' ethical decision-making process demonstrated that several factors that were employed were similar to those found in the existing ethical decision-making models, thus, providing ecological validity to the factors found in the existing models. Some of these factors include identifying situation, defining dilemma, reviewing legal and ethical guidelines, consulting colleagues, etc.

Interestingly, participants also considered factors, such as considering the therapeutic relationship with the client, discussing the ethical dilemma with the client and with other professionals, reviewing organisation guidelines, and considering of the impact of the decision on the community of psychologists at large. These newly emerged factors reflect one of the Asian values, the collectivist perspective, which focuses on social obligations and relations. Similar to other studies, Khairullah and Khairullah (2013) explained that the Chinese, in their process of decision making, reflect the Chinese cultural values deeply rooted in the Confucian philosophy. It emphasises the importance of social obligations and relations based on harmony, cooperation, loyalty, reciprocity, "guanxi", patience, avoidance of risks, and each individual being conscious of his/her position in the society. As described by the founding father of Singapore, Mr Lee Kuan Yew (1990), such Asian value "places the interests of the community over and above that of the individual." Therefore, it is not surprising that the influence of values is evident in the elements of ethical decision-making process. The inclusion of these newly emerged factors provides valuable implications for the psychologists in the decision-making process.

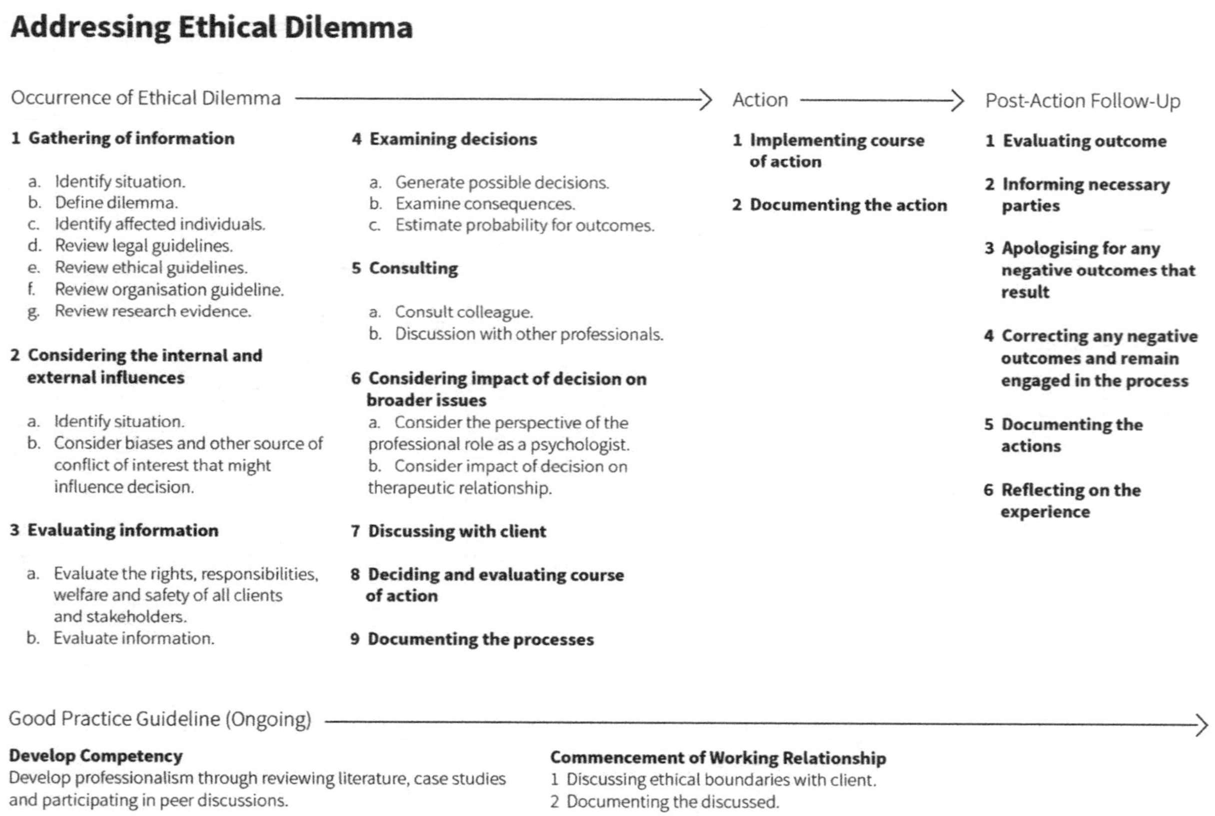

Addressing Ethical Dilemma

Occurrence of Ethical Dilemma ⟶ Action ⟶ Post-Action Follow-Up

1 Gathering of information

a. Identify situation.
b. Define dilemma.
c. Identify affected individuals.
d. Review legal guidelines.
e. Review ethical guidelines.
f. Review organisation guideline.
g. Review research evidence.

2 Considering the internal and external influences

a. Identify situation.
b. Consider biases and other source of conflict of interest that might influence decision.

3 Evaluating information

a. Evaluate the rights, responsibilities, welfare and safety of all clients and stakeholders.
b. Evaluate information.

4 Examining decisions

a. Generate possible decisions.
b. Examine consequences.
c. Estimate probability for outcomes.

5 Consulting

a. Consult colleague.
b. Discussion with other professionals.

6 Considering impact of decision on broader issues

a. Consider the perspective of the professional role as a psychologist.
b. Consider impact of decision on therapeutic relationship.

7 Discussing with client

8 Deciding and evaluating course of action

9 Documenting the processes

1 Implementing course of action

2 Documenting the action

1 Evaluating outcome

2 Informing necessary parties

3 Apologising for any negative outcomes that result

4 Correcting any negative outcomes and remain engaged in the process

5 Documenting the actions

6 Reflecting on the experience

Good Practice Guideline (Ongoing)

Develop Competency
Develop professionalism through reviewing literature, case studies and participating in peer discussions.

Commencement of Working Relationship
1 Discussing ethical boundaries with client.
2 Documenting the discussed.

Figure 5.2 Singapore psychology ethical decision-making model

Furthermore, through qualitative interviews (Toh, 2017), personal and organisational factors that facilitate the decision-making processes were identified.

Personal Factors:

- Openness: To be willing to share concerns with various stakeholders
- Perspective-Taking: To be able to understand the position of various stakeholders
- Protecting Interest of Client: To consciously consider the best interest of the client
- Integrity: To be honest
- Reflective: To be thoughtful about processes
- Analytical: To reason well
- Positive Regards: To accept and support the client
- Non-Judgmental: To refrain from criticising client
- Knowing Boundaries: To be aware of one's limits
- Professionalism: To be competent
- Seek Feedback: To be willing to receive comments and suggestions of others
- Knowing Code of Ethics: To be aware of the current code of ethics
- Self-Care: To ensure that one's health does not affect performance or conduct

Organisational Factors:

- Providing support through peer discussions, supervision, networking and relevant trainings
- Having organisation leaders value code of ethics in psychologist's professional practice
- Having Standard Operating Procedures, a set of step-by-step instructions, to help psychologists carry out routine procedures in the decision-making processes.

Disciplinary Advisory Committee

There was an increased awareness of ethical practice following the launch of the revised code of ethics in 2019, which led to increased complaints received. These complaints related to issues pertaining to professional misconduct, romantic and sexual relationship between psychologist and client, informed consent and discrimination.

The rising concern led to the formation of a Disciplinary Advisory Committee in 2020. The committee led by the Vice-President of the Singapore Psychological Society (SPS), is comprised of individuals with varying experiences that can be helpful in the discussion of ethical concerns. This included a university lecturer in ethics, a lawyer, an executive committee member of the Singapore Association for Counselling (SAC), a psychologist in the government service, the President of the SPS, and the Chairperson of the SRP.

This committee has been handling complaints, conducting informal investigations and providing closure for complainant and complainee. The common ethical issues raised were similar to the findings by Toh (2017) who explored the common ethical issues that the psychologists faced through qualitative interviews. The areas of concerns regarding ethical matters surfaced were

1   confidentiality,
2   competency,
3   conflict of interest,
4   data manipulation,
5   informed consent and
6   multiple relationships.

The Future

The following are some considerations for future revisions of the SPS Code, but are also generic enough to be relevant to other country psychological associations.

Tele-psychology

With significant technological advances and the burgeoning of tele-psychology, it is imperative that future revisions of the SPS code consider detailed discussions on the importance of data security and confidentiality, for instance. Despite the ease of tele-psychology, practitioners must also be cautiously reminded about its limitations.

Dialogue about ethical dilemmas

While the value of a well-written code of ethics cannot be overemphasized, it cannot be denied that taking the code at face value with little to no internalization is not ideal, either. The code needs to come alive and a critical way to achieve this is through regular and lively discourses about real or hypothetical ethical dilemmas. In order to truly foster critical analysis of a code, such discussions go a far way in helping one to methodically address ethical dilemmas – skills that can then be more easily generalised to one's own professional situations. Such work can be subsumed under a Special Interest Group – Ethics, which could also focus on outreach to students studying psychology modules.

Professional Development

In order to ensure that Psychologists continue to be keenly attuned to ethical issues, continuing professional development should make ethics a compulsory topic.

Conclusion

The Psychology profession in Singapore has developed and progressed considerably over the past few decades. Despite the profession being not formally regulated, the community of Psychologists together with SPS have galvanised their efforts to improve professional standards. In a short span of five years, a voluntary-regulatory system is now increasingly recognised, the SPS Code has been revised comprehensively, a locally-relevant ethical decision-making model has been proposed, and a Disciplinary Advisory Committee has been formed to address complaints regarding unethical practices. In the next lap, the challenge for SPS would be to further bring the code of ethics alive. The code cannot and must not remain as simply words on a document, but rather this dynamic set of processes must transcend every aspect of Psychological work so that we then consciously and unconsciously over time, do the right thing.

References

Francis, R. (2009). *Ethics for psychologists* (2nd ed.). West Sussex: British Psychological Society and Blackwell Publications.

Hill, M., Glaser, K., & Harden, J. (1995). A feminist model for ethical decision making. In E. Rave, & C. Larsen, *Ethical decision making in therapy: Feminist perspectives* (pp. 18–37). New York: Guilford Publications.

Khairullah, D., & Khairullah, Z. (2013, February). Cultural values and decision-making in China. *International Journal of Business, Humanities and Technology*, 3(2), 1–12.

Kitchener, K. (1984). Intuition, critical evaluation and ethical principles: The foundation for ethical decisions in counseling psychology. *The Counseling Psychologist*, 12 (3–4), 43–55.

Lee, K. Y. (1990, August 31). Opening of the Singapore Academy of Law. www.sal.org.sg/Lists/Speeches/DispForm.aspx?ID=28

Tan, A.-G. (2002). *Psychology in Singapore*. Singapore: McGraw-Hill.

Toh, A. (2017). *Psychology ethical decision-making process in Singapore* (Unpublished master's thesis). National University of Singapore, Singapore.

Welfel, E., & Lipsitz, N. (1984). The ethical behavior of professional psychologists: A critical analysis of the research. *Counseling Psychologist*, 12, 31–42.

PART 3

Australasian Countries: Australia and New Zealand

6

THE AUSTRALIAN CODE OF ETHICS

Alfred Allan

The Australian Code of Ethics

The development of the Australian code of ethics demonstrates the role codes can play in the professionalization of a discipline. Scholars consider the appointment of Henry Lauri as lecturer of mental and moral philosophy at the University of Sydney in 1886 as the start of psychology as a sub-discipline in Australia (Cooke, 2000; O'Neil, 1987). The sub-discipline thereafter evolved as it did in most other Western countries by developing a scientific focus that became so distinct from academic philosophy that universities eventually formed separate psychology academic departments in the mid-1920s (O'Neil, 1982). The graduates of these psychology departments naturally started looking for ways to apply their knowledge (John, 1985) and this led to the development of applied (also sometimes called technical or consultative) psychology from the early part of the 20th century (Taft & Day, 1988; White & Sarfaty, 1970). Academic and applied psychologists' needs led to the formation of the Australian Overseas[1] Branch (Branch) of the British Psychological Society (BPS) in 1944 (Cooke, 2000). This event accelerated the professionalization of psychology but failed to solve an ethical issue that confronted psychology at the time because the BPS did not have its own code of ethics.

The Beginning

Australian psychologists were concerned about several ethical issues (e.g., confidentiality) at the end of the Second World War, but the issue that was with hindsight pivotal in the development of the Australian code was access to and use of the data they had collected during the War. The Victorian group of the Branch formed a committee to consider this issue and its recommendations led to the development of a code to regulate the communication of all psychological data (Branch, 1960). This 6-page code stipulated what information could be communicated to whom and in what form and prompted members of the various state-based groups within the Branch to actively discuss other ethical issues. The South Australian group consequently developed a draft code of ethics during 1947 and 1948 and after a trial by members it was adopted by the Branch in 1949 (Branch, 1960; Cooke, 2000).

The 1949 Code of Professional Ethics (1949 Code)

The 1949 code was arguably the first national code of ethics for psychologists that was published, but its drafters admitted that they were influenced by an earlier code from Minnesota (Minnesota Society for Applied Psychology, 1947). They also admitted that they had copied sections (Cooke, 2000) and this is especially clear if one reads Principle IV of the code. The 1949 code is nevertheless a document with distinct features.[2] The drafters, for instance, made it clear that psychologists were bound "by the requirements of the law" (Cooke, 2000, p. 112) and this notion has been embedded in subsequent codes, including the preamble of the current code of the Australian Psychological Society (APS, 2007).

The 1949 code that can be described as a narrative that listed the obligations of psychologists, was well received (Cooke, 2000). The publication of this code so soon after the formation of the Branch is remarkable considering Australia's geographical size,[3] population at the time,[4] isolation,[5] and few academic and applied psychologists.[6] The most likely reason is that most, if not all, Australian psychologists at the time worked in the capital cities of the six states and two territories and despite the vast distances between them they were all confronted with common and urgent ethical problems nobody else could solve for them. They did not have the luxury of taking the in-depth intellectual and considered approach that American psychologists (e.g., Bixler & Seeman, 1946; Hobbs, 1948; Sargent, 1945; Sutich, 1944) and the American Psychological Association (APA, 1952) took, but they had to be pragmatic and deal with the problems confronting them and did so by adopting a national code. Those involved in the drafting and publication of the 1949 code nevertheless realized the limitations of the code even before it became operative as their American counterparts realized three years later when they finalized the APA code (see APA, 1952)

Reflection and Consultation

The Branch therefore started discussing the revision of the code in 1950 (Cooke, 2000) and this time the process was more reflective and consultative and therefore took much longer. The review formally commenced in August 1956 when "the Annual General Meeting of the Branch instructed its executive committee (executive) to inquire into the working of the code and to obtain from members suggestions considering its revision and extension to other areas of professional activity" (Branch, 1960, p. 1). The executive appointed a sub-committee to collate the many comments it received, and it submitted a report to the annual general meeting of the Branch in August 1957.

The 1960 Code of Professional Conduct (1960 Code)

The executive responded to the general meeting's instructions and directed the same sub-committee to draw up a reviewed and extended code. Cooke (2000) reports that Frank Simpson prepared the first draft that the sub-committee after further revision sent to Branch groups and university departments for comment in 1958. The sub-committee completed the final draft after it had considered the comments it received, the findings of the Branch's ethics committee and a "publication on ethical standards kindly supplied by the American Psychological Association" (Branch, 1960, p. 1). The reference to ethical standards is most likely to the Ethical standards of psychologists (American Psychological Association, 1953a) or the summary of the document (American Psychological Association, 1953b). The new draft was adopted and published under a new name as the Code of Professional Conduct in June, 1960.

The 1960 code consisted of ten general principles of professional conduct[7] and specific standards. The drafters made it clear that the "primary purpose of the code as a whole, however, is not to set up rigid legalistic rules of conduct but to provide lines of guidance for members" (Branch, 1960, p. 1). Cooke (2000) reported that most of the members did not know what to do with the code because so few of them were in private practice, but it received international attention when the Polish Academy of Sciences asked permission to quote from it in 1963 (Cooke, 2000).

Two watershed events in 1966 nevertheless made the prompt review of the 1960 code inevitable. The first event would have been enough to justify a revision of the code because the Branch opened its doors as the APS on 6 January 1966 after it and the BPS agreed to part ways the previous year (Cooke, 2000; Gray, 1984). The promulgation of the Psychological Practices Act (1965) by Victoria, however, made it essential for the members of the newly formed APS to consider the relevance of its code. The Victorian government passed this Act in an attempt to protect the public from scientology, but it essentially meant that it would in future regulate psychologists (Cooke, 2000; Mills, 1966). Many psychologists feared that other Australian states and territories would introduce similar legislation and that they would lose control of the profession (Cooke, 2000). Some psychologists, however, realized the code was "a public document which can be used by other professions, by the general public, or by the courts, as a yardstick by which to measure the behaviour of psychologists" (Nixon, 1968, p. 89). The APS therefore saw "the formulation of a code as an opportunity for members to regulate and control their own affairs" (Nixon, 1968, p. 92) and this has been a convention since then.

Two later events demonstrated the wisdom of this approach. First, those states that later formed registration boards often gave them the option of using the APS code (e.g., section 21(5) of the Psychologists Registration Act [WA], 1976). Second, courts held that registration boards could use the APS code to judge the behavior of non-APS psychologists because it reflects what psychologists generally regarded as appropriate professional conduct (e.g., Psychologist Registration Board v Robinson, 2004).

The 1968 Code of Professional Conduct (1968 Code)

Professional and public debate regarding the regulation of psychology and the definition of psychological practice in the legislation formed the backdrop to the preparation of the 1968 code (Cooke, 2000). Little is known of the review, but Mary Nixon prepared the first draft (Cooke, 2000), and it is possible that she framed the provisions in the code in such a way that regulators would find it useful because the 1968 code is essentially a shorter version of the 1960 code with 36 principles instead of the 112 of the previous code. The committee that prepared it aimed to produce a code that would cover all possible contingencies without being too restrictive (Cooke, 2000). The revised code was adopted at the APS' second annual general meeting in 1968 (Gray, 1984), but only published two years later (APS, 1970c).

A separate advice to members (APS, 1970a) containing many of the provisions that had been excluded from the 1960 code accompanied the 1968 code and the APS issued another advice to members that dealt with advertising (APS, 1970b) later in the year. The drafters refer to this separate document containing these advices on the first page of the undated copy of the 1968 code in my possession and also gave a list of what was called further relevant references, namely ethical publications by the APA and the BPS and an article by Fox (1968) on the legal aspects of confidentiality. The drafters did not explain the relationship between these documents and the code, but they added editor notes after some of the standards of the code that referred readers to the advices. The 1968 code also had three appendices, one on the communication of psychological information about individuals. These appendices and advices appear to be the predecessors of the ethical guidelines that formed part of some later versions of the code and that have since 1997 been published as a separate document.

The APS' concern about the ethical implications of psychologists working as private practitioners might explain why the 1968 code was published so long after it was adopted. It is uncertain how many psychologists were in full or part-time practice at the time (White & Sarfaty, 1970), but in Victoria only 17 (7%) psychologists were in private practice (Cooke, 2000). The emergence of private practitioners was controversial (John, 1985; White & Sarfaty, 1970) and sometimes the subject of acrimonious debates (Cooke, 2000). Some ideological concerns came from people who did not think psychologists should charge clients for services. Practical concerns arose because many private practitioners were employed psychologists working part-time (see Owens, 1968) and others were sole practitioners working without peer or organizational review. Private practitioners had to be entrepreneurial (Cooke, 2000) and naturally wanted to advertise their services (APS, 1970b). Appendix C suggests that the APS was also concerned that some private practitioners employed unqualified persons or students in their practices.

Consolidation

A charitable explanation for the time it took the APS to publish the next edition of its code in 1986 is that its members were now ready to systematically collect data and undertake the in-depth intellectual deliberation required to consolidate their collective knowledge in a relevant code of ethics. Linda Viney's (1973) article about the need for a more relevant code suggests that debates were already taking place at the APS' annual conference in 1972, but the formal review process only started in 1976 when the APS established a working party to inquire into the ethical practice of researchers and practitioners (Cooke, 2000; Noble, 1984; Sheehan, 1984).

Noble (1980) reported that the working group followed the procedure that the APA (1973) used in the preparation of Ethical principles in the conduct of research with human participants when it asked members to provide instances of ethically problematic research. The APS group, however, went further and in its questionnaire asked members to also provide examples of professional misconduct in applied psychology and other professional areas. The group sent the questionnaire to 100 members they chose at random from the membership directory and 48 of them responded. The group then mailed a further refined questionnaire to 400 randomly selected members of whom 115 responded. The working party identified only minor ethical problems amongst academics, but several grave issues regarding the activities of applied psychologists, such as the lack of respect for client autonomy and privacy. An autonomy issue that was particularly prominent was some psychologists' expectation that employees of clinics and businesses and trainee psychologists should participate in groups and sometimes join other group members in sexual activity (Noble, 1980, 1984). These revelations led to a more general debate about psychologists expecting clients to undress and touching clients (see Cooke, 2000, for a discussion).

The Australian Law Reform Commission's Enquiry on Privacy (1983) was an external instigator for scholarly contributions regarding privacy and confidentiality (Gray, 1984). Fox (1984) for instance undertook a comprehensive review of the notions of privacy and confidentiality in which he consulted the codes of other countries and professions. Nixon (1984) examined who the client is in the context of confidentiality and other authors also examined confidentiality in specific settings such as in the courts (Brown, 1981; Wardlaw, 1984a, 1984b).

The 1986 Code of Professional Conduct (1986 Code)

The little red book as many psychologists from previous generations still fondly refer to the red covered 1986 code was innovative in many respects. It was the first Australian code to provide a clear statement of the general principles that underlie the code (Responsibility, Competence and Propriety). These principles were followed by seven sections dealing with specific professional activities, such as assessment procedures (and five appendices that provided recommendations for persons considering invoking any section of the code); guidelines (e.g., relating to physical contact with clients) and principles relating to research with human participants.

Standard B.7 that was arguably historically the most important new provision provided that:

Personal sexual relationships between psychologists and clients are unethical. When a therapeutic procedure entails some level of physical sexual intimacy with a client, documented informed consent must be obtained from the client or the client's legal guardian prior to the introduction of that procedure. Sexual intercourse between psychologists and clients are unethical.

This standard, however, did not apply to students and trainees because the word client is not defined in the code. There is not a similar standard in the sections on teaching psychology and supervision and training.

The introduction of the Privacy Act (1988) that was arguably the most important legislative change that took place soon after the adoption of the 1986 code did not lead to any amendments, suggesting that the drafters of the code had anticipated what was in the Act. The APS, however, amended the code in 1990 by inserting the word "maintain" in relation to skill and learning in General Principle II and in 1991 by adding provisions to Section B (Consulting Relationships) that required psychologists to make and keep adequate records and reminded them of their responsibilities as custodians of client records, including when they terminate their services. The amended 1986 code was reprinted in 1994 to correct what appears to have been a minor typographical error in General Principle III (Propriety).

The APS further added ethical guidelines relating to authorship, the management of suicidal clients and notably the teaching and use of hypnosis. The guidelines on hypnosis was in response to the debate around hypnosis in general (e.g., Waxman, Misra, Gibson, & Basker, 1985) and in forensic settings specifically (e.g., McConkey & Jupp, 1985; Sanders & Simmons, 1983). This debate commenced before the publication of the 1986 code but increased dramatically thereafter (McConkey, Roche, & Sheehan, 1989; McConkey & Sheehan, 1988a, 1988b, 1992, 1995) as part of the acrimonious debate about repressed memory syndrome in Australia and elsewhere (Cooke, 2000; McConkey, 1995; Thomson, 1995).

The 1997 Code of Ethics (1997 Code)

Several external and internal factors prompted the APS to revise the 1986 code by the mid-1990s (Allan, 2010b). The publication of the APA's revised code (1992a, 1992b) was an external prod (Graham Davidson, personal communication, 19 November 2019), but the internal restructuring of the APS in the mid-1990s was the main reason as it included making changes to its governance structure. The APS reviewed its rules and procedures for dealing with complaints against members (Graham Davidson, personal communication, 19 November 2019) and wanted to clarify the relationship between the code and the ethical guidelines. These guidelines had become very popular and therefore influential, but some of them were dated, others contained material that could have been in the code, and there were guidelines that did not form part of the code (A Garton, personal communication, 9 November 9, 2010). Members also did not know what weight they should give to the ethical guidelines in comparison to the principles and standards of the code; a problem that can be traced back to when the drafters of the 1968 code referred to external documents in the code.

The APS consulted members, representatives of state registration boards and the heads of department and schools of psychology prior to the review (Heywood, 2018). The 1997 code was mostly an editorial revision of the 1986 code, but the drafters nevertheless made some important changes that are still visible in the current code. The most obvious changes were that it was called the Code of Ethics rather than a Code of Professional Conduct and that the drafters defined three constructs, including client and psychologist (APS, 1998). The drafters reviewed the provisions regarding sexual relationships between psychologists and their clients and further proscribed sexual relationships between their psychologists and the former clients for two years after termination of the professional relationship. They, however, in Standard B.11 provided criteria that would be applied to determine whether sexual relationships that psychologists and clients started after two years were unethical.

The drafters explained the function and status of the ethical guidelines in the preamble of the code and warned psychologists that those who act inconsistently with them might be required to demonstrate that their behavior was not unethical. They gave a list of the three ethical guidelines that were current at the time, but the actual guidelines were published in a separate document the next year (APS, 1998). The APS further formed a separate ethical guidelines committee to oversee the drafting and regular revision of the guidelines (Heywood, 2018).

The 1997 code was reprinted on five and reviewed on three occasions, making it difficult for psychologists and those who had to apply it to identify which version of the code they had to work with. Several of these revisions were nevertheless forced upon the APS. The Trans-Tasman Council of Psychologist Registration Boards (Council of Boards) that represented the registration boards of New Zealand and the Australian states and territories objected to the definition and use of the word psychologist in the code (Allan, 2010b). It pointed out that the use of the title psychologist was regulated in all the legislation governing these Boards and the APS consequently changed the word psychologist and its definition in the code to "member" (Definition section). Changes to state health legislation (e.g., Health Records Act [Vic], 2001) similarly compelled the APS to change the time clinical records had to be retained in 2002. The other amendment in 2002 was a reformulation of the solicited testimonials standards and the 2003 revision involved a minor change regarding the use of post-nominals (personal communication, Mick Symons, 18 November 2019).

A Code for the 21st Century

Successive APS ethics committees immediately after the turn of the century questioned whether the 1997 code was still functional in the 21st century (Allan, 2010a, 2010b, 2011). These committees noted the lack of recent in-depth considerations of the code and that despite the many amendments to it, it had not changed fundamentally since 1986. They noted that some psychologists for instance during focus groups questioned whether the code's format and terminology were still functional (see Allan, 2010a) and that several national and international legal, professional and social events had occurred that changed the ethical landscape (Allan, 2010a).

Nationally, amendments to the Privacy Act (1988) in 2001 placed stringent privacy requirements on psychologists, but paradoxically governments introduced security legislation in the aftermath of the terrorist attacks early in the century that gave state agencies powers that appeared to erode the ability of psychologists to keep client information confidential (Allan, 2018). The committees were also aware of discussions among Australian federal, state and territory ministers to create a national scheme of accreditation for health practitioners that included psychologists and they realized that a national regulatory body might develop another code to regulate psychologists (Allan, 2010b). Members of the committee also recognized that Australian psychologists had become more aware of culture and their social responsibility since 1986 (e.g., Davidson, 1988, 1998; Davidson & Sanson, 1995) and that this required a reconsideration of aspects of the code. Internationally the debate around American psychologists' involvement in the interrogation of prisoners was emerging at the time (see Olson, Soldz, & Davis, 2008) raising questions about the relationship between human rights and the code.

The 2007 Code of Ethics (2007 Code)

The APS board of directors in response to a recommendation by the APS ethics committee appointed a group to review the code in April 2005. The group during informal meetings set itself the aim of drafting a uniquely Australian and forward-looking code that would retain the principle-based approach of the past, but emphasize the respect for human dignity as one of the general principles (e.g., Allan, 2013; Allan & Davidson, 2013, 2015). Members also wanted to strike the right balance between tradition and innovation and to consider international developments around codes and stakeholders' views of the code. The group developed a time line that included time to consult internally and externally and invited the Council of Boards to nominate representatives to join it. Members immediately started reviewing relevant documents such as the draft of the Universal Declaration of Ethical Principles for Psychologists (Universal Declaration; Ad Hoc Joint Committee, 2005) and other publications (see Allan, 2010a).

The review of the 1997 code formally commenced with a round table discussion on 16 and 17 February 2006 where members of the group discussed various issues, including the function of codes (Allan, 2011; Allan & Symons, 2010) and the relationship between codes and moral decision-making (Joyce, 2010; Love, 2010). The group tried to give the code an "internal structure that lends itself to ease of understanding and ready adoption by the intended users" (Love, 2010, p. 95) by moving away from the organization of the standards in sections that reflected their functions. They instead grouped standards that flow from general principles together.

The new structure compelled the group to redefine the general principles and the sub-principles falling under them and to reconsider each standard. Alfred Allan with the assistance of Mick Symons prepared the first draft of the code for consideration by the group. Virtually all the standards of the 2007 code were different from those in the 1997 code because the group added and deleted several standards and redrafted those it retained. Standard A.5 is an example of a standard that was added to reflect the legal expectations at the time captured in the 2001 amendments to the Privacy Act (1988) and tribunal decisions (e.g., Re Noble, 2003). The group deleted standards psychologists had, during focus groups, identified as redundant or that were sufficiently dealt with in other codes (e.g., national research codes) or legislation, or that could be put in ethical guidelines rather than the code. Group members nevertheless sometimes retained seemingly redundant standards in the code if they believed they served an important educative function. Among the standards the group retained and redrafted were those regarding sexual behavior where its aim was to combine and formulate these standards more tightly without disturbing existing legal precedents. The group aimed to enhance the functionality of the code for those who had to apply it, including a possible future national registration board. One method they used was to define key constructs precisely enough to be accurate, but general enough to be functional throughout the code.

A particularly vexing issue was how to deal with culture in the code in a way that recognized Aboriginal and Torres Strait Islander (ATSI) people as the first people in Australia whilst at the same time recognizing that the country has become multi-cultural. The group after long deliberations and consulting other codes (specifically the Canadian Psychological Association, 2000) and ethical documents (e.g., Universal Declaration, Ad Hoc Joint Committee, 2005) concluded that the fundamental ethical principle that underlies respect of diversity in general, and culture specifically, was respect for human dignity (Davidson, 2010). The group decided not to define culture in general or any specific culture because doing that would contradict the central idea of humanity that was already embedded in the draft code as General Principle A. Group members also took into account that defining constructs can have unintended consequences (see Tripodi, 2017) and that the APS had an ethical guideline for the provision of service to ATSI people. The group nevertheless wanted to ensure that the description of General Principle A made it clear that psychologists should recognize the humanity of all people. After considering the wording used in the Canadian code at the time (Respect for the dignity of persons) and the draft of the Universal Declaration (Respect for the dignity of all human beings), the working group named the principle "Respect for the rights and dignity of people and peoples" (APS, 2007, p. 9). The use of the word peoples also recognized that ATSI people are not a homogeneous group.

The 2007 code was well received by psychologists and stakeholders and the transition to using it was smooth (Heywood, 2018) even though the APS had to revise the ethical guidelines to take into account the structure, definitions, general and other principles, and standards of the new code. The Psychology Board of

Australia (PsyBA) adopted the code for the profession[8] and it was applied by the courts (e.g., Cook v The Psychologists Board of Queensland, 2015; Psychology Board of Australia v Sullivan, 2017). To the best of my knowledge, only the definition of multiple relationships was questioned by a judge (see Solomon v Australian Health Practitioner Regulation Agency, 2015).

The 2017 Review

Several international and national events after 2007 created new and constantly evolving ethical challenges to psychologists that made a review of the code urgent by 2017. Love and Allan (2010) foreshadowed some of these challenges when they on behalf of the drafters of the 2007 code anticipated what future events and trends might impact on the code. The continued development and expansion of digital technology was one of these challenges. Psychologists had to adopt these innovations for professional purposes because they allowed them to be more innovative and productive and ultimately provide better services to clients. Psychologists who embraced digital technology for professional and social purposes nevertheless faced the challenge of protecting client privacy and setting boundaries in a novel and constantly changing environment. The digital revolution also prompted governments to amend privacy legislation (e.g., Privacy Act, 1988) that required psychologists to reconsider their collection, stewardship, use and disclosure of client information. These amendments changed the circumstances under which psychologists had a legal discretion to disclose confidential client information to prevent harm to individuals and the public. Standard A.5.2.(c) of the code provides that psychologists have a discretion to disclose confidential information without consent in case of an immediate or specific risk, which is stricter than what the amended Privacy Act (1988) required. Coroners (Inquest into the death of Adriana Donato, 2017; Inquest into the deaths arising from the Lindt cafe siege, 2017) noticed this divergence and their recommendations compelled the APS to add a note to the 2007 code to bring this to the attention of psychologists who were subject to section 16A of the Privacy Act (1988).

Governments' ongoing and increasing concerns about the prevention of harm of different kinds further led to legislation that put the privacy of both psychologists and their clients at risk (see Allan, 2018) and required reconsideration of the 2007 code. The most prominent of this legislation was security legislation, but the problem was wider. The Work Health and Safety Act (2011), for example, changed the obligations of chief executive officers of organizations who consequently needed access to files of psychologists working within their organizations. Psychologists often did not realize that Standard B.4 of the code provided guidance to them regarding how to deal with these situations, in part because the construct "third party" was not defined. The Health Practitioner Regulation National Law Act (Regulation National Law Act; 2009) that regulates psychologists further has provisions that impacted on the privacy of clients. Section 141 requires psychologists to notify the relevant regulator if they whilst practicing form the reasonable belief that other health practitioners, including those who are their clients, practiced whilst intoxicated; engaged in sexual misconduct; were so impaired that it placed the public at risk of substantial harm; or practiced in a manner that departs significantly from accepted professional standards. Sections of this Act furthermore compelled psychologists under investigation to release their client files to the regulatory body's investigators.

The potential ethical risks of two developments that were otherwise beneficial to psychologists also became more apparent after 2007. To start with, psychologists' increasing involvement in news, actuality and reality programs enhanced psychology's public profile, but also required these psychologists to be cautious regarding the accuracy and scientific credibility of public statements they made and to consider who their clients are in reality programs. Clients' ability to claim rebates under the Medicare scheme further led to two problems. First, some of the increasing number of psychologists entering private practice were so entrepreneurial that they exploited junior psychologists and put clients at risk. Second, general practitioners were referring clients with complex problems who had previously been served by tertiary mental health services to psychologists in private practice who often did not have the competency or resources to provide services to them.

The review group identified these and other issues at its first meeting on October 25, 2017. The other issues included problems with some of the definitions (e.g., that of a client) and a lack of guidance to psychologists working with couples, families and groups. The group decided that it was unnecessary to make major changes to the code and that it could respond to these issues by making specific additions, deletions and amendments to specific definitions and standards. The final draft of the code was therefore like the 2007 code in structure and format, but with some notable differences. The changes in the definition section included amending some (e.g., of multiple clients), removing the definition of psychologist because it is defined in the National Law Act (2009), replacing some (e.g., moral rights with human rights) and adding a definition for third party that had not been previously defined. The group amended too many standards to write about, but important changes were to the confidentiality standard (A.5) that was substantially rewritten to bring it in line with the changes to the Privacy Act (1988) and the amendment of Standard B.7 to clarify psychologists' responsibilities when they delegate tasks to people who provide professional, business and support services. Many amendments were editorial, but the committee added several standards, such as Standard C.6.5 that requires psychologists to ensure that their contracts allow them to act consistently with ethical principles and standards of the code.

The group submitted the final draft of the code to the APS Board in September 2018 who requested the group to amend the clauses relating to sexual activity with clients, former clients and those closely related to their clients. The Board particularly requested the group to remove the standard that stipulated the process psychologists can follow if they want to engage in such sexual behavior after two years. The working group considered the history of the relevant provision in the Australian code, 46 other codes of other psychology organizations and relevant literature (e.g., Allan & Thomson, 2010; Capawana, 2016; Manning, 2014;

Surgenor, Diesfeld, & Rychert, 2019). The group further examined the body of legal precedents about the relevant provisions in the Australian code that had developed over several decades. Group members concluded that whilst it fully supported the adoption of a zero-tolerance policy by the APS, it deemed it unpractical to embed such a policy in the code of ethics and recommended that the relevant standard should be retained. The group in making this decision considered the arguments of its predecessor (see Allan & Thomson, 2010) and the risk that new provisions would attract legal testing and that the PsyBA would be at a higher risk of challenges that might be successful thereby disturbing the legal precedents that had been established. The APS Board has not made a final decision regarding the code at the time of writing.

Conclusion

One could argue that the code has been the cornerstone of the profession's existence in Australia. Psychologists' ethical concerns was one of the important factors that led to the formation of the Branch and the drafting of the 1949 code. This code was one of the first concrete internal and external signs of the emerging profession of psychology in Australia. The code led the professionalization process in Australia in contrast to many other countries where the profession was well-established when psychologists developed their first codes.

The first Australian code was therefore a pragmatic document that was drafted in the beginning without the luxury of reflection, but when the profession was more mature such in-depth intellectual reflection and consultation took place in preparation of the 1960 and 1968 codes. The drafters of 1986 code consolidated the knowledge generated by their predecessors with insights gained from public debate and quantitative studies and the drafters of the 1997 code continued this consolidation. The drafters of the Australian codes up to this time appear to have been influenced by the APA codes (e.g., Leach & Harbin, 1997), but the drafters of the 2007 code deliberately tried to change this. They endeavored to develop a code that aligned with other codes (including that of the APA) and ethical documents such as the Universal Declaration, but was nevertheless distinct, forwarding looking, and true to the conventions of previous Australian codes.

One of these conventions was the recognition that ethical decision-making takes place within the parameters of law. Drafters therefore understood that if they wanted Australian psychologists to use the code as their first reference point when they faced ethical problems it had to be compatible with the law in all the Australian jurisdictions. Another convention is that the standards of Australian codes are often abstract and general with clear definitions of key constructs in recent codes. One reason for this is that drafters wanted to encourage regulators to use the code and wanted to provide guidance to all psychologists irrespective of the work they do or the settings they work in without being unduly restrictive.

The APS realized that Australian codes were therefore more legalistic than most other codes and dealt with this in two ways. First, it provided practical and educative information in an extensive set of ethical guidelines that complement the code by providing more concrete and specific guidance to psychologists. There are currently 29 sets of them (APS, 2019) and the ethical guidelines committee regularly review existing ones. Second, it tells psychologists that the standards only set out the minimum requirements psychologists' professional behavior must meet in order not to be unethical and that the profession expects them to be more aspirational. Drafters of Australian codes have therefore since 1986 followed a principle-based approach. This involved them setting out three general principles that indicated to psychologists what professional behavior the profession wanted them to aspire to and simultaneously gave them constructs they could use to make ethical decisions when the standards of the code failed to provide guidance to them.

The Australian code is therefore unique in many respects and reflects Australian culture's emphasis on justice, equality, inclusiveness, consultation and doing the right thing for the group. It has since 1949 evolved and it will keep on doing so as legal, professional, social and technological changes create new ethical challenges to psychologists. The challenge for the drafters of future codes will be to draft codes that can meet these challenges following the conventions of their predecessors.

Acknowledgments

I wish to thank Maria Allan and Anthony Cole for their comments on earlier drafts of this chapter. I also thank Graham Davidson, Alison Garton, Mick Symons and Clive Williams for the information they provided to me.

Notes

1　The word overseas does not appear on some of the documents produced by the Branch and some authors such as Cooke (2000) and Heywood (2018) do not use it. I will, however, use the word in this chapter because it appears on contemporary sources like the mimeograph copy of the 1960 Code that is in my possession and O'Neil (1961), and senior psychologists like Don Thomson (personal communication, 15 November 2019) and Clive Williams (personal communication, 17 November 2019) assured me the word overseas (and sometimes oversea) was part of the official name of the Branch.
2　A copy of the 1949 Code is reproduced in Cooke (2000) on p. 112.
3　Australia land mass is 7,692,024 km^2, i.e., about 78% of the USA landmass of 9,833,517 km^2 www.ga.gov.au/scientific-topics/national-location-information/dimensions/australias-size-compared
4　About 7,391,000 people in 1947 census www.abs.gov.au/
5　The flight distance from Sydney to New York is 9,934 miles and to London is 10,556 miles.
6　The Branch had 54 members in 1945 (Cooke, 2000).
7　A copy of these principles appears in Cooke (2000), on p. 113.
8　www.psychologyboard.gov.au/Standards-and-Guidelines/Codes-Guidelines-Policies.aspx

References

Ad Hoc Joint Committee. (2005). *Draft: Universal declaration of ethical principles of psychologists*. International Union of Psychological Science and the International Association of Applied Psychology.

Allan, A. (2010a). The functionality of the Australian Psychological Society's 1997 and 2007 Codes of Ethics. In A. Allan & A. W. Love (Eds.), *Ethical practice in psychology - Reflections from the creators of the APS Code of Ethics* (pp. 25–39). Chichester, United Kingdom: John Wiley & Sons.

Allan, A. (2010b). Introduction. In A. Allan & A. W. Love (Eds.), *Ethical practice in psychology - Reflections from the creators of the APS Code of Ethics* (pp. 1–11). Chichester, United Kingdom: John Wiley & Sons.

Allan, A. (2011). The development of a code for Australian psychologists. *Ethics and Behavior*, 21(6), 435–451. doi:10.1080/10508422.2011.622176

Allan, A. (2013). Are human rights redundant in the ethical codes of psychologists? *Ethics and Behavior*, 23(4), 251–265. doi:10.1080/10508422.2013.776480

Allan, A. (2018, 26 June). *Jean Pettifor Distinguished Lecture on Ethics: The professions' response to the changing expectations of a society fearful of the risk of violent harm*. 29th International Congress of Applied Psychology. Montreal, Canada.

Allan, A., & Davidson, G. R. (2013). Respect for the dignity of people: What does this principle mean in practice? *Australian Psychologist*, 48(5), 345–352. doi:10.1111_ap.12012

Allan, A., & Davidson, G. R. (2015). Respectful professional behaviour: What does it mean? In S. Morrissey, P. Reddy, G. R. Davidson & A. Allan (Eds.), *Ethics and Professional practice* (2nd ed., pp. 25–39). Melbourne: Australia: Cengage.

Allan, A., & Symons, M. (2010). The development of the 2007 Code. In A. Allan & A. W. Love (Eds.), *Ethical practice in psychology – Reflections from the creators of the APS Code of Ethics* (pp. 13–24). Chichester, United Kingdom: John Wiley & Sons.

Allan, A., & Thomson, D. M. (2010). The regulation of sexual activity between psychologists and their clients and former clients. In A. Allan & A. W. Love (Eds.), *Ethical practice in psychology – Reflections from the creators of the APS Code of Ethics* (pp. 149–160). Chichester, United Kingdom: John Wiley & Sons.

American Psychological Association (1952). Discussion on ethics. *American Psychologist*, 7(8), 425–455. doi:10.1037/h0057724

American Psychological Association (1953a). *Ethical standards of psychologists*. Washington, DC: Author.

American Psychological Association (1953b). *Ethical standards of psychologists: A summary of ethical principles*. Washington, DC: Author.

American Psychological Association (1973). Ethical principles in the conduct of research with human participants. *American Psychologist*, 28(1), 79–80. doi:10.1037/h0038067

American Psychological Association (1992a). Ethical principles of psychologists and code of conduct. *American Psychologist*, 47(12), 1597–1612.

American Psychological Association (1992b). Ethical principles of psychologists and code of conduct. Retrieved from www.apa.org/ethics/code2002.pdf

Australian Law Reform Commission (1983). Enquiry on privacy: 1976–1983. Retrieved from www.alrc.gov.au/inquiry/privacy-1976-83/

Australian Overseas Branch of the British Psychological Society (1960). *Code of professional conduct*. Melbourne, Australia: Author.

Australian Psychological Society (1970a). Advice to members. *Australian Psychologist*, 5, 89–95.

Australian Psychological Society (1970b). Advice to members. *Australian Psychologist*, 5(2), 207–209. doi:10.1080/00050067008259891

Australian Psychological Society (1970c). The Australian Psychological Society Code of Professional Conduct. *Australian Psychologist*, 5, 75–88.

Australian Psychological Society (1998). *Ethical guidelines* (1st ed.). Melbourne: APS.

Australian Psychological Society (2019). *Ethical guidelines* (15th ed.). Melbourne: APS. retrieved from www.psychology.org.au/for-members/publications/news/2019/APS-Ethical-Guidelines-15th-Edition-now-available

Australian Psychological Society (2007). *Code of ethics*. Retrieved from www.psychsociety.org.au/

Bixler, R., & Seeman, J. (1946). Suggestions for a code of ethics for consulting psychologists. *Abnormal Social Psychology*, 41, 486–490.

Brown, P. F. (1981). The psychologist in the courts. *Australian Psychologist*, 16(3), 423–432.

Canadian Psychological Association (2000). *Code of ethics for psychologists* (3rd ed.). Retrieved from https://cpa.ca/docs/File/Ethics/cpa_code_2000_eng_jp_jan2014.pdf

Capawana, M. R. (2016). Intimate attractions and sexual misconduct in the therapeutic relationship: Implications for socially just practice. *Cogent Psychology*, 3(1), 1194176. doi:10.1080/23311908.2016.1194176

Cook v The Psychologists Board of Queensland [2015]. *QCA 250*. Retrieved from www.austlii.edu.au/cgi-bin/viewdoc/au/cases/qld/QCA/2015/250.html.

Cooke, J. S. (2000). *A meeting of minds: The Australian Psychological Society and Australian psychologists 1944–1994*. Melbourne: Australian Psychological Society.

Davidson, G. R. (1988). Ethnicity and cognitive assessment: Australian perspectives. In G. Davidson (Ed.), *Some social and cultural perspectives on cognitive assessment* (pp. 7–14). Darwin: Institute of Technology.

Davidson, G. R. (1998). In pursuit of social responsibility in psychology: A comment on Butler (1998). *Australian Psychologist*, 33(1), 47–49.

Davidson, G. R. (2010). Exploration of psychologists' social responsibilities: How does the 2007 APS code of ethics measure up? In A. Allan & A. W. Love (Eds.), *Ethical Practice in Psychology – Reflections from the Creators of the APS Code of Ethics* (pp. 103–121). Chichester, UK: John Wiley & Sons.

Davidson, G. R., & Sanson, A. (1995). Should the APS have an ethical code of social action? *Bulletin of the Australian Psychological Society* (October), 2–4.

Fox, R. G. (1968). Legal aspects of confidentiality. *Australian Psychologist*, 3(2), 53–75.

Fox, R. G. (1984). Ethical and legal principles of confidentiality for psychologists and social workers. In M. C. Nixon (Ed.), *Issues in Psychological Practice* (pp. 147–187). Melbourne: Longman Cheshire.

Gray, K. C. (1984). The Australian Psychological Society. In M. C. Nixon (Ed.), *Issues in Psychological Practice* (pp. 3–25). Melbourne: Longman Cheshire.

Health Practitioner Regulation National Law Act (2009). Queensland. Retrieved from www3.austlii.edu.au/au/legis/qld/consol_act/hprnla2009428/

Health Records Act [Vic] (2001). Victoria. Retrieved from www5.austlii.edu.au/au/legis/vic/consol_act/hra2001144/.

Heywood, J. (2018). *The power of minds*. Melbourne, Australia: Australian Psychological Society and Bounce Books.

Hobbs, N. (1948). The development of a code of ethical standards for psychology. *American Psychologist*, 3, 80–84.

Inquest into the death of Adriana Donato. (2017). Coroners Court of Victoria. Retrieved from www.coronerscourt.vic.gov.au/home/coroners+written+findings/findings+-+inquest+into+the+death+of+adriana+donato

Inquest into the deaths arising from the Lindt cafe siege. (2017). State Coroner of New South Wales. Retrieved from www.lindtinquest.justice.nsw.gov.au/Documents/findings-and-recommendations.pdf

John, I. D. (1985). The identity prescription of the "the psychologist." *Australian Psychologist*, 20(2), 123–142.

Joyce, M. R. (2010). Reviewing the APS Code of Ethics with young people in mind. In A. Allan & A. W. Love (Eds.), *Ethical practice in psychology - Reflections from the creators of the APS Code of Ethics* (pp. 123–134). Chichester, United Kingdom: John Wiley & Sons.

Leach, M. M., & Harbin, J. J. (1997). Psychological ethics codes: A comparison of twenty-four countries. *International Journal of Psychology*, 32, 181–192.

Love, A. W. (2010). The APS Code in relation to professional ethics education. In A. Allan & A. W. Love (Eds.), *Ethical practice in psychology – Reflections from the creators of the APS Code of Ethics* (pp. 93–102). Chichester, United Kingdom: John Wiley & Sons.

Love, A. W., & Allan, A. (2010). Looking forward. In A. Allan & A. W. Love (Eds.), *Ethical practice in psychology – Reflections from the creators of the APS Code of Ethics* (pp. 161–169). Chichester, United Kingdom: John Wiley & Sons.

Manning, J. (2014). Changing disciplinary responses to sexual misconduct by health practitioners in New Zealand. *Journal of Law and Medicine*, 21, 508–515.

McConkey, K. M. (1995). Guidelines relating to the reporting of recovered memories. *Bulletin of the Australian Psychological Society*, 17(1), 20–21.

McConkey, K. M., & Jupp, J. J. (1985). Opinions about the forensic use of hypnosis. *Australian Psychologist*, 20(3), 283–291. doi:10.1080/00050068508256173

McConkey, K. M., & Sheehan, P. W. (1988a). Forensic hypnosis: Current legislation and its relevance to practice. *Australian Psychologist*, 23(3), 323–334. doi:10.1080/0005006880825561 5

McConkey, K. M., & Sheehan, P. W. (1988b). Hypnosis and criminal investigation: An analysis of policy and practice of police in Australia. *Criminal Law Journal*, 12(2), 63–85.

McConkey, K. M., & Sheehan, P. W. (1992). Ethical issues in forensic hypnosis. *Australian Psychologist*, 27(3), 150–153. doi:10.1080/00050069208257602

McConkey, K. M., & Sheehan, P. W. (1995). *Hypnosis, memory, and behavior in criminal investigation*. London: The Guilford Press.

McConkey, K. M., Roche, S. M., & Sheehan, P. W. (1989). Reports of forensic hypnosis: A critical analysis. *Australian Psychologist*, 23(4), 249–272. doi:10.1080/00050068908259565

Mills, J. D. (1966). The Victorian psychological practices act 1965. *Australian Psychologist*, 1(1), 30–38. doi:10.1080/00050066608256206.

Minnesota Society for Applied Psychology (1947). A proposal for a code of ethics for professional psychologists. *American Psychologist*, 2, 246.

Nixon, M. (1968). Enforcement of the code. *Australian Psychologist*, 3, 92.

Nixon, M. (1984). Confidentiality and the notion of "client" in psychological practice. In M. C. Nixon (Ed.), *Issues in Psychological Practice* (pp. 188–194). Melbourne: Longman Cheshire.

Noble, W. G. (1980). Psychologists and ethics: Report of a working party. *Australian Psychologist*, 15(3), 393–411.

Noble, W. G. (1984). Ethics, psychologists' practices, and psychological theory. In M. C. Nixon (Ed.), *Issues in Psychological Practice* (pp. 50–67). Melbourne: Longman Cheshire.

O'Neil, W. M. (1961). The Australian Oversea Branch – Trails and triumphs. *Bulletin of the Australian Psychological Society*, 17(1), 15–16.

O'Neil, W. M. (1982). *The beginnings of modern psychology*. Sydney: Sydney University Press.

O'Neil, W. M. (1987). *A century of psychology in Australia*. Sydney: Sydney University Press.

Olson, B., Soldz, S., & Davis, M. (2008). The ethics of interrogation and the American Psychological Association: A critique of policy and process. *Philosophy, Ethics, and Humanities in Medicine*, 3(3).

Owens, A. G. (1968). Salaried psychologists in full time employment undertaking part-time practice for a fee. *Australian Psychologist*, 3(2), 81–88.

Privacy Act [Commonwealth]. (1988). Retrieved from www.legislation.gov.au/Details/C2021C00024

Psychological Practices Act [Victoria]. (1965). (Victoria). 7355. Retrieved from www.austlii.edu.au/au/legis/vic/hist_act/ppa1965238.pdf

Psychologist Registration Board v Robinson. [2004] QCA 405. Retrieved from www.austlii.edu.au/au/cases/qld/QCA/2004/2405.html

Psychologists Registration Act [WA]. (1976) Retrieved from http://classic.austlii.edu.au/au/legis/wa/repealed_act/pra1976338/

Psychology Board of Australia v Sullivan. [2017] ACAT 104. Retrieved from www6.austlii.edu.au/cgi-bin/sign.cgi/au/cases/act/ACAT/2017/104.

Re Noble. [2003] VPSRB 2. Retrieved from www.austlii.edu.au/au/cases/vic/VPSRB/2003/2.pdf

Sanders, G. S., & Simmons, W. L. (1983). Use of hypnosis to enhance eyewitness accuracy: Does it work? *Journal of Applied Psychology*, 68, 70–77.

Sargent, H. (1945). Professional ethics and the problems of therapy. *Abnormal Social Psychology*, 40, 47–60.

Sheehan, P. W. (1984). Psychology as a profession and the Australian Psychological Society. In M. C. Nixon (Ed.), *Issues in Psychological Practice* (pp. 26–49). Melbourne: Longman Cheshire.

Solomon v Australian Health Practitioner Regulation Agency. [2015] WASC 203. Retrieved from http://decisions.justice.wa.gov.au/supreme/supdcsn.nsf/PDFJudgments-WebVw/2015WASC0203/%24FILE/2015WASC0203.pdf.

Surgenor, L. J., Diesfeld, K., & Rychert, M. (2019). Consensual sexual relationships between health practitioners and their patients: An analysis of disciplinary cases from New Zealand. *Psychiatry, Psychology and Law*, 26(5), 766–782. doi:10.1080/13218719.2019.1640801

Sutich, A. (1944). Toward a professional code of ethics for psychological consultants. *Abnormal Social Psychology*, 39, 329–350.

Taft, R., & Day, R. H. (1988). Psychology in Australia. *Annual Review of Psychology*, 39, 375–400.

Thomson, D. M. (1995). Allegations of childhood abuse: Repressed memories or false memories. *Psychiatry, Psychology and Law*, 2, 1.

Tripodi, V. (2017). *Discrimination in philosophy Rivista di estetica*, 64(1), 3–17.

Viney, L. L. (1973). Toward a more relevant code of professional conduct. *Australian Psychologist*, 8, 106.

Wardlaw, G. (1984a). Confidentiality, the courts and psychologists. In M. C. Nixon (Ed.), *Issues in Psychological Practice* (pp. 195–204). Melbourne: Longman Cheshire.

Wardlaw, G. (1984b). The Psychologists in Court: Some guidelines on the presentation of psychological evidence. In M. C. Nixon (Ed.), *Issues in psychological practice* (pp. 133–143). Melbourne: Longman Cheshire.

Waxman, D., Misra, P. C., Gibson, M., & Basker, M. A. (1985). *Modern trends in hypnosis.* New York: Plenum Press.

White, J., & Sarfaty, P. (1970). A report of the Division's Working Party on private practice in clinical psychology. *Australian Psychologist*, 5, 184.

Work Health and Safety Act. (2011). Retrieved from www.austlii.edu.au/cgi-bin/viewdb/au/legis/cth/consol_act/whasa2011218/

7

THE CODE OF ETHICS FOR PSYCHOLOGISTS WORKING IN AOTEAROA NEW ZEALAND

John Fitzgerald

To understand the development of the *Code of Ethics for Psychologists Working in Aotearoa New Zealand* and the broader socio-political context within New Zealand during recent years, one must begin with *te Tiriti o Waitangi* (the Treaty of Waitangi). Te Tiriti was signed by representatives of the Queen of England (the 'Crown') and Māori leaders (the indigenous people of Aotearoa New Zealand) in 1854 and is rightly identified as the founding document of our nation. Whether due to purposeful or accidental misunderstanding te Tiriti has been the focus of division and dissension over many years. This is despite the three principles of the Treaty appearing straightforward in their expression and interpretation, these principles being; *Partnership* (between the Crown and Māori on all issues*), Protection* (of Māori knowledge, language, standing, processes, culture, etc., and according to them equal rights and benefits), and *Participation* (ensuring equal participation at all levels).

At the time when te Tiriti was signed, Aotearoa (the Māori name for New Zealand) was already accustomed to settlers, seafarers and traders from a number of European nations who had been arriving since the 1770s. However, in response to increasing unruly behaviour the indigenous people invited the Crown to take responsibility for their citizens. To achieve this the British proposed a formal treaty which the authors (the British) understood to give them sovereignty, effectively making all Māori British citizens, according them citizenship rights, but also making them subject to the rule of the Crown. There is clear evidence that this was not the view of Māori chiefs at the time, and that what those people sought was for the Crown to exercise control over its own people (Huygens & Nairn, 2016), not open the door to colonisation.

Since the signing of te Tiriti the internal history of Aotearoa New Zealand has been characterised by a struggle between cultures. For *pakeha* (the collective noun now used by New Zealanders to signify people from another place) this has been from a position of privilege and dominance, for Māori (*tangata whenua*, meaning 'the people of the land') this has been a fight (sometimes literally) for survival. Over recent decades there has been a growing sensitivity to bi-cultural issues, the special relationship between the Crown and Māori which has seen a growing awareness and acknowledgement of historical injustices, and a desire to correct and compensate for these. This movement can be seen everywhere in Aotearoa New Zealand, although the changes made to date remain well short of those required.

The journey to full and fair bi-cultural engagement can also be seen in the development of the Code of Ethics which provides a foundation for the practice of professional psychology in Aotearoa New Zealand.

A History of New Zealand's Code of Ethics for Psychologists

Academic psychology in Aotearoa New Zealand has its roots firmly located in traditional Western psychology, originally based on the institutions of the United Kingdom, but now also heavily influenced by academic psychology practice in the North America and other international centres. Thomas Hunter established New Zealand's first psychology laboratory in 1907 at Victoria College, which has since become Victoria University of Wellington, located in the country's capital city (Kemp, 2007).

In 1947, psychology in New Zealand was formally recognized by the British Psychological Society when their board recognised New Zealand as an overseas branch of the Society. In 1967 the New Zealand Psychological Society (NZPsS) was established as an independent organisation. The New Zealand College of Clinical Psychologists (NZCCP) incorporation document was signed in 1989.

The first legislative framework focused on the practice of psychology was the Psychologists Act (1981). This act was passed to provide for the registration and discipline of psychologists by establishing a Psychologists Board who would advise on registration, training, and the promotion of high practice standards. Guidance documents were developed to assist the Board in regulation of profession and to provide a framework/context for responding to complaints about psychologists, although there is no point in the Act where ethical or competent practice is mentioned as these are assumed based on the possession of confirmed qualifications. These guidance documents were formalised into the first substantive Code of Ethics in 1986. The 1986 Code followed those of the professional psychological societies in Britain, Australia, Canada and USA.

The 1986 Code of Ethics was developed by the NZPsS with three purposes in mind,

1   to unify the practices of the profession,
2   to guide psychologists, and
3   to make a statement about the professional standards of psychologists available to the public.

This iteration of the Code was managed by the Council of the NZPsS. Section 10 of the Code stated that, "Psychologists abide by the rulings and decisions which are made by Council concerning ethical behaviour and standards of professional conduct". The definitions contained within the 1986 Code do not define the meaning of 'psychologist', but do define a 'practitioner' as a psychologists engaged in applying their knowledge and skills in applied settings. The title of practitioner is not used elsewhere in the document. This suggests that within the code psychologists were assumed to be primarily academics, and that the application of psychology to applied areas was a relatively new endeavour. This fitted well with the character of the NZPsS as a scholarly society.

The 1986 Code contained ten sections covering; responsibility, competence and accountability, description of services, confidentiality, professional relations, research with humans, teaching and research using animals, publications and public statements, psychological assessment, and decisions of council. With the benefit of hindsight it is clear that a number of the specific clauses within that Code have little to do with ethics and made little contribution to the stated purposes of the Code. For example, Clause 1.2 (Responsivity) stated that, "Psychologists engaged in teaching help students to acquire knowledge and skill, to achieve high standards of scholarship, and to develop independent thought." This clause contributed little to unifying the profession, guiding psychologists in making ethical decisions, or informing the public about standards or practice. Lindsay (2012) identifies the purposes of a code of ethics as being; educative about ethical practice, supportive of ethical decision-making, an aid to regulation, and informative for members of the public. Reviewing the 1986 version of our Code suggests that at that time it primarily focused on establishment of the profession and aiding regulation, and addressed few of the areas Lindsay (2012) mentions.

The most striking feature of the 1986 Code was its complete omission of any direct reference to te Tiriti o Waitangi. Although psychologists were required to "respect the cultural environment in which they work" and demonstrate sensitivity to "cultural and social diversity," the absence of reference to te Tiriti was seen as a gap that had to be filled (Dixon, 1993).

The review and subsequent revision of the 1986 Code commenced in 1995. The impetus for this was recognition that the existing Code was overly oriented towards rules and regulations, did not provide enough guidance on ethical practice and ethical decision-making, and did not express the cultural aspirations rising in the consciousness of psychology and New Zealand generally. As a model the profession took the 1991 Canadian Code of Ethics, which adopted a more principle-based and aspirational approach to ethical practice than the previous Codes. The start of the review also coincided with the adoption of the European Meta-Code of Ethics by the European Federation of Psychologists' Associations in 1995.

While the 1986 Code clearly identifies its origins within the codes of UK, Australia, Canada and US there is nothing in the 2002 Code to acknowledge its influences. Seymour (2016) states that the development work for the 2002 Code was heavily influence by the 1991 Canadian Code *"because* it represented quite a radical departure from their previous code and the codes of other countries" (italics added) suggesting that at that time there was substantial dissatisfaction with the previous Code and a desire to strike out in a new direction and develop a Code which was more aspirational and less reminiscent of a Code of Conduct.

The process used to revise the Code was led by the NZPsS and included members of the NZPsS, the National Standing Committee on Bi-Cultural Issues (NSCBI; a sub-committee of the NZPsS), and the Psychologists Board. The revision of the Code took a number of years as the views of psychologists and other stakeholders were widely canvassed. An analysis of the complaints against psychologists was also undertaken to better understand those areas of ethical practice where psychologists were experiencing greatest difficulty. The new Code was developed within the context of innovative legislative developments in the areas of privacy (Privacy Act 2003) and consumer rights and protections within the health sector (Health & Disability Commissioner Act 1994).

The current iteration of the Code, the *Code of Ethics for Psychologists Working in Aotearoa New Zealand* (2002), is starkly different from its predecessor. It is more easily recognizable as a document focused on ethical practice and aligns more closely with the four purposes identified by Lindsay (2012). The 2002 Code was adopted by members of the NZPsS and NZCCP at their respective Annual General Meetings in 2002, and by the Psychologists Board in December 2002.

In contrast to its predecessor the 2002 Code is clearly focused on enhancing ethical practice rather than simply providing a regulatory framework. The explicit purposes for the document are specified as

1   unifying the practices of the profession,
2   guiding ethical decision making, and
3   establishing guidelines which inform the public about the ethical practice of psychology.

The 2002 Code is based around the four ubiquitous principles which are also found in the Universal Declaration of Ethical Principles promulgated by the International Union of Psychological Sciences (2008). These principles relate to respect, competent caring, integrity, and professional responsibilities to society, and each has a short preamble outlining the rationale and applicability of the principle. In the New Zealand Code each of the principles has associated value statements, and there is a total of 22 such statements within the Code. The value statements are associated with specific practice implications (113 in total) and many of these have comments to further aid interpretation and application.

Another innovation within the 2002 Code was the inclusion of a suggested process for making ethical decisions. There are six recommended steps which are closely aligned with, although generally briefer than similar frameworks outlined in other international codes and guidance. For example, the current Code of the Canadian Psychological Association (4th edition) has ten such steps.

The Code also includes a *te reo* (Māori language) translation, *Te Tikanga Matatika Mā ngā Kaimātai Hinengaro e mahi ana i Aotearoa/New Zealand*. While the *te reo* translation of the Code was developed and included in the current Code it is a translation of English words and generally Western concepts of ethical practice that may not accurately reflect indigenous notions of ethical practice amongst Māori practitioners, or which may not be fully applicable to Māori service users. However, Pehi (2011) observes that having a careful translation of the Code is important because New Zealand has already learned from bitter experience how a poorly translated document can have catastrophic consequences. Every effort was made in drafting the Code to ensure the principles and spirit of te Tiriti are recognized and applied.

As indicated above, the 1986 Code made no mention of te Tiriti o Waitangi. Between 1986 and the adoption of the new Code there was a period of growing awareness that the Crown and its agencies and organisations was not meeting its obligations under te Tiriti. These omissions have resulted in significant disparities between Māori and pakeha on a broad range of social indicators. The placing of te Tiriti obligations (literally) at the front of the new Code suggests that this was a major driver of the changes. The first page of the Code begins with a Declaration that, "In giving effect to the Principles and Values of this Code of Ethics there shall be due regard for New Zealand's cultural diversity and in particular for the provisions of, and the spirit and intent of, the Treaty of Waitangi." The words "spirit and intent" are especially important given there are discrepancies between the original text versions of te Tiriti. It is clear that the intention at this time is to honour the Treaty principles of Partnership, Participation and Protection.

The professional practice of psychology in Aotearoa New Zealand is also subject to a framework of professional core competencies, which are developed and maintained by the Psychologists Board. At their most specific level these relate to particular scopes of professional practice, for example, core competencies for clinical psychologists, educational psychologists, neuropsychologists, etc. However, there is also a set of competencies relevant to all psychologists (referred to as the General Scope of Practice), and a set of competencies related to cultural awareness, sensitivity and competence, which are required of all registered psychologists. Therefore, engaging in culturally imbedded and informed practice is not just an ethical obligation, it also forms a basic competence requirement for all psychologists.

There has been mounting interest in reviewing and revising the *Code of Ethics for Psychologists Working in Aotearoa New Zealand* in recent years. The current version of the New Zealand Code is one of the most enduring within the international psychology community. The impetus for a review came initially from psychologists working in private practice who do not find the practice implications and further comments provided in the Code adequately address a number of the issues they have to deal with, for example, issues arising in the management of the financial and commercial arrangements they dealing with. Over the last two decades there has been a steady increase in demand for private or independent practitioners offering services. The principles and values within the current Code are not dependant on the mode of working, but it has been accepted that further guidance on the interpretation and implementation of these may be helpful. Another area of practice development has been the rapid increase in the use of digital and on-line resources across many aspects of the work of a psychologist.

Again, while the principles and values of the current Code are applicable it would be helpful to consider those aspects of ethical practice which impinge on these topics.

There are a number of specific issues to consider when reviewing and revising our Code, however, there are some important framing issues which will provide general context even before the review team explores the content of the Code.

1   Ethical colonisation – While the 2002 Code of Ethics Review Group went to great lengths to ensure the Code was explicit in recognizing the central importance of te Tiriti o Waitangi, and we have a Māori language translation of the full Code, it is undeniable that the Code and its conceptualisation of professional ethics is based within a Western paradigm. It would be interesting to explore whether Māori psychology practitioners would draft a code of ethical practice for their work with Māori clients which is different from the Code we currently have. Huygens and Nairn (2016) provide a thoughtful exposition of views on this topic and conclude that our current Code is not what limits ethical bi-cultural practice, but rather it is the lack of cultural awareness and knowledge amongst practitioners. One of the challenges facing the current Code of Ethics Review Group is to ensure the changing world views of New Zealand pakeha and Māori and both fully encompassed within our Code.

2   Ethics and legislation – An obvious motivating factor supporting a review of the current Code is the significant legislative and social changes that have occurred since the last iteration was drafted. Rather than having a single statute covering the activities of psychologists we now have the Health Practitioners Competence Assurance Act (HPCA Act 2003), which covers 17 health professional groups, including psychotherapists, doctors, nurses, dentists, podiatrists, chiropractors, and others. Regulation of each professional group is devolved to a Responsible Authority (regulation board). Under the Psychologists Act (1981) regulation of psychology practice was the responsibility of the NZPsS. Our current Code pre-dates the passing of the HPCA Act. We have also had time to further develop our understanding of the Trans-Tasman Mutual Recognition Act (TTMRA; 1997) which allows psychologists trained and registered in Australia to register and work in New Zealand and vice versa, despite the significant differences in service structures and cultural awareness/knowledge. It seems timely to reflect on the impact of these changes on the way professional psychology is practiced in Aotearoa New Zealand.

3   Ethics and regulation – While aspiring to an approach based on excellence and virtue (*aretaic* ethics) the fact that our Code is also used as part of a regulatory framework requires reduction to a framework of rules/duty oriented *deontological* ethics. As in many international jurisdictions our Code has no independent standing in law, however, it is a cornerstone of the work the New Zealand Psychologists Board undertakes to protect the health and safety of the public under the HPCA Act. Regulation of the profession is not listed as one of the stated purposes of the Code, but it is cited as a general purpose

by Lindsay (2012) and it is used in this way before the Health Practitioners Disciplinary Tribunal. Because of this the regulator is a co-owner of the Code and will play a part in any review and revision activities. This creates a possibility that the defining of ethical practice is aligned to make it easier to regulate the profession rather than being an accurate reflection of virtuous practice.

4   Ethical decision-making – While the six-step decision-making process has been embraced by psychologists in New Zealand it has been observed that this represents a formal process that is not feasible in all situations and does not reflect the processes used in all cases of ethical decision-making (Clark, 2012). It is also observed that many overseas codes have more detailed or broader recommendations regarding how decisions are made when ethical issues are the focus. For example, the current code of the Canadian Psychological Association (2017) suggests a ten-step process which prompts for the consideration of factors such as personal values and best interests, and the exploration of personal biases and external pressures, in addition to a focus on professional ethics.

5   Changing work practices – When the previous Code was produced there was little private practice of psychology in New Zealand. The Accident Compensation Corporation, the agency that funds and supports the rehabilitation of citizens who are injured in accidents, was founded by legislation passed in 1974. In 1992 sexual assault was added to the list of events referred to as *accidents*, implying no-fault on the part of the victim. This has generated an increasing demand for independent (private) psychological and counselling services for those who had experienced sexual assault. Most court work, e.g., psychological reports for the Family Court or Youth Court, are undertaken by private practitioners rather than those working in government agencies. Finally, primary healthcare in New Zealand is largely organised around General Practice, that is, community-based family doctors who largely own their practices and receive per capita funding via Primary Health Organisations (PHO). Psychological services delivered within this context are funded via private contracts with a PHO rather than being provided by government funded secondary providers via a primary-secondary collaboration. Each of these opportunities has seen the gradual expansion of private practice opportunities for the practice of psychology.

The Importance of a Bi-Cultural Approach

As indicated above most people living in Aotearoa New Zealand would accept that the foundational document of our nation is te Tiriti o Waitangi. Te Tiriti sets out the three principles which guide the relationships between Māori and pakeha. The history of honouring Te Tiriti has not been auspicious and in 1975 the government of the day passed the Treaty of Waitangi Act, which established the Waitangi Tribunal. The Tribunal is a standing commission which hears claims and makes recommendations relating to legislation, policies, and actions or omissions of the Crown in relation to their commitments under te Tiriti. By 2015 there had been 2,500 claims lodged with the Tribunal, a number of which have impacted on New Zealand at a national level.

In 2016 the Tribunal commenced a Health Services and Outcomes Inquiry which collected together a large number of claims concerning grievances about health service and outcomes which were considered to be of national significance. One of the claims which has been added to this Inquiry is claim WAI 2575 which relates specifically to the obligations of the Crown to

a   deliver culturally compliant psychological services to Māori, and
b   ensure that psychologists acknowledge and give effect to non-Western systems of psychological assistance.

This claim draws attention to the substantial disparities between Māori and pakeha across the full scope of social indicators, such as health status, educational attainment, employment, incarceration rates, and suicide rates (Cunneen & Tauri, 2019; Houkamau, 2019; Marriot & Sim, 2014). It suggests that this has resulted, in part, from a lack of diversity in the workforce, general refusal to incorporate Māori models of health and wellbeing within basic training and practice of psychologists, and the provision of services which fail to meet the cultural needs of Māori to such a degree that they are often effectively excluded from receiving psychological assessment and interventions. Within the claim, there is an implication for psychologists that this is not simply a failure in planning, resource allocation, instructional practice and so on, but a fundamental failure of human rights and ethical obligations.

Although there is much work to be done in ensuring the undertakings of te Tiriti are honoured, the movements which have been initiated in recent decades, including the substantial shift in emphasis in our Code of Ethics, can be seen as an indication that the tide may be starting to turn. The WAI 2575 claim makes it clear that we still have a long way to go, but the fact that such a claim can be lodged and the response to it has been one of support from the profession, before the Tribunal has even decided how it is going to hear the claim, suggests that there is a high level of acceptance of the basic premise of the claim. Specifically,

a   the importance of ensuring practice in psychology is sensitive, respectful and informed about culturally derived knowledge and approaches,
b   actively supports cultural diversity in training and practice, and
c   builds evidence-based practice, which encompasses and values indigenous and broader cultural perspective.

Running under the surface of the national discourse in this area is a lack of agreement about the nature of psychology, what constitutes psychological knowledge, how data about psychological matters can/should be collected, and how psychology can be applied for the benefit of individuals, groups, communities, and society in general (e.g., Waitoki, Dudgeon, & Nikora, 2018). This is simply demonstrated by examining a basic model of Māori health, *Te Whare*

Tapa Wha (House with Four Walls; Durie, 1994, 2001). This model identifies four interdependent elements that are required for the maintenance the wellbeing, in the same way that four interdependent walls are required to support the roof of a building. The elements of this holistic model are:

- *taha hinengaro* (mental and emotional wellbeing, including capacity to communicate);
- *taha tinana* (physical wellbeing);
- *taha whanau* (family and social wellbeing, including connection to ancestors);
- *taha wairua* (spiritual wellbeing, related to beliefs, values, traditions, identity).

This more holistic vision of health and wellbeing presents difficulties when we attempt to integrate it with a Western approach to psychology that is embedded within an understanding of science as being the systematic study of the structure and behaviour of the physical and natural world, and where evidence is only available via controlled observation and experimentation. Te Whare Tapa Wha requires non-Māori health practitioners to seek understanding outside of the text books and scientific journals, referring instead to indigenous knowledge and practices. More than this, we are challenged to consider whether it is even possible for non-Māori practitioners to develop enough knowledge of Māori ways (*mātauranga Māori*) necessary to practice safely with Māori service users.

Rather than responding with inaction in the face of this challenge many Māori and pakeha thought leaders have developed ways of working together. One such innovator is Prof Angus Macfarlane who has taken the approach of indigenising that discipline of psychology within the field of special education (Macfarlane, 2012). Macfarlane emphasises the importance of honouring others, listening to what they have to offer, listening to culture, and then allowing the convergence of streams, or braiding of rivers. This approach acknowledges that both indigenous and Western approaches have something to offer, and captures the essence of our current Code of Ethics, one that respects multiple perspectives and requires openness and flexibility based on cultural awareness, sensitivity and knowledge amongst practitioners.

How our Code is Used

The New Zealand Psychologists Board only regulates Registered Psychologists. As the HPCA Act identifies registered professionals under the Act as 'Health Practitioners' the Board's activities relate primarily to clinical, counselling, neuropsychologists, and some educational psychologists, as well as a range of psychologists registered under the General Scope of Practice. Those with psychology qualifications who work in academic or research, organisations (e.g., human resources) are less likely to be registered and, therefore, cannot refer to themselves as a 'Psychologist' as this is a protected term under the Act. As indicated above the Code constitutes a part of the regulatory framework for Registered Psychologists and informs the widely accepted values base on which all psychologists practice in

New Zealand. Breaches of the Code are usually a significant feature of disciplinary action taken against psychologists by the Psychologists Board and Health Practitioners Disciplinary Tribunal when there is a perceived need to protect members of the public from a psychology practitioner.

While assisting in the regulation of the profession is an important aspect of the Code, this only comes into play in a formal way when egregious errors have been made, recognized, and cannot be remediated via other routes, such as engagement in competence improvement plans. The way most psychologists experience the Code is as a framework which supports excellence in practice, encouraging reflection and framing discourse around competence and responsible caring. Psychologists in Aotearoa New Zealand are rightly proud of our Code, its commitment to te Tiriti, and the trust it places in practitioners to 'do the right thing' based on shared principles and values.

Concluding Comments

The development of the Code of Ethics for psychologists working in Aotearoa New Zealand can be traced through a number of distinct stages, which have been highlighted here. The first stage was the establishment of the discipline and its first steps towards independence from the influences of the Old World. Once psychology was established the next stage was to define the boundaries of the discipline though the application of rules providing guidance and regulation, this was achieved via the 1986 Code. The most recent stage has seen a greater focus on the professional and social environment. This is reflected in the principles and values expressed in the 2002 Code and is in keeping with international developments in this area. It is exciting to consider what will come next for psychologists working 'at the end of the world'. There is no ethical map for this work, no detailed step-by-step route marked out, but we will need a reliable compass to keep us pointing in the right direction. As the discipline of psychology in Aotearoa continues to review the merits of Western approaches to psychology and the promise of indigenous psychologies we will need to ensure we have developed an ethical compass that is fit-for-purpose.

References

Clark, C. (2012). Individual moralities and institutional ethics: Implications for the Canadian Code of Ethics for Psychologists. *Psychotherapy and Politics International*, 10(3), 187–204.

Code of Ethics for Psychologists Working in Aotearoa New Zealand (2002). Retrieved from www.psychology.org.nz/journal-archive/code-of-ethics.pdf

Cunneen, C. & Tauri, J. M. (2019). Indigenous peoples, criminology, and criminal justice. *Annual Review of Criminology*, 2, 359–381.

Dixon, B. (1993). *Ethics systems in the New Zealand Psychological Society*. Presentation at the 1993 Annual Conference of the New Zealand Psychological Society. Retrieved from http s://researchcommons.waikato.ac.nz/bitstream/handle/10289/3320/Dixon%20-%20Ethics %20systems.pdf?sequence=1&isAllowed=y

Durie, M. (1994) *Whaiora Māori health development* (2nd ed.). Oxford University Press.

Durie, M. (2001) *Mauri ora: The dynamics of Māori health*. Oxford University Press.

Health & Disability Commissioner Act (1994). Retrieved from http://legislation.govt.nz/act/p ublic/1994/0088/latest/DLM333584.html

Health Practitioners Competence Assurance Act (2003). Retrieved from www.legislation.govt.nz/a ct/public/2003/0048/latest/DLM203312.html

Houkamau, C. (2019). Maori identity and economic wellbeing. In C. Fleming & M. Man-ning (Eds). *Routledge handbook of indigenous wellbeing* (pp. 209–220). London: Routledge.

Huygens, I. & Nairn, R. (2016). Ethics and culture: Foundations of practice. In W. Waitoki, J. Feather, N. Robertson, & J. Rucklidge (Eds). *Professional practice of psychology in Aotearoa New Zealand* (pp. 15–26). Wellington, New Zealand: NZ Psychological Society.

Kemp, S. (2007). The history of early psychological research in New Zealand. In A. Weatherall, M. Wilson, D. Harper, & J. McDowall (Eds.), *Psychology in Aotearoa/New Zealand* (pp 1–6). Auckland, New Zealand: Pearson.

Lindsay, G. (2012). Ethical decision making. In M. M. Leach, M. J. Stevens, G. Lindsay, A. Ferrero & Y. Korket (Eds), *The Oxford handbook of international psychological ethics* (pp. 74–89). New York: Oxford University Press.

Macfarlane, A. H. (2012). "Other" education down-under: Indigenising the discipline for psychologists and specialist educators. *Other Education*, 1(1), 205–225.

Marriot, L. & Sim, D. (2014). *Indicators of inequality for Māori and Pacific people*. Working Papers in Public Finance. Wellington, New Zealand: Victoria University Business School.

Pehi, P. (2011). Translating the Code of Ethics – Part II. *Psychology Aotearoa*, 2011(1), 23–26.

Privacy Act (2003). Retrieved from www.legislation.govt.nz/act/public/1993/0028/latest/ DLM296639.html

Seymour, F. (2016). Ethics: The foundation for practice. In W. Waitoki, J. Feather, N. Robertson, & J. Rucklidge (Eds). *Professional practice of psychology in Aotearoa New Zealand* (pp. 5–13). Wellington, New Zealand: NZ Psychological Society.

Trans-Tasman Mutual Recognition Act (1997). Retrieved from www.legislation.govt.nz/act/public/ 1997/0060/latest/DLM410793.html

Universal Declaration of Ethical Principles for Psychologists (2008). Retrieved from www.iupsys. net/about/governance/universal-declaration-of-ethical-principles-for-psychologists.html

Waitoki, W., Dudgeon, P., & Nikora, L. W. (2018). Indigenous psychology in Aotearoa/ New Zealand and Australia. In S. Fernando & R. Moodley (Eds), *Global psychologies: Mental health and the global south* (pp. 163–184). London: Palgrave Macmillan.

PART 4

European Countries: Hungary, Slovenia, the UK, and the EFPA's Meta-Code

8

THE FIRST "HALF OF HUNDRED" YEARS OF THE HUNGARIAN PSYCHOLOGISTS' ETHICS CODE

Judit Szimethné Galaczi, Éva Kovácsné Vajger and Ibolya Oláh

English translation by Zoltan Jakab

> In my experience moral and ethical norms have with decreasing force in guiding our life. There are less than optimal generally accepted cornerstones. We often relativize although we are obviously aware of the frameworks. The Code of Ethics, as a mediator of values, plays a key role in ensuring that the psychological profession has a solid ethical, moral foundation. Without a solid ethical foundation, this profession cannot be practiced.
>
> *(an influential member of the Ethics Committee)*

At present there are several systems of ethical rules in force in Hungary that apply to psychologists or affect their activities (codes of ethics for training institutions, sectoral chambers, professional NGOs etc.). The most significant of these is the Professional Ethics Code for Psychologists (hereinafter: Code), which is a joint document of two main professional non-governmental organizations, the Hungarian Psychological Association (HPA) and the Hungarian Association Protection of Psychologists' Interests (API).

The outstanding importance of this document is due to several factors:

- This Code is historically the first, its original version created nearly fifty years ago. To date, it is the only one in Hungary that is special, i.e., it only applies to psychologists. The other codes, together with other professions, regulate the operation of psychologists, with which they carry out their activities in the same field, purpose or nature (e.g., the code of the chambers of forensic doctors, teachers).

- This Code is the only one created through broad professional cooperation and consensus. Historically, the publication of the wording of the first and second versions has aroused keen interest among contemporary Hungarian psychologists, which has manifested itself in hundreds of comments (critical remarks, suggestions etc.). At the professional social event aimed at its adoption, the affirmative vote of a large number of participants legitimized the final document.

- The scope of the Code is limited to the membership of associations that have established or operate a joint Ethics Committee to enforce the ethical requirements set out in the Code. However, its authority and guiding role go far beyond its personal scope, both in the professional and in the wider social public consciousness.

In our study, we focus primarily on the presentation of this document: its history, characteristics, operation, and the historical, economic, social, professional, cultural, and national characteristics that affect them.

The Story with the Historical Background

The need to formulate ethical expectations for practicing the profession of psychologist first arose in 1968. This is also relatively early in the international context, and coincides with the proliferation of Psychology in Hungary after a long period of rejection.

In the last decades of the 19th century, Psychology, which appeared as an independent discipline, soon made its way to Hungary. At that time, Hungary was in a state union with Austria (Austro-Hungarian Monarchy), so it developed as an active part of the lively intellectual life of Europe, mainly in interaction with the scientific and cultural peculiarities of the German-speaking area. The interest in Psychology and the scientific activity in this field was already indicated by the publications of well-known Hungarian doctors, philosophers and pedagogues before the turn of the century (of course it approached from other different disciplines for the time being). The first experimental Psychology laboratory founded at the Faculty of Medicine of the university of Budapest (1899) can be considered the beginning of institutionalization. At the beginning of the 20th century, the number of organizations established for the theoretical and practical activities of psychology increased. The first application of Psychology was in the fields of special education (1902), child Psychology (1907), and career choice (1908).

In treating mental illnesses psychoanalysis played an important role at the time. A newly formed discipline and movement, psychoanalysis – originated from the Monarchy's capital – had an important group of followers in Budapest who formulated a specific approach named the "Budapest School." The activity of the Hungarian psychoanalytic movement is indicated by the founding of their association (1913) and the establishment of the first, albeit very shortly-existing, university psychoanalytic department in the world (1919).

The end of World War I brought significant changes for Hungary. The Austro-Hungarian empire disintegrated, and the Hungarian Kingdom became independent. The country's social and economic system changed several times: a few months of democracy were followed by a few months of proletarian dictatorship, after which kingdom returned; it was, however, headed by a governor instead of a king. The long-time multiethnic country was disintegrated into several successor nation-states with borders determined by peace treaties ending the war; as a result, Hungary's territory and population were both reduced to roughly one third of their original figures.

The history of Psychology in Hungary was multiply affected by these radical historical changes and their political and ideological consequences. The system of academic and cultural institutions was necessarily restructured. Some professionals of outstanding importance were forced to emigrate for political reasons. Theoretical and practical Psychology shifted them in part due to the social and political shock and in the context of the raising nationalist spirit in many countries of post-war Europe. Pluralist and progressive tendencies that had characterized Psychology in Hungary were largely disrupted.

The development of psychological theory, the spreading of its practical applications and with it, institutionalization gained momentum in the late 1920s and early 1930s. At that time, the statist aspiration of the existing power played a decisive role in the development of Psychology's destiny.

A consequence of this political context was that Psychology's acquiring independent academic status made little progress. Despite the establishment of an Institute of Psychology at a university in a rural town (Szeged, 1929), its task was only to assist teacher training, and there was no independent vocational training in psychology in the country. Obtaining qualification in Psychology was only possible at foreign universities. In Hungary, the spreading of psychological knowledge took the form of public lectures, written publications and training courses.

In contrast, applied Psychology spread and flourished. It entered the working world: the first psychotechnical institute for professional aptitude testing was established by the public transportation company of the capital (1925), and then an ability testing station was founded by the Institute of Social Insurance (1929), later by the Army (1933), the Post (1934), and the railways company (1936).

The state supported the use of psychological expertise in schooling, education, and child-welfare. In addition, authorities expected psychology to assist their nationalist endeavor including "improving the quality of the population," to resolve social problems such as poverty, crime, alcoholism, and political deviancies, and also to contribute to the large-scale education reform aiming at a system to include the whole child population, taking into account the specificities of childhood. To this end the government supported institutional development: institutes for educational and career counseling, and mental health were established.

Due to its boom, Psychology has become increasingly known and popular in the wider society as well. Beyond the state framework, many charitable initiatives, civilian associations and movements provided psychological expertise. An increasing number of publications appeared for general audiences. The spreading of applied Psychology in everyday practice had caused worries in the scientific public. The professionals worried that the activities of "benign dilettantes and profiteers" would undermine the credibility of Psychology. There were no legal or ethical means available to address this.

As Psychology diversified, and the number of its practitioners increased, the need arose for an independent scientific organization. This led to the foundation of the Hungarian Psychological Association (HPA) in 1928. The association's goals were to facilitate the collaboration of psychologists, the support of psychological research and practice, and a broadening of international connections, in order to make psychology's scientific status recognized, and to further professionalize the field, especially vocational training and applied areas. This was a milestone in the development in the history of Hungarian Psychology. One of the first moves of the Association was to start a periodical named *Review of Hungarian Psychology*.

In the period pre-WW II, and especially in its initial stages, the spread of nationalism and fascism (which penetrated the ranks and leadership of the HPA, with the central theme of "the Psychology of the Hungarian people") again forced some psychologists to emigrate from Hungary. Many of the psychologists who decided not to leave the country become sufferers or victims of anti-Semitic measures that had been gradually introduced since 1938. The development of Hungarian Psychology underwent a break again.

At the end of WW II, Hungary's form of government changed from kingdom to republic, led by a coalition government (involving the Social Democrats, Communists, the Small-holders' Party, and the Peasants' Party). The following years were marked by the drafting of a peace treaty, reconstruction to repair the damages caused by the war, and, in the political sphere, the parties' competition for power.

In the first years of post-war peace, during the coalition period, Psychology suddenly began to develop in Hungary. Applied areas that had formed between the two wars continued functioning (for example professional aptitude testing, mental health and therapeutic activities). The recovery was due to a change in social functions.

The State set itself the goal of transforming the social structure in order to resolve the existing serious social tensions. It intended a strategic role for public education in achieving the necessary mass social mobility (catching up, elite exchange). The development and implementation of education policy reform required the participation of scientific experts, which the State expected from Psychology. It has invested significant resources in providing progressive and practical expertise.

In addition to university-level education in psychology that started at the University of Budapest (Psychology was an elective course in Liberal Arts), the Institute of Psychology has become an important center of theoretical Psychology and research. The state established further independent research institutes with psychological profile which, in addition to the research, also provided services in applied areas such as educational counseling, psychotherapy, and lectures to the general public. The former organization of the mental health movement was also re-established to deal with traumas and emotional problems caused by the war. In sum the coalition period, which lasted only a few years, was of outstanding importance for Hungarian Psychology, in terms of institutionalization and social participation.

Hungary as one of the defeated States in WW II had been under Soviet occupation and control from 1945. This contributed to the fact that the competition between the parties of the coalition era was eventually won by the Communist Party (1948 was the "year of the turn"). The country set off down the road to Socialism (private property was seized by the State; planned economy was introduced, and Marxist ideology became predominant), and the Hungarian People's Republic was formed (1949). In the first half of the 1950s, following the example of Soviet Stalinism, adopting its institutional system and practice, a totalitarian state developed in Hungary (including violent nationalization, cult of personal, conceptual lawsuits, and penal camps).

Psychology could not avoid its fate in the reign of the Soviet model in Hungary. Within a short time, its preferred and supported status ended, becoming a rejected and banned discipline. In particular, Psychology's concept of human development was incompatible with the contemporary voluntarist political approach, that proclaimed the rapid, unlimited, and irreversible formability of people, which allows for deep-running change of the society. Psychoanalysis in particular qualified as a dangerous theory due to the fact that it does not limit human functioning to the conscious factors. Psychology, considered a product of bourgeois ideology, which is inherently hostile to communist ideology, was stigmatized and persecuted by Communist power. Its role in public policy was taken over by Pedagogy.

The network of psychological institutions, the system of education and applied services formed during the coalition years, the scientific association (HPA) and the scientific periodical were quickly liquidated by the government. Experts who held important positions during Psychology's boom were suspended from office, and they were banned from continuing to work in their profession. For one decade, Psychology in Hungary (almost) ceased to exist.

Following the death of the Soviet dictator (1953), his successor initiated political and ideological relief. However, it took years for the effects to materialize in the countries under Soviet influence.

In Hungary this change realized through a social crisis. The crisis was a revolution towards democratic transformation and autonomy (1956), its suppression by Soviet military intervention, and subsequent retaliation (until 1963). The socioeconomic situation consolidated in the 1960s when power and political control began to soften over time, and the period has been marked by modernization efforts, with the increasing openness required for this.

In Hungary only a few psychological institutions survived the "decade of silence." Subsequent milestones in the process of revival were the formation of the Psychology Committee within the Hungarian Academy of Sciences (HAS; 1958), the re-opening of professional forums for publication (1958, 1960), the re-foundation of the scientific association (HPA 1962), starting university-level education in Psychology (1958), and the formation of the Institute of Psychology of the HAS (1965) – which created the possibility of professional unity and scientific rank.

The liberation of Psychology from the status of "forbidden science" was facilitated by the fact that during these times the Cold War competition between the superpowers had already taken place in the area of scientific and technological developments, in which Psychology, previously discredited by the Soviet side, had once again become important.

In Hungary, however, the development of Psychology did not continue at the point where it stopped before the dictatorship. Those in power at that time did not require its social-shaping contribution – because they envisaged other means to solve social problems.

The attitude of psychologists who have been battered several times throughout history has also become more apolitical ("neutral expert"). The international scientific achievements and connections made available by the opening ("Westernization" in general) have helped to strengthen the autonomy of Psychology rather than the role of the reformer of society, and the psychologist to become the "agent of the individual." The transformation of personal motivations in welfare societies has slowly resulted in a change of mentality in Hungary as well. The model of the "socialist type of person" serving the community has been replaced by the appreciation of privacy, the pursuit of well-being and self-fulfillment (individualization) also in public services.

The changing role of Psychology has contributed to the fact that the increase in the development of science, training, the number professionals, the differentiation of applied areas and the increase in user needs were together able to shape the recognition, acceptance and fate of Hungarian Psychology. The "central will", i. e., the intention to develop the contemporary centralized state power based on a comprehensive concept, played little role in this. Institutionalization and professionalization were developed based on psychologists' own discretion and ambitions, as a result of the prestige and relationship (lobbying) of individuals ("caring for Psychology is the job of psychologists"). This informality (the legalization of a bottom-up initiative through informal means of personal or political bargaining) has generally characterized the power decision-making mechanism of these decades.

Influential characters of Psychology in Hungary have achieved significant successes in this way: the discipline, the practice, the professional society and the system of psychological institutions have developed intensively and become more and more differentiated since the Sixties.

The later dominant "flag bearer" generation of Hungarian clinical Psychology grew up in an informal workshop organized and operated under the guidance of a charismatic person. In this workshop, a number of methods from abroad (mainly group therapies) were adapted and professionals were trained for their application. With the help of his students, the "Master" inspired, organized and implemented the theoretical and methodological foundations of Hungarian clinical psychology ("textbook" 1974, later a series of publications introducing diagnostic tools), its institutional acceptance and wide recognition in health care, the development and implementation of specialist training (postgraduate programs at university 1980).

In 1960, 12 people worked in Industrial Psychology in the country. Thanks to a kind of informal marketing activity of some psychologists, by 1965, 40 industrial companies implemented their respective occupational psychological laboratories (and by the 1980s they already had 68 locations). Initially, their main activity was the vocational selection and subsequent checks of suitability and competence, then ergonomics emerged, and from the 1970s onwards a more complex approach, which also paid attention to the safety, protection and well-being of the workers, began to deal with the organizations. The growing importance of Industrial Psychology was also fostered by the attempt to change the concept of the economy (introduction of a "new economic mechanism", market processes instead of planned economy, 1968). A career choice guidance institute was established in the capital (1967), with the support and coordination of which a national career counseling network was established (1972) and operated successfully, as a result of which Industrial Psychology became widely known. An analysis of the situation of Hungarian Psychology was made in 1979–80, and based on its results, the Industrial Psychology Coordinating Council was established. The Council, among its numerous tasks, created (1982) and operated for nearly 20 years, the Psychologists' Register of Hungary (which ceased without successor in 2001).

In the field of education, a few institutions survived the 1950s. One of them (the child psychotherapy division of a clinic) established a child psychotherapy institute in the capital (1968). This center served as a supportive and informal professional foundation for the development of a network of parental counseling and child guidance centers first in Budapest (1968), and then throughout the country (1972). Through the work of educational counseling centers – especially due to the compulsory school readiness tests (1972) – Psychology became available to a significant part of the population, the awareness and acceptance of which was increased during these times by regular appearances in the media (mainly TV and radio shows, articles in popular magazines). The growing social demands on the profession are illustrated by the shortage of child psychologists in the 1970s.

A smaller group of professionals who studied Psychology as part of Pedagogy (following 1958) started their career in the early 1960s. The only university that provided a major in Psychology as such (paired with Hungarian language and literature) produced a few graduates in 1968 for the first time. In the following years, this number was no more than a few dozen per year. Initially, training in Psychology included specialization from the third academic year on, in one of three possible directions: Clinical Psychology, Educational Psychology or Industrial Psychology. Psychology became a single-major program ten years later (1972), and it became more theory-oriented. The specialization was moved to the level of postgraduate education. After that, a rural university joined the training (Debrecen, 1974).

Due to the slow process of system development, the training of psychologists was unable to keep up with consumer needs for a while. In the absence of trained professionals, the positions created for psychologists were initially filled mainly by non-psychologists who either took advantage of retraining or not (retraining was available for a longer period in the form of evening and correspondence courses with reduced study time for people who graduated in other subjects). These employment conditions, as training progressed and volume increased, became an obstacle to the employment of real psychologists. At the same time, typically neither the employer institutions nor the clients were sufficiently informed to be able to adapt their expectations to the realistic possibilities of Psychology. In part, results beyond their competence were expected from psychologists, in part, information or interventions that were inconsistent with the psychologist's commitment to the client.

A well-known situation emerged from the 1930s, when "charlatanism" posed a real threat to the prestige and success of the psychologist profession, which, in the absence of legal and formal means, could at most stand against the personal action of individual professionals. In this situation, the need for explicit professional ethics regulation arose, mainly for reasons of profession and experts' protection. In the end, it took almost a decade to develop it, and it has required constant care and renewal ever since.

The idea was first represented by Imre Molnár[1] at the general meeting of the HPA in 1968. Despite the positive reception, due to other tasks, actions took place only after several repeated initiatives (1970). It was then that the HPA established a five-member committee to develop a Code of Professional Ethics for Psychologists.

As a first step, the committee developed the concept of a Code to be established, and decided that the Code should include:

- the ethical principles and, in addition, the most important rules of conduct that can serve as a guide by making the expected professional conduct clear to professionals and users;
- a general part for all psychologists and specific additional parts for the three areas of application that employ most psychologists (Clinical, Pedagogical and Industrial Psychology), which help to interpret at a specific level and emphasize the importance and realization of individual expectations, especially for lay persons (employers, clients).

It took another three years before the actual work on the elaboration of the Code could begin (because of acquisition and translation of foreign Codes).

The work took place in several phases: the study of foreign codes was followed by the analysis of domestic practice, from which the first wording of the general part could be prepared, which was discussed and further developed by three ad hoc committees. Among the sectors, the team of representatives of Industrial Psychology was the most active – among them Péter Simon,[2] who was not only a team member of the Industrial Psychology group, but also a long-term central player in the creation and development of the whole Code. This additional part was prepared and discussed first, by full membership of a specialized professional association (120 people), later by company executives as employers of occupational psychologists. The draft was then sent to all members of the HPA, after which it was adopted by the General Assembly with minimal modification (1975), and the Code entered into force.

Meanwhile, the clinical sector had worked to develop another regulatory option: initiating (1966) and achieving (1976) the legalization of professional requirements for psychologists. The "Qualification Regulation" stipulated that psychological activity could only be pursued with a degree in Psychology and defined who qualified as a professional psychologist. Although the implementation of the decree has stalled, the codification itself was nevertheless another milestone in the Hungarian profession of Psychology.

Despite these achievements, however, the issue of the Code of Professional Ethics had not been removed from the HPA's agenda. Not only because the section containing the special rules of the clinic and the pedagogical field was still missing, but also because it became clear in a few years that the Code could fulfill its function only if the professional community was able to respond in case the rules were not followed. Once again, Imre Molnár was the initiator of the HPA's establishment of a new committee (1980), whose basic task was not only to develop the Code of Ethics but also to operate it in practice.

During the further development of the Code (1980–84), great care was taken to acquaint as many professionals as possible with the text, and encourage them to contribute with their suggestions to the document being prepared. The volume of the work is illustrated by the following data: the process lasted a total of four years, approximately 20 experts regularly participated, 51 more professionals exercised the right to propose, 458 proposals were discussed, of which 109 amendments were implemented. At the delegate meeting, which adopted the finished material, 116 people participated and voted.

Serving the common cause with such activity and devotion was an indication of interest and sense of responsibility by the professional community. The new, completed version of the Code entered into force in 1984, binding on all members of the HPA.

By the 1980s, Socialism was in crisis at the international level (in the economic, social and ideological spheres). Soviet power was weakening, there was a generational change in positions of power, opposition political groups strengthened in Hungary and society's advocacy activity increased. In Hungary, the "change of regime" took place peacefully (1988–90). The party-state Socialist system was transformed into a pluralist, democratic, republican, market-economy European State by legislative means (new constitution and related laws), which was named the Republic of Hungary (1989).

The change of regime and the transformed legal environment also triggered changes in the situation of Hungarian Psychology. Independent NGOs of psychological approaches and methods began to proliferate, enriching the specialization of methodological training and practice. The Hungarian Chamber of Psychologists (HCP 1989) was established, with the hope that it could gain official authority as an advocacy organization for psychologists, which has not been realized since then (its successor organization is the MPÉE, which still operates today).

As a result of the privatization of the economy, large industrial companies, together with the occupational psychology laboratories, have disappeared, but some new areas of application have emerged (e.g., "head-hunting" for highly qualified jobs, career counseling, mental aptitude testing for possessing and carrying firearms), only some of which are available in public services. Currently, the public administration is the area where occupational psychology activities are carried out (Tax and Customs Administration, Hungarian Army, Police, Disaster Management, public space supervision) and nowadays also employs a relatively large number of psychologists for repeated training of drivers (for drivers whose driving license has been revoked for a traffic offense).

The financing of the health care system has changed, in which the activity of psychologists is markedly underestimated, therefore it is not profitable for hospitals and clinics to employ such a specialist (it does not "produce" their own salaries), so there are only a few psychologist jobs in public health institutions. Psychologists have come into private practice.

The countrywide service networks set up under the old regime (educational counseling, career counseling, psychiatry and neurology centers) have been partially maintained, and recently significantly developed areas of school and kindergarten psychology and psychological services in child welfare institutions.

A professional protocol has been developed in a number of areas, which has been a huge step in the development of professionalism, supporting the professional in acquiring internship and in practice, promoting the transparency of the profession for outsiders.

Non-psychological mental services have diversified and differentiated, new occupations have emerged, and a number of helping activities have become widespread (more than 20 new helping professions were introduced in the early 1990s). The activities of the churches have been renewed and become significantly more active in the field of education and mental health services.

The book market has risen, private publishers have begun to offer out volumes about scientific and popular psychology and provide a wide variety of products that promise to support lifestyle, self-knowledge, mental health, mental well-being, and personality development.

The system of higher education and procedures of scientific qualification changed a few times; at the same time, the popularity of psychology kept increasing (has become "fashionable"). At the present time, seven Hungarian universities offer Psychology programs in the Bologna system, that is, at BA, MA, and PhD levels (since its introduction in 2005). The annual number of new Psychology graduates averages around 500.

In this diversified and accelerated continuous process of development, the psychological profession was at a great loss: in the legislative process of the change of regime, when the previous legislation was repealed (deregulation 1990), the regulation on the qualification of psychologists was repealed also. Since then, no legislation has been adopted that would generally define the concept and content of psychological activity. Prominent representatives and organizations of the psychological profession have made numerous attempts to solve this problem, without much success so far. In this unfortunate situation when official regulation is not available, psychological ethics regulation bears heavy responsibilities. The HPA and the HCP have entered into an agreement to cooperate in the area of ethics, which still exists since then (currently with the HCP's successor organization, the API).

Ethical regulation seeks to keep pace with the development of Psychology in Hungary. One way of doing this is to formulate resolutions in principle on issues that are not yet covered by the Code. Another way is to completely rethink the code within the framework of the occasional reform, to include the necessary amendments and additions.

Most recently, the revision and transformation of the Code took place in a long process in the 1990s. The then renewed Code entered into force in 2004 and has been in force ever since. Preparations for the next reform are in progress. The aim of the reform is to update the Code, to respond better to current challenges in psychology's internal situation and improve harmonization with international requirements.

Characteristics of the Hungarian Ethics Code

Regarding the *sources* of the Hungarian Ethics Code, it was a distinctive Hungarian feature that at the time of preparing the first draft of the Code, many psychologists had graduated abroad, therefore they made a great effort to be familiar with foreign psychological literature (Rajnai, 2020). However, it was not easy to access foreign documents at the time (1970) from which to start framing the national code. The first source obtained was a discussion about the French ethics code, in the form of journal publications by the French psychological associations. By the time a Hungarian translation of these publications was prepared by the HPA, the ethics code of the American Psychological Association and that of the German Psychological Society were also acquired. These documents served as a basis for compiling the first version of the Code. A few years later when expanding the Code became necessary (1980), further sources were also available: the ethics codes of Britain and Holland, as well as more recent versions of the American, German, and French codes (Molnár, 1985). Finally, preparing the present version was also aided by the Scandinavian code of psychological ethics.

Since 1980, the HPA is a member of the European Federation of Psychologists' Associations (EFPA) which compiled general guidelines called a *meta-code* (2005) to be followed by the ethics codes of its member organizations. An earlier version of these guidelines (1996) helped to attain the current form of the Code. The preparation of the Code mainly relied on domestic psychological practice and experience. Foreign ethics codes mostly served as a background against which to recognize and analyze similarities and also differences in psychological practice in Hungary.

Differences between the source documents made it clear in the beginning that all countries formulated somewhat different ethical rules, presumably due to variations in legal context, working conditions and attitudes toward psychology within the society, which together determined what aspects of psychological practice needed to be regulated and how.

The *declared goals and objectives* of the Code are essentially unchanged from the way they were at the outset: specifying the fundamental rights and obligations associated with psychologists' professional activities, and emphasizing ethical responsibility.

At an earlier stage of professionalization of psychology in Hungary, when the Code was created, no guide or reference was available to psychologists practicing their profession to justify their decisions and activities in situations involving ambiguity or conflict. Comprehensive regulation of the psychological profession in Hungary has been partial up to the present. In a number of areas specific procedures and protocols have been prepared, while legislation governing psychologists' professional activities is still missing. For this reason, the Code and its proper use are of crucial importance. To fill the void in existing regulations, the Code contains the most important standards of conduct, in addition to ethical principles.

Compared to similar documents in other countries, our Code places a stronger emphasis on informing institutions employing psychologists about professional and ethical standards. At present this aspect is still relevant in ensuring proper professional activities of psychologists, in particular, to protect them from demands contrary to the Code's rules and principles. Unfortunately, the scope and limits of psychological competence are still not part of common knowledge in Hungary, and there is no other authoritative source to promote their entrenchment. Information from reliable sources for employers and clients is especially important with respect to novel areas of applied psychology.

In its introduction, the code enumerates *fundamental values* which are to be observed and affirmed by psychologists throughout their professional career: the respect for and the protection of human dignity; a striving for a high level of professional competence and an awareness of its boundaries; and the protection of the psychologist's professional role and integrity. These universal values were specified in the 1984 version, and are still present in the most recent one.

Beyond enumerating values, the present Code also explicates the most important *general principles* in a separate chapter, in a structure similar to other ethics codes. These principles include respect for human dignity; fidelity and responsibility; integrity; competence and beneficence; which correspond to the approaches of other codes, mostly of the EFPA meta-code and of the APA code. These values and principles are essential norms that are unavoidable while performing work centered around interpersonal relationships.

The general rules of the Hungarian ethics code address all of the main topics that figure in codes of other countries. In some places there is verbatim adoption, especially from the APA Code: if an idea was discussed and considered necessary to be included in our Code, and upon thorough scrutiny, its formulation in the source document was found suitable, then their priority was not deviation from the source but clarity and precision.

The first chapter of the ethical standards of our Code addresses the issue of *competence*. Compared to other codes that we are aware of, this is a distinctive characteristic. As explained in the history section above, in the last 120 years in Hungary – with the exception of the 1976–90 period – psychology as a profession lacked legal regulation. However, psychologists and their employers do need definitions of professional competencies, therefore the issue has been included in the Code. At present when our profession is already accepted by society, defining competencies still plays a role in delineating borders with related fields and parallel areas (like coaching or training) (Rajnai, 2020).

When the 1975 Code was created, most Industrial Psychologists worked at state-owned industrial companies, factories or plants, while clinical and educational psychologists were employed by healthcare and public education institutions. This fact was represented in the first Code thus: "Psychologists' activities are carried out in, and commissioned by, public or social organizations or organs. Private individuals' commissions may only be fulfilled if one is entitled by the law." The later shift toward the emerging private sector was reflected by the following regulation: "Private practice may only be pursued by specialists of psychology, in their own area of specialization" (1984). In the present code we find: "In their professional work psychologists consider the Ethics Code regardless of the professional field and the legal framework in which they work" (2004).

Like a number of foreign codes, our Code also emphasizes *responsibility* as a general rule. Responsibility should be taken for psychologists' professional decisions, methods and procedures employed, their expected outcomes, psychological interventions, and in the course of all these, for the protection of interests of individuals and society. This chapter prescribes that psychologists' professional activities be done at the highest standards and in line with their convictions. In the Code, emphasis is placed on the individual responsibility of psychologists as employees (Rajnai, 2020).

The chapter on *professional competence*, similar to the American code, addresses the issues of professional development (making ongoing efforts to improve one's knowledge and competence), boundaries of competence, personal problems and obstacles to performing professional duties, and activities which may or may not be performed without a degree in Psychology. It is emphasized that non-psychologists should not conduct psychological examinations and interventions; to ensure this, tests, assessment and therapeutic instruments must not be passed on to non-psychologists, nor can non-psychologists be trained to use such instruments. Our Code, unlike the American one, in no case allows psychologists to perform activities for which they lack official training or education – not even in urgent cases where competent service is unavailable. The fact that our Code protects competence boundaries so strongly is related to the local history of education and professionalism in Psychology.

Official forms of professional *cooperation* were also less elaborate and less well-regulated legally in the past, including training routines and internship (Rajnai, 2020). For this reason, our Code, in the chapter on professional competence, discusses in detail cooperation with colleagues and professionals of related professions including supporting the development of subordinate colleagues (psychologists, interns, assistants), helping psychology students and professionals starting their career, and consultation with medical professionals.

The 1975 and 1984 versions of our Code had another peculiarity: unlike other codes that we know of, an entire chapter used to be devoted to providing suitable *working conditions*. At the time of creating these earlier versions, professionals had substantial struggles for satisfactory conditions and equipment for their work. Later development of the profession, extending knowledge about psychology in society, and the growth of private practice made it unnecessary to discuss working conditions in a chapter of its own; this topic is now part of the requirements of professional competence.

The chapter on *client relationships* is in accordance with the corresponding chapter of the American code in a number of ways: it addresses the issues of discrimination, multiple relationships, service made for a third party, avoiding exploitation, and informed consent. This chapter also prescribes informed consent as necessary for voice or video recordings, appropriately provided information about fees in private practice, and the requirement that, with a few reasonable exceptions, diagnostic statements, reports, and therapies can only be based on in-person meetings and procedures. Coincidence with the content of foreign codes at this point follows from the nature of these activities, and that of services based on trustful interpersonal relationship and communication (Rajnai, 2020).

Issues of *privacy and confidentiality* are also presented in accordance with foreign codes, especially the American one; the only difference is that minimizing intrusions on privacy is not discussed. On the other hand, our code discusses thoroughly two subclasses of confidential information: prominent psychological information and data of personal identification, in compatibility with Hungarian law. Regarding the handling of personal data, assessment and therapeutic documents, our code makes reference to the law concerning the protection of personal data. The explication of these features is important because, even though protection of the rights of the individual plays a more and more important role in our society, these rights are not yet sufficiently built into common knowledge (Rajnai, 2020).

Within the topic of *research*, a distinctive characteristic of our Code is that it requires the collaboration of a veterinary surgeon in experiments involving interventions affecting the health of animals. In addition, the placement, care, and feeding of experimental animals must also be supervised by a veterinarian or some other professional with comparable competence. This emphasis on animal protection is related to the fact that earlier, the importance of animals used to be based mostly on their utility, and considering animals as individuals is another relative newcomer to Hungarian common knowledge in recent decades (Rajnai, 2020).

In the topic of *public statements and advertising* a Hungarian peculiarity is that the first two versions of the Code did not discuss advertising at all, only professional publications and appearances. As private practice became more common, the latest version was supplemented with paragraphs on advertisements of psychologists' services and the associated fees.

The closing section of our Code discusses the *resolution of ethical issues*. In its contents, it is similar to its American counterpart. There are two issues presented in the American code that are not included in ours: *Improper Complaints*, and

Unfair Discrimination Against Complainants and Respondents, due to the fact that such cases had been quite infrequent in Hungary.

Our Code repeatedly stresses that psychologists should *communicate clearly*, using a language appropriate to the age, education, and mental status of the persons involved (including clients, colleagues in other professions more or less closely related to psychology, co-workers of other professions, employers, and general audience of lectures). Another important expectation is that psychologists should strive to earn *trust and respect for their profession* through their professionally and ethically correct conduct. The history of Psychology in our country, with its relatively slow progress and temporary declines, makes individual responsibility for psychology's social status and acceptance an important issue up to the present.

A distinctive *structural characteristic* of our Code is that the authors of the first two editions decided to add supplementary collections of area-specific ethical rules for the three main areas involving the highest number of psychologists. We did not find a similar structure in any of the foreign codes we studied, even though the ethics codes published by the British, American, and German societies are accompanied by separate documents that specify the rules for specific areas. The authors of our code aimed at constructing a comprehensive document itself including area-specific rules, for the sake of the employers of psychologists who found concrete regulations more cogent than general ethical principles. This is how supplementary professional requirements of Industrial and Organizational Psychology came to be added to the 1975 code, and those of clinical and educational psychology to the 1984 one (Molnár, 1985).

The present Code contains generally applicable rules equally effective for each area. The reason for this different approach is that in the twenty-year period between the last two versions, the special areas within psychology underwent substantial differentiation; as a result, the Code's focus shifted from specialities of the areas to general characteristics of work done within the framework of inter-personal relations. Special rules for special areas migrated to the ethics codes of method-specific associations operating as professional NGOs (Rajnai, 2020).

Regarding its *language and style*, our code resembles the German, French and Dutch codes in that it uses subjunctive mood expressing obligation or requirement. On the contrary, the American code describes, in indicative mood, what psychologists *are like* – and not what they *should be like*. The indicative form presumably comes from the tacit assumption that best practices in Psychology have developed in compatibility with the *right* ethical principles, and this factive view is properly expressed by indicative mood in third person singular. On the contrary, the British ethics code uses only subjunctive mood expressing obligation.

Authors of the first Hungarian code started from the premise that this document contains normative rules of behavioral conduct, therefore the proper formulation is to use demands and requirements specifying what psychologists should be like, e.g., "is obliged to," "must do," "should proceed so and so," although at some places indicative mood is used to express the same normative approach ("acts in such a way that ..."). However, since not each particular requirement carries the same level of force, nor are they equally possible to comply with, sometimes we use less categorical forms like "strives to ...," "takes into account that..." (Molnar, 1985). These stylistic features of the code have been essentially unchanged up to the present time.

The Ethics Code and the Ethics Committee: Functioning and Influences

It was one year after the creation of the Code that the so-called "training statute" took effect (1976); it was intended to resolve anomalies of employment in the psychological profession. This plan, however, did not materialize as no associated implementing regulations were published. Therefore, psychologists had to face the frustrating fact that legal sanctioning of unauthorized use of professional titles remained impossible, which, among other things, also affected their sources of living. Still only ethical objections could be raised against spurious psychological practices. At this point the HPA established its Ethics Committee (1980; hereafter EC) as an official body to endorse and enforce ethical norms and to sanction their violation. The EC has been functioning since then.

Each section and division of the HPA delegates one member to the EC, thereby each subfield of psychology is represented in its membership to assure that any ethical problem or conflict encountered be treated involving relevant expertise.

Members of the Committee volunteer their professional services motivated by their sense of responsibility and professional conscience. Being delegated to the EC is an honor – a recognition of performance and moral stance by the nominating division or section. The Committee has two leaders; initially these were the chair and the secretary. More recently, since the HPA and the API cooperate in ethical matters (1992), both organizations delegate one member who fills the chair and co-chair position respectively, with a rotation in every second year. The mandate of EC members and leaders is for four years. In the last ten terms the number of members of the EC varied between ten and 33; the total number of members over the 40 years of its operation is 98. One of the members has continuously been active since 1980! Their work is supported by a legal expert who is a full member of the Committee.

Duties and rules of operation of the EC are defined in two documents: the Statute and the Regulations. These were prepared at the time of the Committee's formation and – similarly to the Code – they were subsequently renewed a few times (1987; 1990; 2002) to incorporate experience accumulated over the years of operation.

The Statute defines the Committee as a body of protection for the psychological profession which works to promote the accordance of work in psychology with ethical and professional norms, thereby assuring moral conduct in professional life, and protects the interests of the society related to Psychology, and the membership of the two associations operating the Committee against unjustified demands and expectations. The Committee is not a patron of psychologists, nor is it their educator, therapist, attorney, or accuser. Its role is guidance toward morally right action. Its principal means of operation is emitting resolutions which are to reinforce professionals who proceed according to the relevant norms of their profession, and to correct those psychologists who violate them.

Resolutions of the EC can take the following forms:

- *Rulings* are formulated in response to particular ethical conflicts or complaints submitted to the Committee
- *Guidance* is provided upon request in cases where the party seeking advice has doubts about the correct conduct
- A *stand* is taken either upon request or on the Committee's own initiative when its necessity is recognized. It reflects on some current event or phenomenon with the aim of specifying (or fine-tuning) relevant principles that figure in the Code only in a more general form short of providing accurate guidance for the situation in question.
- *Opinions or proposals* are formulated upon request or upon the Committee's decision. Their purpose is to contribute to, or influence, legislation affecting the psychological profession, and to amend or extend the Code.

The Committee performs its work at regular meetings between which cases and other matters are handled by the president. In particular cases information necessary for reaching a conclusion (e.g., hearing of the complainant and the complained, processing of relevant documents) is collected by a fact-finding commission which is an ad hoc group comprising a few volunteer members of the EC assembled for purposes of a given case. The collected information is presented at Committee meetings followed by discussion and decision-making. In cases where an ethical violation is established, the EC applies sanctions. Depending on the severity of the violation, the sanction can be a warning, an admonition or an initiation of expulsion from the HPA.

Over the 40 years of its existence the EC handled several hundred ethical conflicts. In each case the first step is to determine competence or lack thereof, with respect to the persons involved and the character of the situation. The EC takes itself to be competent only in cases which involve one or more members of the HPA (the association is its personal domain of operation), and in which the issue is ethical in nature. Quite often the filed complaint is either legal, purely professional or employment-related, therefore it falls in the scope of ruling of other official bodies. In such cases the complainant is directed to the appropriate organization accompanied by a justification to assist them in their future choices.

The most frequent type of complaint is objection to psychologists' unacceptable behavior. Within this category one can find violation of secrecy, unprofessional conduct, partiality by forensic experts, superficial approach, and abandoning the general framework or ground rules of psychotherapeutic practice. A wide variety of cases have been encountered including unauthorized use (of titles, tests or other methods etc.), plagiarism, copyright infringement, or employer inspection illegitimately accessing personal information.

The EC prepares a summary report of its work in every year, and submits it to the two associations (HPA and API). The report is also published on the association homepages and in the form of newsletters for the members. Stands that are to further specify some principles (see above) are also published on the HPA homepage for professional and general audience; members receive them as news-letters in a more detailed form accompanied by interpretive explanations.

In its early period of operation, the EC published anonymous summaries about each case in the newsletters; this no longer happens due to changes in data protection and personal privacy laws. In 2008 the Committee introduced a new column in the newsletter in order to raise and analyze ethical problems. With this move the EC intended to offer a better view of its operation, to enhance the sensitivity of profes-sionals to ethical matters, and to make norms and requirements more transparent and better understood – in sum, to promote sophisticated ethical thought.

In developing and strengthening the influence of professional ethics, the HPA–API EC has long-term companions. Starting in the early 1980s undergraduate programs in psychology have included *Ethics for psychologists* as a subject (a mandatory course). In 2014 an ethics reader was published which presented and analyzed cases from vir-tually all subfields of psychology. As the closing act of their education, psychology students take a professional oath to strengthen their identity as psychologists, and to motivate them to observe ethical principles in their work. The ethics of scientific research became a responsibility of universities and research institutes as the Science Ethics Code of the Hungarian Academy of Sciences was published. This code was subsequently adopted by a number of universities in the country.

Following the change of regime in 1990, a number of professions have formed their own chambers with statutory authority. Psychologists are involved in some of these organizations; for example, clinical psychologists are mandatory members of the Hungarian Medical Chamber, forensic psychologists are members of the Hungarian Chamber of Forensic Experts, and psychologists working in education join the National Chamber of Educators. The ethics codes of these organizations apply to their psychologist members as well.

Psychologists' increasing involvement in the private sector following 1990 (including economic organizations, and professional NGOs) created another con-text from the point of view of ethics, as these organizations also provided for their own codes of conduct to gain the trust of their clients and customers.

At the time of founding the EC and compiling the Code the community of psychologists in Hungary comprised a few hundred people, hardly anyone of whom was *not* a member of the HPA. Therefore, practically all psychologists were at the time subject to the ethical requirements therein. Despite the mild sanctions, the Code exerted a strong influence on the profession; within such a small and socially densely interconnected group following the norms was a substantial pressure.

Today the number of psychologists in Hungary is approximately 15,000. The overwhelming majority of them of them are affected by the rulings of more than one ethics code, depending on their field of work and expertise. The specific requirements of different codes are not identical; having a clear view of all the relevant ones is difficult, let alone complying with each.

For a while now the HPA membership has fallen behind the overall psychol-ogist population in number. In addition, publicizing ethical issues in professional circles is no longer a usual practice. As a result, the enforcing power of the Code has lessened to some extent. Still the number of cases filed in recent years, and the willingness of involved professionals to cooperate together suggest that it still has substantial authority and respect.

Concluding Comments

We can conclude that one of the Hungarian Ethics Code's specialities is that the authors, despite the difficult circumstances, aspired to create a state-of-the-art Code that meets international standards. Beyond the universal characteristics of a profession that relies on interpersonal skills, the different versions of the Hungarian Code reflect the country's historical background and the state and development of the psychological profession. The most important Hungarian characteristics are maintaining competence, and the intention to enhance psychological knowledge and the prestige of the psychological profession in society.

Ethics for psychologists in Hungary had come a long way in fifty years, however, it has not yet reached a reasonably stable point. We expect the coming years to bring suitable legislation and institutions of protection for our profession; in other words, that representatives of professional ethics be able to focus on ethical issues in an efficient system thereby preserving the prestige of the psychological profession.

Notes

1 Imre Molnár (1908–1996): His professional activity is related to Pedagogical and Industrial Psychology. He was a specialist with outstanding activity and influence in Hungarian psychological public life, the initiator and manager of the ethical regulation of the profession until decades, the founder of the Ethics Committee and its chairman for 16 years (1980–96). For his exemplary oeuvre, he was awarded the HPA "Corporate Commemorative Medal" (1983).
2 Péter Simon (1943–): Industrial Psychologist, who, in addition to his central role in shaping the Hungarian Ethics Code, he was the co-chair of the Ethics Committee for 16 years. His outstanding work was recognized by the HPA as a "Corporate Commemorative Medal" (2011).

References

Bagdy, Emőke (2010) *Quo vadis magyar klinikai pszichológia? Avagy mit tudjon az, aki ma e hivatás szolgálatára vágyik?* [Quo vadis clinical psychology in Hungary? What should one know to serve in this profession?] *Alkalmazott pszichológia* [*Applied Psychology*] 2010(3–4).

Dienes, Erzsébet (2020) *A magyar munkalélektan története* [History of Industrial Psychology in Hungary], manuscript

Kovai, Melinda (2016) *Lélektan és politika* [Psychology and Politics]. Budapest: L'Harmattan Kft.

HPA – AHP (1975, 1985, 2004) *Ethical Principles and Code of Conduct for Psychologists.*

HPA archives 1985–2009, reviewed by Hazag Anikó és Nagy Anett

HPA archives 1980–2010, reviewed by Sz.Galaczi Judit

Molnár, Imre (1985) *Az etikai kódex kialakulásának története* [History of the Ethics Code], *Magyar Pszichológiai Szemle* [Hungarian Review of Psychology], 1985(1).

Pléh, Csaba (2010) *A lélektan története* [History of Psychology]. Budapest: Osiris Kiadó.

Pléh, Csaba (2008) A pszichológia alakulása a hivatások rendszerében [The history of psychology in the context of other professions]. In E. Kiss (Ed.), *Nyolc évtized: Tanulmányok a*

Magyar Pszichológiai Társaság életéből [Eight Decades: Studies of the history of the Hungarian Psychological Association]. Budapest: MPT.

Pléh, Csaba (2016) *Intézmények, eszmék és sorsok a magyar pszichológia fél évszázadában* [Institutions, Ideas, and Lives in 50 years of Hungarian Psychology: 1960–2010], *Magyar Pszichológiai Szemle*, 1916(4–5).

Rajnai, Nadinka (2020) A Kódex társadalmi összefüggései [social context of the code]. Personal communication.

Simon, Péter (2020) A Kódex története és a sajátosságok motivációi [history of the code, and the motivations for its specialities]. Personal communication and reviewer comments.

Szabó, Mónika (2019) *Tanulmány vázlat és munkaterv* (Study outline and work plan), manuscript

Focus groups

2019.11.26. Participants: Czigler István, Dulin Jenő, Komlósi Annamária, Pléh Csaba, Rajnai Nadinka, Torma Kálmán, moderators: Kaló Zsuzsa and Sz. Galaczi Judit.

2020.01.16. Participants: Boros János, Dienes Erzsébet, Pataki Ilona, Szakács Ferenc, moderator: Sz. Galaczi Judit.

9

ETHICS FOR PSYCHOLOGISTS IN SLOVENIA

Vita Poštuvan

Ethical codes and ethical awareness are inter-linked with the development and organization of the profession in specific cultural and social environments. Therefore, if one wishes to understand the development of ethical codes for psychologists in Slovenia, a historical aspect needs to be explained.

The Slovene Psychologists' Organization

Slovene psychologists were initially organized under the umbrella of the Yugoslavian Psychologists' Association. The branch of Slovene members was formed in 1954 and is considered as one of the starting points for the Slovene psychologists' movement (DPS, 2019). At that time, its emphasis was on linking with the umbrella organization and work was done in cooperation with psychologists from other countries of ex-Yugoslavia. An independent Slovene professional body was established later on and registered in the Slovene business register in 1976 as the Slovene Psychologists' Association (DPS, 2019; AJPES, 2019).

Nowadays, the Slovene Psychologists' Association represents around 200 members and is a voluntary professional organization. There is an estimation that only around 10% of educated psychologists are its members, even though it is the only psychological association in the country not related to a specific field of work. Moreover, the Slovene Psychologists' Association is also a member of European Federation of Psychologists' Associations (EFPA) and the EuroPsy certificate is awarded under its supervision. It has several boards addressing different fields of psychology (such as counselling and psychotherapy, organizational psychology, psychology in education, social work, etc.) and committees, among which there is also an Ethics committee. The low ratio of members compared to the number of educated people can be partly explained because many graduates do not work in the field of psychology. But the ratio is still low compared to other similar organizations abroad and this is probably due to the voluntary status of the association: as described below, there are no legal or license-related rules that would require membership status.

Lack of Legal Measures or Licensing for Psychologists

There is no professional law that regulates the profession of psychologists in Slovenia, even though there have been ongoing attempts to provide such measures since Slovene independence in 1991. Several working groups have been formed since then and the draft of a law was presented to different governmental bodies, also to the parliament (Zupan & Bucik, 2000). The biggest obstacles in this process so far have been the complexity and broad areas of work of psychologists, which are apparently difficult to combine under a unified legal umbrella. However, there also seems to be a lack of governmental motivation, and probably a lack of awareness as to why having such a law is important for our society. For some, the current situation seems to be convenient too, as it gives space for avoiding responsibilities that would involve the law (Matjan Štuhec, 2011).

The lack of a common law causes problems in specific aspects of psychologists' work, but the biggest issue is that the quality of psychological services for lay public is hard to maintain. For example, the title "psychologist" is not protected, so anyone, without specific training, can claim to have competence in psychology and to provide psychological services. This is especially relevant for the private sector, as in several public sectors there is a greater level of regulation, with internal rules. Even more, in the current system it is difficult to distinguish those who have the basic education of psychology from those who have the required additional trainings or specific competencies.

The main criteria for employing someone as a psychologist is their education: nowadays this means having a masters level degree in psychology. Supervised practice is required in most of the public sector services. Unfortunately, once one requires these conditions, there is no licensing system where competencies can be reassessed and professional work reevaluated within specific time frames. An additional problem is that, at the moment, the supervised practice implemented in everyday practice in Slovenia does not include the gatekeeping function as it is understood in the EuroPsy model,[1] with the exception of a small number of specially trained supervisors. So, once someone gets a title of a psychologist by finishing his masters level degree, this is (more or less) a formation for a lifetime.

Moreover, the Slovene Psychologists' Association does not have any legal power, neither is an order, union or other government consulting body relevant for the maintenance or regulation of best practices. It does not have the power to enforce any regulations outside of its members. Consequently, a psychologist who is not a member of the association is under no specific external regulation if they break ethical or professional standards. It is, of course, different if a psychologist breaks other laws, such as The Data Protection Act, or is involved in any criminal behavior etc. – then they are prosecuted according to general legal standards.

The situation regarding ethical evaluation is different for those who are members of the Slovene Psychologists' Association: namely, membership status anticipates that members can be evaluated regarding their use of professional and ethical standards and judged and sanctioned according to the internal rules and codes. The most serious sanction of the association is to lose the membership status. However, since the membership is low and voluntary, this sanctioning does not represent a big threat. Moreover, the association's honorary court of arbitration is responsible for the implementation of the sanctions, but while its functions are weak in practice, it was also not operational in the past. Overall, this shows that the association does not serve as a legal authority to regulate the profession and it has only limited power to regulate the behavior of psychologists. Therefore, its vision is focused on providing networking for psychologists and raising the public recognition of the profession. Nevertheless, in order to protect oftentimes vulnerable clients of psychological services, the situation should be improved.

The Role of Ethics

Ethics is of a high importance for the work of Slovene psychologists, but there is a challenge to maintaining high standards. With the lack of any law and the previously described vague role of the association, ethical awareness does not rely on the possible sanctions imposed on someone breaking the principles, but rather on internal awareness of the correct way of work. Therefore, we have aspirational rather than enforceable ethical codes.

Nevertheless, an ethics code has a very central role in the education process of prospective psychologists. At the moment, three public universities provide the education of psychologists that is recognized by EuroPsy in Slovenia. All have either specific subjects referring to the teaching of ethics (University of Maribor, University of Primorska) or address it within several different subjects (University of Ljubljana). No private university providing psychology education so far complies with the EuroPsy standards.

There are not many studies addressing the ethical issues of Slovene psychologists. A study by Zupan and Bucik (2000) showed several areas where problems or doubts are frequently noticed in the professional work of psychologists. These were areas of record keeping, breaking the confidentiality, access to personal data, the content of informed consent, feelings of incompetence, unauthorized copying of literature and diagnostic instruments, questionable participants in psychological research, and lack of information on ethical aspects of students' supervised practice. Another important finding of this study was that psychologists often reported conflicts between law and ethics, incorrect reports in the media, and felt a lack of control over professional ethics. Moreover, the study concluded that the knowledge of the students on ethics is very satisfactory, but that in the cases of ethical violation psychologists do less than they should. Even though the study was published 20 years ago, its recommendation of having more awareness training and education in the field of ethics is still very relevant.

Slovene Ethics Codes

So far, there have been three versions of the Slovene psychologists' ethics codes, dating from 1982, 2002, and 2018.

First code: 1982

The first code was accepted at the general assembly of the Slovene Psychologists' Association in 1982 after more than two decades of working without one (DPS, 1982). According to the historical report of Matjan Štuhec (2011), some psychologists at that time even claimed that the code was not needed because *people in the profession of psychology are ethical per se.* However, the code was, of course, more than necessary in order to unify and follow ethical standards among professionals.

When reading the first code, the vocabulary and content reflect the cultural, social and political situation of the period: self-governing socialism is mentioned in the code several times, which was the political system of Yugoslavia at that time. It is interesting to note that, in the preamble to the code, self-governing socialism was explained as a process of fulfilling the ancient human tendency for having free will and making decisions according to it. Furthermore, this tendency is described as the fundament for human development recognized by psychological science (Polič, 1982). Hence, the political system of the time was rationalized and claimed to be supported by the psychological science. Also, other words used in the text reflect the cultural, social and political context of the period: socialists' humanism, democratic self-governing relationships, etc.

As regards to the content of the code, ethical standards at that time were not grouped, but rather presented in 14 articles, which seemed to follow from broader topics to narrower principles describing areas of ethical behavior in specific situations. The articles addressed the following topics: the code, ethics, humanity, professionalism, psychological help, professional secrecy, language, relationships among psychologists, professional independence, relationship towards public, research, psycho-diagnostic tools, implementation of the code, and responsibility. The code also had an appendix that further defined specific terms, which in some parts became an integrated part of the future codes.

Even some professional terminology is interesting to observe from today's point of view. For example, *psychological help* refers to the professional work that encourages the development of the person as a whole. Today we would probably use a term psychological support or even psychological interventions to describe the similar and not to suggest the explicit pathology of clients (who are in need of help). Words like interventions or support would broaden and reframe psychologists' work to include prevention and promotion of psychological knowledge. Besides the content related to defining psychological help (or work) it is unusual that this article describes also the relationship of psychologist and the client, importance of psychologist's care for his integrity, and a part about informed consent. The title *psychological help* for sure does not wholly represent the content. What is more, the informed consent is portrayed in a very vague and descriptive way.

Second code: 2002

The second version of the ethical code was accepted in 2002 (DPS, 2002). The code expanded to 57 articles and compared to the first version these were structured in line with the Meta Code of ethics that was accepted in 1995 at the European Federation of Psychologist' Associations. The code addresses

1   respect for the human rights and dignity,
2   competences,
3   responsibilities and
4   integrity.

The principles are ordered according to their significance (Matjan Štuhec, 2011).

Also, this version of the code reflects the social, cultural and political circumstances of the period. The reference to the constitution and the laws of The Republic of Slovenia is made in the preamble of the text, as well as to the professional organization of European psychologists, which is the European Federation of Psychologists' Associations. That gave credibility and broader international perspective to the text. What is also important to note is that this version was evaluated and confirmed by the EFPA Board of Ethics and was used and referred to in the processes of implementing the EuroPsy model in Slovenia.

Analyzing the vocabulary and the content of the text gives interesting insights. Only three areas of work are mentioned where a psychologist is developing his/her professional relationship with clients: psychological help, research and teaching. From today's perspective, we could broaden this, especially in line with the previously mentioned discussion about psychological help (not including any prevention, promotion or other related non-pathological aspects of work). Also, some phrases and content of the code were used in a non-systematic way or could nowadays be replaced by other more appropriate wording. Otherwise, the content of this version of the code can still be understood as very relevant.

Third code: 2018[2]

The most recent version of the ethical code was accepted at the general assembly of the Slovene Psychologists' Association in May 2018 (Arzenšek, Boben, Erce Vratuša, Kavšek, & Poštuvan, 2019). The motivation to update the previous version of the code merely came from the awareness that many social changes happened during the period of 16 years that had an impact on the professional work of psychologists. Moreover, codes from other countries (such as the British, Australian, Canadian) and specially the international documents prepared by EFPA (the Meta-Code of Ethics and especially Model Code of Ethics) were additional inspiration.

The preamble of this code's version is much longer than in the previous versions, as well is the content of the code. It has 82 articles, many of them having additional sub-articles. This suggests that the current version of the code is much more elaborated, as compared to the previous ones. The code, similarly to the second version, takes into consideration the guaranteed rights of the Constitution and laws of the Republic of Slovenia, and also all international documents in the field of human rights approved and accepted by the Republic of Slovenia, as well as refers to European Federation of Psychologist' Associations (EFPA). For the first time the Meta-Code of Ethics and Model Code of Ethics are mentioned, and they influenced the structure as well as the order of the articles.

Ethical principles are defined in four chapters arranged by their significance: principles of respect for human rights, principles of professional competence, principles of psychologists' responsibility and principles of integrity of the profession. When it comes to the areas of psychologists' work, these are defined in an open way, referring to psychological support, research, teaching, as well as other social activities. Moreover, in the preamble the self-actualization of the person is mentioned: the work of psychologists contributes to it so that a person can manage all areas of his life as efficiently as possible. It is also stated that psychologists contribute to the welfare of groups or organizations, to the public good, the quality of everyday life of the society in which they live and work, as well as to the development of the psychological profession, social and economic development and to the common good.

As stated before, the content of both the preamble and the code is more developed in this version. This is in line, on the one hand, with a broader understanding of psychologists' working areas, not limited only to offering help, but instead considering psychological interventions at the level of prevention, promotion, policy building, public good etc. On the other hand, more detailed description of several principles was requested when the draft of the first version of the updated code was sent to a year-long public debate. Psychologists expressed dilemmas in understanding some articles and wished for a clear guidance for those more vaguely described principles. Moreover, more elaborated text is probably also a consequence of the changed social circumstances that shape the ways psychologists work, the use of internet being just one of them. Despite the details, this version of the ethical code is still written in an aspirational way.

Commonalities of the Three Versions

Despite the mentioned differences of the three codes' versions, there are more commonalities between them. All of them express the most important standards or principles that serve as a framework for psychologists' work in specific time frame. In all of the cases, social, cultural and political systems influenced the development of the codes, but at the same time the basic principles of psychologists' ethics (e.g., respecting human rights) remained stable throughout (maybe only having different expressions to describe them).

All versions of the code propose the detailed definitions of specific terminology in the appendixes, but only the first version actually had this. The lack of this in the second version was also noticed by Matjan Štuhec (2011), who refers to it as unfinished work. The appendix for the current version is being prepared within the present work of the Ethical committee of the Slovene Psychologists' Association. Also, all versions of the codes mention the sanctions in cases of misuse, which are further defined under the honorary court of arbitration of the association. There is also the potential for misuse of the code by legal authorities to judge the work of a psychologist.

All three versions of the codes are based on the European cultural background, with the emphasis on respect of all people without discrimination. According to the research of Musek (1993) the most important values of Slovenians can be clustered under social, safety related, democratic and traditional principles, so being considered as a "[morally] good person" is of high importance in Slovene society. The codes reflect that – as, for example, respect for human rights and psychologist's responsibility – are the most developed parts of the latest version of the code. There is great concern in the codes that the psychologist takes his social responsibility and responsibility towards the clients very seriously and helps the person in need by all means. Moreover, this expressed expectancy of a high level of responsibility and discipline is in line with one of the Slovenes' self-stereotype, namely that they are hardworking, disciplined, and productivity driven (Musek, 1994). Another stereotype is that Slovenians tend to be submissive to higher authorities or nations (Musek, 1994), which might be reflected in the processes of code development, where relying on other (inter)national codes is considered an advantage, rather than an uncritical influence.

Other Challenges

Slovene psychologists still have several challenges regarding ethical issues. Recent round table discussion at the eighth congress of the Slovene Psychologists' Association addressed the updates in the third version of the code (Poštuvan, 2019) and several issues were raised, such as the lack of power of the ethical committee and honorary court of the association and a need for further discussions about ethical dilemmas in different settings.

There is clearly a lack of guidelines on ethical behavior in specific fields of work in the Slovene language. So far, no specific guidelines have been developed within the scope of the association, but the EFPA's guidelines for psychologists who collaborate in media were translated. With limited resources the reference to the European association is very important, but at the same time the work of the Board of Ethics within EFPA needs further promotion.

Conclusion

Whilst there is no legal arrangement of the profession of psychology in Slovenia, the ethical principles remain the main source of guidance and evaluation for psychologists. Ethics, therefore, has a very important role, but its everyday implementation is based on aspiration rather than enforcement.

Appendix: Code of Psychologists' Professional Ethics[3]

Introduction

The Code of Psychologists' Professional Ethics (hereinafter referred to as the Code) is a document containing most important principles by which psychologists conduct their work. The purpose of the Code is to provide a more detailed explanation of the range and content of ethical principles that are integrated into the psychological profession and psychological activities and have a significant influence on the psychologists' professional work and the professional development. Code particularly represents a support for psychologists in decision-making and dealing with ethical dilemmas as well as provides a framework for protection of users of psychological services against inappropriate and harmful treatment. Implementing ethical principles strengthens the psychologists' obligation to follow the high standards and ensure quality of psychological work. This also raises public confidence into psychology as a profession.

The text of the Code uses terms written in the male gender, which is considered (in Slovene language) as a neutral form for both sexes. Besides this, a general term "a client" is used in the text, which refers to the person or persons with whom the psychologist is in the occupational or professional relationship, for example, an individual (such as a patient, a client, a student, a user or a participant), a couple, a number of people or an organization.

Psychologists are employed in all working areas of the Republic of Slovenia. In their scientific and professional work, they are establishing professional relationships with individuals and groups in the field of psychological support, research, teaching and other social activities. They treat individuals and/or groups in their personal, familial, educational, organizational, occupational, economical and other matters and/or goals, as well as participants in research, students, employers, employees, colleagues, other users of psychological services and the general public (hereinafter referred to as clients). Work of psychologists at the individual level contributes to the self-actualization of a person so that he can manage all areas of his life as efficiently as possible. Similarly, psychologists contribute to the welfare of groups or organizations and to the public good. Psychologists contribute directly and indirectly to the quality of everyday life of the society in which they live and work. Their work contributes to the development of the psychological profession, social and economic development and to the common good.

The professional ethics of psychologists is based on the principles of ethics and morality of a democratic, legal and social society. This Code takes into consideration the guaranteed rights of the Constitution and laws of the Republic of Slovenia and all international documents in the field of human rights approved and accepted by the Republic of Slovenia. The Code is also in coherence with the documents of the European Federation of Psychological Associations (EFPA), in particular with the Meta-Code of Ethics and the Model Code of Ethics. From the latter it also assumes content and structural changes (compared to the previous version of the Code (DPS, 2002)).

In the Code of Professional Ethics of Psychologists, ethical principles are defined in four chapters, which are arranged by their significance: principles of respect for human rights, principles of professional competence, principles of psychologists' responsibility and principles of integrity of the profession. An integral part of the Code is an annex with additional explanations and definitions of terms from this Code, which is intended to assure more accurate understanding of ethical principles and the specifics of psychological work.

Psychologists are obliged to respect the professional identity of a psychologist, the psychological profession, and the ethical principles written in this Code.

Dr. Vita Poštuvan

27. 8. 2019

1 Principles of Respect for Human Rights

Respect for human rights is a fundamental principle of psychological ethics and is the central guideline of psychological treatment, with the exception of such circumstances that undoubtedly imply a direct threat to a known or unknown individual and by considering the rule that the rights of an individual or group limit rights of another individual and groups.

In psychological treatment, protection of the means of psychological assessment and in carrying out research, respect for human rights is implemented in such a way to ensure dignity, respect, equivalence, equality, being informed, privacy, confidentiality, professionalism of treatment and freedom of choice and possibility of selection. All of this also refers where appropriate to research and work with animals.

A psychologist respects every individual and his rights. He is particularly concerned with the preservation of human dignity and equality in a professional work relationship.

1.1. A psychologist respects all people with whom he comes into a professional relationship and respects the dignity, personality, knowledge, experience and profession of all persons in contact with him.
1.2. In his work, a psychologist respects and protects the rights of the clients to their privacy, self-determination and autonomy.
1.3. In his work, a psychologist makes sure that the client decides for himself as much as possible to, which includes the decision on the beginning and completion of psychological treatment.
    1.3.1. Before psychological treatment, a psychologist is obliged to familiarize the patient with the necessary professional procedures, activities, ethical dilemmas, professional relations, the way of protecting personal data, protecting the psychological report and the possible consequences of the treatment, and has to be sure that the client has understood the given information and explanations.
    1.3.2. In the introductory part of the treatment, where a client gets acquainted with necessary information about psychological treatment, a psychologist has to also inform him about exceptions of protection of psychological data.
    1.3.3. A psychologist must obtain client's consent for treatment. When changing the scope or content of the treatment, the consent must be verified. The client can revoke consent at any time and might request a redefinition of treatment's content.
    1.3.4. A psychologist clarifies with the client any misinterpretation of the treatment, and at the same time maintains client's understanding and consent regarding the treatment.
    1.3.5. In case where aim and outcome of the treatment relates to several clients, the psychologist must obtain consent of all directly and indirectly involved clients.
    1.3.6. In the event that the client has a legal representative, a psychologist is obliged to inform the latter with necessary information about the treatment and has to obtain representative's consent for psychological treatment of the person concerned, except in cases which are determined by the regulations of the Republic of Slovenia.
1.4. A psychologist should use only those procedures and such activities with which he informed the client and who has stated that he accepts them and consents with them.

1.5. A psychologist informs a client about possible types and methods of psychological treatment. At client's request a psychologist also provides information about possible similar psychological treatments by colleagues or other organizations in the public and private sectors.

1.6. A psychologist in no way harasses his client (e.g., sexual harassment, extortion, intimidation, etc.)

1.7. A psychologist in his work should not behave (physically, verbally or non-verbally) in a way to create frightening, hateful, humiliating or offensive environment.

1.8. A psychologist refuses to participate in proceedings that violate the legal and moral rights of other people.

1.9. A psychologist refuses counseling, training, or the provision of information to someone for whom he reasonably assumes will use this knowledge or data in a way that might constitute a violation of human rights.

1.10. A psychologist establishes a confidential relationship with an individual, group or organization. In this relationship he strictly respects the principle of professional secrecy.

1.11. A psychologist performs his work as much as possible in such a way that prevents intentional or unintentional misuse of psychological skills and knowledge.

1.12. A psychologist keeps a documentation about the course of psychological treatment (hereinafter referred to as the record) and is the owner and manager of the record. The client has the right to inspect that part of the record which contains his personal information and has restricted access to those data that are defined as a professional secret.

1.13. As a professional secret, a psychologist has to protect the psychological and health status of a client as well as the causes, circumstances and consequences of his condition. People who can access this information due to the nature of their work should also protect them as confidential.

As a professional secret a psychologist must also protect a psychological archive which contains psychological assessment instruments and psychological records.

A psychologist must with the help of his employer provide appropriate conditions for storage and protection for all documents and information that are considered a professional secret.

1.14. Before a psychologist uses the information from the record, he is obliged to inform the client with the purpose of using the data and has to obtain his consent.

1.15. A psychologist at the request of the client or his legal representative alters or excludes the information from the record which are inaccurate, incomplete or is not in accordance with the purpose of psychological treatment or integrates information which are incomplete. Along with that he makes a note about the request, what and when the record was changed.

1.16. The client alone, his legal representative and officially authorized persons under the conditions and in the manner prescribed by the regulations of the Republic of Slovenia have the right to inspect the record of psychological treatment in the presence of a psychologist.

1.17. A psychologist knows and adheres to the rights, principles and measures that prevent illegal and unjustified intrusion of personal integrity, his personal and family life that would occur for sake of collection, processing, storage and transmission and use of personal data.

1.18. When a psychologist uses examples from psychological treatments for the purpose of teaching, supervising or publishing in the media or in scientific journals, he must ensure the complete anonymity of the clients.

1.19. When a psychologist reports, informs, explains, or publishes anything that concerns the client, in order to ensure his anonymity, a psychologist will provide reasonable data limitations.

1.20. In order to publish data according to which it could be possible to identify the client, a psychologist must first obtain client's written consent.

1.21. A psychologist should not, regardless of client's consent, publish data that could harm the client.

1.22. A psychologist treats all people equally regardless of race, ethnicity, gender, religion, political affiliation, sexual orientation or other personal circumstances. He does not allow, justify, conceal, facilitate or participate in any discrimination.

1.23. A psychologist rejects and prevents procedures and treatment that discriminate against people.

1.24. A psychologist especially considers client's rights and common well-being, where the informing and explanation of the psychologist and obtaining consent before the beginning of the psychological examination is impaired because of objective reasons (e.g., the health of the client, the chronological or mental age of the client, the limitation of court proceedings, etc.)

2 Principles of Professional Competence

These principles define the ethical awareness of the psychologist, his knowledge of professional competences and the limitation of these competences, as well as the knowledge and limitation of psychological procedures, methods and techniques, and the acceptance of the necessity of continuous professional development for professional work.

The psychologist strives to achieve and maintain the highest level of professional competence in his work and is aware of its limitations. Therefore, he performs only such psychological activity and only uses those psychological procedures, methods and techniques for which he is educated and trained. During training, however, these methods and techniques can be used under the supervision of a mentor.

2.1. A psychologist works professionally within the limits of his education, competence, experience, ethical principles and responsibilities of the workplace or role in psychological treatment.

2.2. A psychologist in his work uses those psychological procedures, methods, techniques and instruments for psychological assessment, which were evaluated and accepted by the psychological profession.

2.3. A professional complexity of individual specific fields of psychological work binds the psychologist to master this field profoundly.

2.4. When choosing psychological procedures, methods, techniques and instruments for psychological assessment, a psychologist is independent and autonomous and takes into account the guidelines and recommendations of the profession in his field of work.

A psychologist always strives to choose most suitable instruments for psychological assessment that corresponds to the purpose and target group.

A psychologist adheres the accepted categorization of instruments for psychological assessment according to the complexity of use and uses only those for whom he is appropriately qualified.

2.5. In his work, a psychologist performs only those psychological procedures, methods, techniques and psychological assessment instruments that are optimal for the purpose and course of the treatment and professional results.

2.6. In his work, a psychologist uses standardized and high quality psychological assessment tools that meet international standards and guidelines.

Psychologist must critically use psychological procedures, methods, techniques and means for psychological assessment which he translates from a different social and cultural environment, and which are not yet standardized for use in his work environment.

2.7. The psychologist keeps orderly, systematic and time-perfect professional record about the course of psychological treatment, thus ensuring the quality and transparency of professional work and professional relationship.

2.8. A psychologist keeps his personal notes about treatment separate from the record and these notes are not part of the record or archive and are in no way accessible to anyone.

2.9. In case of a legal request or justified need to disclose the information from the case record, the psychologist limits and only discloses the content which is directly related to the need or request.

2.10. A psychologist may refuse the client's request to access his personal psychological record, notwithstanding the fact that he has the right to inspect a part of the record with his personal data, when he professionally justifies that the inspection may have harmful consequences for the client.

2.11. A psychologist may deviate from the obligation of complete protection of psychological treatment data only in exceptional cases, and only if he obtains during the treatment information that:

- the life of a client is endangered,
- the life of another person is at risk,
- violence and abuse of children is carried out,
- there is justified likelihood of causing greater social damage and with that associated general danger.

2.12. Psychological record is part of a protected psychological archive. This archive can be separately protected at various locations of the psychologist's working environment.

2.13. A protected psychological archive contains records of treated clients and used and/or unused psychological assessment instruments, the dissemination of which would significantly harm the profession, an individual or society.

2.14. The professional work binds a psychologist to continuously improve his professional skills, engage in the supervision of psychological practice and attend professional meetings of psychologists and related professions.

2.15. A psychologist takes over and performs professional work when he is physically and mentally healthy, which allows him to be professional able and prudent.

3 Principles of Psychologists' Responsibilities

These principles define the responsibilities of a psychologist to ensure a high level of professional and scientific work, responsibilities for avoiding doing harm and responsibilities for ensuring the integrity of the treatment, responsibilities of the treatment itself, responsibilities to the clients, and responsibilities of a psychologist to solve ethical dilemmas in his professional activities.

A psychologist is aware of his professional responsibilities towards the clients, to the organizations where he is employed, and to the community and society in which he lives.

A psychologist avoids doing harm and is fully responsible for his professional activity. As much as possible he takes care that his professional work is not misused.

3.1. A psychologist is responsible for the professionalism, quality and integrity of psychological treatment and for the consequences of his professional activity.

3.2. During his professional activities a psychologist strictly follows the principle of professional secrecy. The duty to respect this principle also applies after completion of psychological treatment.

3.3. A psychologist is responsible for obtaining and communicating to the client only the information that is related to the objectives of the treatment.

3.4. Due to the nature of psychologist's work the main focus of his responsibilities is on directly involved clients in psychological treatment, because they are more vulnerable (e.g., a client, a student, a worker). Therefore, the professional responsibility for them is bigger than for the indirectly involved clients (e.g., a public, a work team, employer).

3.5. In case that the psychologist's work anticipates treatment of clients who cannot be informed about the treatment beforehand and their consent cannot be obtained, a psychologist will check all possibilities for not doing such treatment. If there is a suspicion that the intervention may cause harm, discomfort or other dangers, a psychologist will refuse to carry out such work and/or participation in such work.

3.6. In the event that the psychologist includes in treatment clients who cannot be informed about his activities beforehand and their consent cannot be obtained, a psychologist is personally responsible for them. He conducts these kinds of treatments only when the goals serve the common good and common good of clients themselves or in the event of significant progress of mankind. In case that he carries out such psychological treatment, he is also responsible that all of his co-workers follow ethical principles and are obliged to protect clients against physical and mental discomfort and from danger and harm, that can be caused by the treatment until the end, and also after the conclusion of the treatment.

3.7. A psychologist is responsible for possible mistakes and misuse of psychological information and psychological assessment instruments, if it turns out that they have arisen with his work and his actions.

3.8. A psychologist is responsible for safe and confidential storing and using all information about the client in any form.

3.9. A psychologist is obliged to ensure that the psychological assessment instruments are handled as confidential material according to the regulations and that these materials are stored in a protected psychological archive.

3.10. Psychological assessment instruments are used and stored in such way so they can be accessed by appropriately qualified psychologists or psychologists in the mentoring process.

3.11. A psychologist, when using psychological assessment instruments, respects copyrights, legislation and agreements about these instruments, accepted in psychological professional circles.

3.12. A psychologist is aware that mismanagement of psychological assessment instruments (application, evaluation, interpretation of results) can cause irreparable harm to the individual, profession and society, and therefore in the event when he is allowed to use a certain appropriately categorized psychological assessment instrument, he is obliged to estimate whether his theoretical and practical knowledge, understanding, work experience and additional qualifications make him competent to use certain psychological assessment instruments. In case of a dilemma, he has to estimate the use of a psychological assessment instrument with a professional competent colleague who uses this instrument in his professional activities.

3.13. With his professional knowledge and work a psychologist should not cause harm to the clients. He tries as much as possible to mitigate the consequences of the inevitable damage or the unpredictable harmful consequences of psychological treatment.

3.14. A psychologist is responsible for full conclusion of the treatment even when he cannot conclude it himself for objective reasons. In this case, the treatment should be provided in cooperation with a colleagues or work organization in which the treatment started. A psychologist who carries out professional work as an individual is obliged to refer the case to a colleague with whom he agrees in advance on the possible acceptance of the client.

3.15. If the client turns to a psychologist in case of the original treatment, a psychologist remains responsible for assisting the client even after when the treatment is over, unless if there are circumstances in which the psychologist is obliged to refuse the treatment (e.g., the medical condition of the psychologist, replacement of the work area of the psychologist, the conflict of roles, the prohibition of pursuing the profession of a psychologist), and refer the case to another psychologist.

3.16. When a psychologist conducts a project, teaches, mentors or supervises, he is responsible for the correct scientific and professional activity of all participants and for adhering to professional ethical principles.

3.17. A psychologist is attentive to ethical dilemmas, recognizes them, and endeavors to resolve these dilemmas in accordance with the principles of this code. When dealing with ethical dilemmas, he is consulting with colleagues in his field of work and/or contacting the Slovenian Psychologists' Association.

4 Principles of Integrity of the Profession

The principles in this chapter include respect for psychological profession, the honesty and credibility of the psychologist, the openness and transparency of psychological treatment and the situation of conflicts of interest and unethical work.

A psychologist strives for the integrity of psychological science and the profession and for the mutual development of theory and practical experience.

In professional activities, the psychologist is fair, just and credible.

4.1. A psychologist develops and maintains a high scientific and professional level of his professional activity and acts honourably in accordance with the principles of this Code.

4.2. A psychologist must be aware of his personal and professional limitations and the limitation of his workplace, research or role in psychological treatment.

4.3. In case of professional dilemmas, psychologists must help each other.

4.4. A psychologist does not introduce his personal, ideological, political and religious belief into his professional work.

4.5. A psychologist presents his professional competence and experience objectively and fairly to his clients, co-workers, fellow psychologists and the general public.

4.6. A psychologist raises awareness about the possibilities and limitations of psychological treatment, as well as about data protection.

4.7. A psychologist prevents the conflict of interests. He is aware of the negative consequences caused by the double or multiple relationships, therefore, if he considers that such a relationship is too burdensome, he proposes his exclusion from one of the working roles (e. g., the simultaneous role of counseling and decision-making).

4.8. When a psychologist in dealing with the client has also a private or social role, he maintains a professional role and avoids other roles in connection with the client. In the events that such an avoidance is not possible, he informs the client about the incompatibility and directs it to a colleague or other organization.

4.9. A psychologist does not exploit the professional relationship and psychological data for ideological and other types (e.g., political, status) interests or for material benefits at his personal level or at the level of other associations of which he is a member.

4.10. During the treatment a psychologist does not exploit the inequality of power that arises from the professional relationship, and even after the completion psychological treatment.

4.11. A psychologist creatively contributes to the development and usefulness of the profession, and provides findings and lessons to the professional and general public.

4.12. A psychologist has an active attitude towards the public and strives that the public is objectively informed about the contributions of the psychological findings for the development of the individual and society. He avoids sensationalism.

4.13. A psychologist who works privately is obliged that before the treatment he informs the client about the prices, as indicated in the price list of his activity. Any changes in labor costs may be agreed with the client.

4.14. A psychologist respects the rules of his workplace within the organization where he works, including the communication paths, administrative tasks, the service price list and, when necessary, about that he informs the client.

4.15. A psychologist in principle does not accept the client's gifts for his professional work. When a client insists that he accepts a gift, a psychologist can do that only when this is in accordance with the regulations of the Republic of Slovenia.

5 Enforcement and Respect of the Code of Psychologists' Professional Ethics

5.1. The Code of psychologists' professional ethics is mandatory for all psychologists. It equally applies to students of programs in the field of psychology.

5.2. A psychologist becomes acquainted with this Code during the course of education in the context of study processes, supervised practice and informal forms of education and through the Slovenian Psychologists' Association.

5.3. In the event of a doubt or a reasonable suspicion of a violation of this Code from other colleague, a psychologist must take action and warn the offender himself and discourage him from doing so. If he continues with the violation a psychologist informs the Slovenian Psychologists' Association in order to assure the enforcement and respect of the code.

5.4. The Committee for Psychodiagnostic Instruments of the Slovenian Psychologists' Association determines the use and list of instruments for psychological assessment and competence requirements of psychologists and students of programs in the field of psychology.

5.5. The Committee for Ethical Issues of the Slovenian Psychologists' Association is responsible for the Code of Psychologists' Professional Ethics. The Committee deals with complaints from individuals linked to alleged violations of ethical principles by psychologists and also helps when psychologists are in doubts about their ethical behavior. It also informs psychologists about ethical dilemmas through public events and publications.

5.6. The Honorary Court of Arbitration of the Slovenian Psychologists' Association deals with suspected violations of ethical principles of this Code by the psychologist.

5.7. For violations of ethical principles from this Code there are penalties, which are defined in the acts of the Honorary Court of Arbitration of the Slovenian Psychologists' Association.

5.8. Slovenian Psychologists' Association is responsible for raising awareness of the ethical principles of the psychological profession and providing access to the contents of the Code through the various communication channels in the professional and nonprofessional public.

6 Transitional Provisions

6.1. The Code of Professional Ethics of Psychologists is accepted at the General Assembly of the Slovenian Psychologists' Association and is valid from the day of its acceptance.

6.2. An integral part of this Code is the Annex, which provides explanations of individual articles of the Code with examples from practice, List of rules, and procedure manual of the Committee for Ethical Issues of the Slovenian Psychologists' Association and the procedure manual of Honorary Court of Arbitration of the Slovenian Psychologists' Association.

6.3. The acts of the Slovenian Psychologists' Association bound to the Code of Psychologists' Professional Ethics, to the work of the Committee for Ethical Issues and to the work of Committee for Psychodiagnostic instruments, shall be accepted at the General Assembly of the Slovenian Psychologists' Association and shall be valid on the date of its acceptance.

Marko Vrtovec, President of Slovenia Psychologists' Association

Maribor, 11. 5. 2018.

Notes

1 EuroPsy is a European Certificate in Psychology, and a qualification standard developed by the European Federation of Psychologists' Associations (EFPA, 2019)

2 See Appendix to this chapter: Code of Psychologists' Professional Ethics.

3 Arzenšek, Boben, Erce Vratuša, Kavšek, & Poštuvan (2019).

References

AJPES (2019). *Slovenian Business Register*. Retrieved from www.ajpes.si/podjetje/drustvo_p sihologov_slovenije?enota=130107&EnotaStatus=1#

Arzenšek, T., Boben, D., Erce Vratuša, M., Kavšek, N., & Poštuvan, V. (2019). *Kodeks poklicne etike psihologov*. Ljubljana: Društvo psihologov Slovenije.

DPS (1982). *Kodeks psihološke etike*. Ljubljana: Društvo psihologov Slovenije.

DPS (2002). *Kodeks poklicne etike psihologov Slovenije*. Ljubljana: Društvo psihologov Slovenije.

DPS (2019). *Društvo psihologov Slovenije*. Retrieved from www.dps.si/2018/11/drustvo-p sihologov-slovenije/

EFPA (2019). *What is Europsy?* Retrieved from http://www.efpa.eu/EuroPsy

Matjan Štuhec, P. (2011). Kodeks psihološke etike nekoč in danes. *Panika*, 15(2), 32–34.

Musek, J. (1993). *Osebnost in vrednote* [Personality and values]. Ljubljana, Educy.

Musek, J. (1994). *Psihološki portret Slovencev* [Psychological Profile of Slovenians]. Ljubljana, Znanstveno.

Polič, M. (1982). *Za človeškost psihologije* [Uvodnik: Kodeks psihološke etike]. Ljubljana: Društvo psihologov Slovenije.

Poštuvan, V. (2019). *Renewal of the Psychologists' Professional Ethics Code – What's New?*Eighth Congress of Psychology. Zreče.

Zupan, T. & Bucik, V. (2000). Etični problemi pri praktičnem delu psihologa [Ethical issues in the professional work of psychologists: state of affairs in Slovenia]. *Psihološka obzorja* [Horizons of Psychology], 9(4), 25–43.

10

PROFESSIONAL IDENTITY, BEHAVIOUR AND VALUES

A Partial and Provocative History of the Code of Ethics of the British Psychological Society

Richard Kwiatkowski and Claire Jackson

Introduction

We aim in this paper to trace the development of the British Psychological Society's code of ethics and describe where that development has led it to today. As a membership organisation internal rules exist – for example rules about members undertaking work on behalf of the Society, and how members are to treat each other; additionally external rules apply; thus members are bound by normal ethical and legal codes (for example the law, social norms) and finally the code of ethics and conduct of members in their professional roles or their work as psychologists is an important part of professional and social identity as a psychologist. This final set is the code we are (mostly) interested in in this chapter.

To signpost our conclusion, we will suggest it was the campaign for professional recognition through regulation and the advent of chartering that really drove the development of these particular values, rather than a typical rule-based approach to ethics and conduct across psychology, and in particular has impacted applied psychology and regulation.

Since the British Psychological Society is not currently a regulator (The Health and Care Professions Council and other bodies perform that function) we are left with interesting questions about the future development of this area for the British Psychological Society, and the role of its Code of Ethics.

We seek to show that as the code has become more pared down and values-based it may actually be performing an unexpected function, not of prescribing and proscribing behaviour, but rather creating a higher-level understanding of the shared beliefs underpinning what it is to be a psychologist. The initial BPS drive towards rules, and the control of psychology may have, then, actually resulted in something unexpectedly more abstract yet potentially more important and enduring.

Beginnings

The British Psychological Society was founded in 1901. Luminaries gathered at University College, London to establish what they fervently hoped would be a renowned learned society. Beginnings can be very important in shaping subsequent developments. Historically we might suggest that here there was no hesitation in creating a body that was exclusive. Inevitably most members were (and perhaps still are) professional and middle class.

There have been many accounts of these early days; the reader is referred to Lovie (2001) who emphasises the initial early exclusivity of the British Psychological Society, and how the opening up of the Society to a wider membership took many years and a good deal of political, social and psychological capital. (For example, as is still the case with some London clubs, the prospective member's name was displayed and all it took was for one objection from a current member to be received for that person's application for membership to fail).

Thus, for many years, and whilst a lot of the work of the British Psychological Society was theoretical or experimental, the development of specific codes of ethics and conduct were, it seems, somewhat peripheral to the core interests of the senior members. As Bunn (2001a) has eloquently stated in his writings about C. S. Myers after those early elite days, the aims of the British Psychological Society became focused on a desire to expand its membership, its influence, and to delineate a field that might properly be called psychology, rather than mentalism, philosophy, spiritualism, psychoanalysis, or any of the other adjacent fields that were flourishing at that time. In passing, and possibly significantly, we should note that due to C. S. Myers' reforms, a number of the members of the Society were not "psychologists" as we would recognise them – they were often doctors or interested professional people. The early psychologists were engaged in trying to harness the contemporaneous confidence in science, and perhaps its prestige, and seeking what was at the time the criteria for academic credibility amongst their peers. They would not, perhaps, have wished to open up a potential Pandora's Box of differentiating ethical concerns, if, indeed, they were particularly conscious of them.

We can speculate on the reasons for this. Many of the medical members will have had their own codes of ethics (sometimes based on the Hippocratic oath) but the impression we have is that once someone had been accepted into the British Psychological Society at that time the understanding was that they were "a good egg" (we use the anachronistic English phrase deliberately) and could therefore be trusted. A system of personal recommendations by proposers – and then ratification by the governing body – the Council – and then a final round of ratification at a general meeting of the members of the Society was developed. As (Lovie,

2001) noted it was actually hard to become a member if you were not already well "known" to the existing members. We will return to the topic of what it means to be a "psychologist" later in this chapter, since it has implications for psychological ethics in the United Kingdom to this day.

We cannot allow the context of these beginnings to pass without comment. At this point in history the British Empire was all-powerful. Queen Victoria had just died and, for the rich, the Edwardian era was a time of plenty. What has been termed "the imperialist project" had been largely successful. A level of confidence existed politically and scientifically in the United Kingdom that has rarely been seen before or since. This meant, of course, that many of the injustices, and much of what we now view as an astonishing lack of respect for other cultures and civilisations was often present. Some famous expeditions (for instance the famous Torres Straits expedition of 1898) would strike us now (at the very least) as odd; some of the aims, concerned checking out the hypotheses that visual and sound perceptions would somehow vary on the basis of race, might make us now feel rather uncomfortable. If a contemporary ethics committee were to receive such a request they would, we would suggest, especially in the era of "Black Lives Matter" be much more acutely aware of a possible hidden agenda or particular assumptions. Nevertheless, a key point here is that psychology sought to make itself "scientific", and in those pre-Popperian days science implied measurement and objectivity, which is perhaps why, as (Lovie, 2001) suggests, early psychology was often very interested in physiology and psychophysics. We don't discount the influence of those coming from a medically qualified background in the emphasis in topics being considered.

For the first few years of its existence the BPS sought to start journals, have meetings, carry out experiments, set up committees, encourage research and generally to busy itself in just the ways one would expect a new organisation to behave. We will not rehearse here what Bunn et al. (2001b) have already covered. However, there was still no sign of a distinct ethical code.

The First World War

Part of the reason for the move from an experimental, physiological and philo-sophical bent to something perhaps more applied, (and this is speculation), was that a number of the prominent psychologists of the time had experienced (the horror of) the First World War. For example, Charles Myers, perhaps the most influential early member (and first President) of the British Psychological Society, had actually coined the term "shell shock" to indicate the psychological trauma that could take place in soldiers who had not actually been physically injured. Again, one can see the overt link to ideas of physiology here; for example, one might be able to postulate the hypothesis that the physical concussion created by the impact of a shell might create physical neurological disturbance. In fact, Myers later came to regret the term, because a number of soldiers who we would now recognise as suffering from post-traumatic stress disorder were, nevertheless, shot for cowardice in the face of the enemy because they had not actually been specifically subject to shelling near the time of the particular incident that led to their charge. (Indeed, Myers was so appalled by the way that soldiers had been treated, against his advice, that, fearing a cover-up, he refused to give evidence to the subsequent Royal Commission.)

There were numerous other developments related to psychology in the First World War; for example, psychologists were involved in psychophysiological measurements that allowed good sonar operators to be selected. The industrial fatigue board brought in regulations that meant that excessively long days were avoided (and the incidence of tragic accidents, for example in the munitions industry, were reduced). And, perhaps most notably, clinical psychologists treated "neurotic" soldiers returning from the front with what we would identify as a humane talking therapy, rather than using electric "sporadic brushes", which we would, nowadays, probably put into the category of torture, but which were, nevertheless, utilised to deal with "hysterical" soldiers in some hospitals.

As noted, this period in psychology was inhabited by key figures including Myers, Rivers and Smith who had all come back from the dreadful experience of mass death, tragic and pointless waste of human life, themselves forever changed. The jaunty Edwardian complacency and confidence was replaced by something perhaps more cautious, and that extended itself to a realisation of the importance of life, work, and of the value of each individual. But, although that is speculation, we do have some first-hand accounts of how psychologists such as Myers were never the same after the First World War experiences (NIIP Jubilee Issue, 1970).

However, whilst this might, to an extent, explain some of the moral, ethical, and philosophical positions undertaken by specific psychologists in their writing and in their work, again we do not, perhaps surprisingly, have anything that we would recognise as a code of ethics or conduct at this point.

Between the Wars

There was a flourishing of psychology in Britain between the wars. The influence of Freud and psychoanalysis which had been a major topic of interest on the eve of war was still significant. Medical, Educational and Industrial special interest "Sections" developed within the British Psychological Society. Similarly, in organisational psychology the National Institute of Industrial Psychology conducted numerous investigations on the behalf of significant employers. Some of the early accounts in this area contain heartfelt thanks from people on the shop floor and from trade unions as well as the industrialists themselves.

However, Clinical psychology, and what was then called Industrial psychology it was claimed, began to influence much experimental psychology (Myers, 1911, p. 1), and, as we will see, control of variables and consistency of behaviour in an experimental context became very important in the scientific project. It has been argued elsewhere (Kwiatkowski et al., 2006) that these early forays into what we would identify as applied psychology had an implicit humanistic bent, and that the project here was the betterment of the human experience, and these developments were actually based on broadly humanistic shared values and ideas (and some religious ones, for instance stewardship), which were, nonetheless, rarely articulated. However, perhaps because such values were not made explicit, there is little mention at this stage of a code of ethics or of conduct.

It could be argued that the presence of an unwritten and uncodified constitution in the United Kingdom, coupled with the idea of "doing the right thing", as well as the importance of precedent may have had some sort of influence here; this is rather in contrast to the experience, we might suggest, in North America and other countries, where a written constitution and a particular approach to the rule of law created a very different milieu?

The Second World War

Psychology was active during the Second World War, as has been well documented, for example by Sylvia Shimmin in relation to occupational psychology (Shimmin, 1994). There was significant development in other areas, especially, as one would expect, clinical psychology. In common with many other professions, the technical contribution to the war overrode other considerations: the British Psychological Society itself did not develop significantly (though the Social Psychology section was formed in 1940).

In relation to a code of ethics, Beatrice Edgell (1947) mentions that

> In 1937 during the Extended General Meeting at Manchester a morning session was occupied with a discussion of the question, *"What is a Qualified Psychologist and for What Work should he (sic) be Qualified?"* There was a general feeling that the Society ought to protect the interests of trained psychologists, and that by requiring a high standard of professional training from everyone admitted to a certain category of membership, it would enable the public who made use of the services of such members to "be ensured against *inefficiency and charlatanism*. The existing [membership] register might be regarded as providing a first step towards differentiation in the qualification of members, but the Council realized that, if the Society was to accept the function of safeguarding professional interests, it would require to alter its constitution." [our emphasis]

Interestingly, in 1941, at the height of the war, perhaps as a result of the 1937 debate, the BPS changed its legal status to become a limited company, the first step, it had been advised, in obtaining a Royal charter, and it hoped regulation (Jackson, 2019). The limited emphasis on the strategy and policy, role and ethics of the profession was not surprising given that survival is a higher order need than psychology. Although many BPS members were in the forces the Society published a number of thought-provoking papers and hosted meetings on evacuated children, bombing, war neuroses, morale, hatred of the enemy, post war planning, vitamin deficiency, anti-Semitism, racism, and finally rehabilitating Germans (by coincidence some involving "de-Nazification," work that a future member of the BPS Ethics Committee was involved in, with the honorary rank of General – Prof Peter Rickman).

However, we can point to specific professional developments, such as the Northfield experiment, where combatants who had the equivalent of the First World War "shell shock" were sent, and were treated in a much more humane fashion, including what we would today recognise as group psychotherapy. Similarly, officer selection involved a large number of psychologists working on the War office selection boards which would, after the war, morph into the civil service selection boards which continue to this day. In each case, the best scientific practice was applied, we would argue, often in an implicitly ethical and respectful way. Yet there was still no generally accepted overarching ethical code.

Post-War Development

Perhaps linked to their existence within a radically different milieu, the American Psychological Association created a formal code of ethics before the British Psychological Society. Indeed, in 1938 the APA started seriously considering implementing a code of ethics. As already noted, one might speculate that this was due to a perhaps more legalistic (collective) frame of mind; the existence of a written constitution; variations in state-level legislation; and the primacy of written laws rather than an unwritten or uncodified constitution in Britain, (and for historical and cultural reasons the legal primacy of precedent). in America the legitimacy of a written code of ethics was accepted, and therefore the need for one was seen earlier than in the United Kingdom. As with a number of other professional areas, we would suggest that there was at that time very little acknowledgement of the possibility of professional unethical behaviour, particularly, as we now know, of utilising position to perpetrate abuse, and so the notion of protecting the public did not actively emerge.

Some small steps along the path to a code were taking place in the United Kingdom; according to the by-laws of the newly incorporated Society printed in 1941 – the British Psychological Society was obligated to keep a register of members, their qualifications and appointment. There were, by then, two forms to be completed when applying for membership – one with name of proposer, seconder and name and address of applicant. Applicants were further asked to provide their date of birth, academic qualifications as well as whether psychology was included as part of the qualifying examination for their degree or diploma and whether psychology was part of any thesis. Other information included positions held: academic, medical, administrative or any other; psychological publications and membership of offices held. Once elected a member had to sign a form agreeing to abide by the rules.

Our impression is that these were internal "club" rules rather than anything that we might recognise as a code governing or guiding the profession's interaction with the public. One possible point of controversy was that "grandparenting" meant that previous members were transferred across; this included a number of the more medically qualified members. Some more "pure" psychologists were worried about this and there were some threats of defection to the Experimental Psychology Society, which, neatly calls to mind the relationship between the American Psychological Association and the American Psychological Society.

148

Interestingly, it was a group of Australian psychologists (then a branch of the British Psychological Society) in 1950 who were first off the mark in creating a code of ethics. As a consequence, the British Psychological Society Council appointed a subcommittee to report on "the professional problems of psychologists." There seemed to be an idea that this would lead to the development of a code. However, this code was limited in scope – it was entitled "*a code of professional ethics governing the disclosure by qualified psychologists of psychological information about individuals.*" This focus on the importance of nondisclosure of "medical" information would be familiar to a number of those grand-parented. At this time the British Psychological Society was still concerned, as it had been before, and, as could be argued it is still is, in pursuing its project of delineating an area of "psychological" professional expertise and keeping control over that area. Similarly, the strict delineation of the range of convenience and the application of this code (from a paternalistic position) left much to be desired.

That code was published in the Quarterly Bulletin of the British Psychological Society (British Psychological Society, 1950). Responses were invited, but no record exists of any comments received. The code runs to seven pages and it is striking in that it seems to be mostly concerned with a very specific context, namely where a psychologist is "examining" a "subject". Some of the time, the code seems to want to have its cake and eat it, for example: "it is the psychologist's duty to be guided by conscientious concern for the welfare of both the individual subject and of society, and to respect the subject's rights to choose his (sic) own course without interference" (3.2). However, "the rules set out hereunder do not bind any psychologist the communication of data in any particular case" (3.41). Some of it we would view from our own position as amazingly paternalistic, for example "the subject-no matter in what relationship he stands to the psychologist-has no proprietary right over the psychologist's record of his case. What is divulged to him as a matter for the psychologist's discretion" (5.11). We would baulk at this today, raising all sorts of human rights, GDPR and ownership concerns. In other parts, what we would perhaps consider to be fairly sensible recommendations are made, for example that the reliability of the information, adequacy and comprehensiveness, and the circumstances under which data is obtained should be taken into account (6.7). However, what is puzzling is that this code seems to have been almost treated as a matter of interest, rather than a recommendation for conduct; it appears to have no mechanisms or sanctions associated with it; it is almost as though the Society has taken an interest in having a code, but in a fairly arm's length and abstract manner. It is not at all clear what happened to it. Perhaps it was not seen as a useful tool in the broader project.

Almost the First Code

It was not until 1954 that the Society's Charter committee prepared a first draft of an ethical code – a "statement on the standards of professional conduct". In Appendix 1 to this chapter for historic reasons we reproduce the statement in full.

The existence of the Charter Committee indicates that, once again, the British Psychological Society was interested in creating legitimacy for itself. According to

Edgell (1947) it had been a request for an *authorised* list or register of British psychologists from the organisers of International Psychological Congress, held at Yale in 1929 that had, at least in part, alerted the Society for the need to be regulated.

Indeed, in the 1954 Annual report (British Psychological Society, 1954) the purpose of the Charter Committee is stated as "To confirm the prestige of the Society as a scientific organisation capable of giving a service to the community and as the responsible body in Britain concerned with the standards and conduct of psychologists." The idea seems to have been that having a Royal Charter would enable psychology to make a claim for an area of knowledge, but more than that an area of professional practice – thus we see at this time a distinction between the idea of ethics and conduct. In part this may also reflect the behaviourism prevalent then within psychology; this position could be caricatured as "we cannot know someone's motives, after all, but we can certainly observe their behaviour or their conduct." The thinking of this Committee was published as an appendix to the annual report of 1954/55. Bizarrely it was emphasised that this code was confidential to members. We have no real explanation for why this should be; their position is that this is a draft whose final form will be shorter than that which is being suggested and that they are waiting for comments. One would suppose the wider the consultation the better. In fact, the Committee recommended that these ideas should be incorporated into the new bylaws, but after a good deal of discussion this proposal was not passed by the annual general meeting. We don't know why.

What immediately strikes us is that the first principle is "it is an obligation for members to discourage the practice of psychology by unqualified persons"; This very much ties in with the terms of reference (as we would term them) of the Charter Committee quoted above which talk of "prestige" of being a scientific organisation and therefore being a "responsible body" for standards and conduct of psychologists. So, as so often in its history, The British Psychological Society seems to us to be here seeking to emphasise its importance and possibly equivalence to other professional e.g. medical bodies. We cannot know, since so many of the protagonists are now dead, what the balance of motivation here was. Nevertheless, the striving for legitimacy and prestige (then as now) seems to us to be, at least in part, the driving factor here.

Turning to the suggestions themselves, many of the principles are ones we would recognise today; for example

- respecting codes of other professionals,
- confidentiality,
- avoiding plagiarism,
- not claiming qualifications not actually held,
- anonymity,
- onward referral,
- avoiding harm,
- the importance of training,

- privacy,
- the importance of appropriate interpersonal relationships.

Given that most of this is uncontentious it is a real mystery (as in much of the story) as to what had happened to stop this being adopted. Was there a fear that psychologists were acting unethically? Or perhaps a fear that drawing attention to a code would make people realise that psychologists had not had one before? Or the move away from a learned society to a professional representative body? Or was it just taken for granted (as at the beginning of the century) that all psychologists were good? Unfortunately, we just don't know unless and until a cache of hitherto unknown contemporary letters comes to light!

Professional Conduct

However, ethics was not a topic that was going to go away. Between 1957 and 1960 a senior committee comprised of Past Presidents considered standards of professional conduct – they recommended the creation of a Standing Committee on Ethics; plans for this were begun in 1958. This would be a committee to which questions of professional conduct could be referred and which would take responsibility for drawing up rules which could be appended to the proposed Bye-Laws, as well as to advise on their subsequent "interpretation and modification". They say that they hope to be able to use the rules drawn up by this committee on a *solvitur ambulando* by which they seem to mean on a case-by-case basis. (Incidentally, The British Psychological Society, again probably in an attempt to appear learned became fond of using phrases like this. Of course, this does not actually mean on a case-by-case basis, but rather solved through experimentation. Until recently the phrase "ultra vires" was regularly used to try to stop members of the society doing anything contentious. Is it mere speculation to suggest that the use of Latin is another mechanism for exclusion?) Strangely, the British Psychological Society appointed a "Standing Advisory Committee on Professional Misconduct" in 1961 seemingly before it actually had an agreed corporate definition on what misconduct might be.

This was a period of considerable development within psychology; new departments were springing up, many with experimental or practical arms. This meant that the need for a code of ethics was becoming more of an obvious requirement. At the same time the British Psychological Society was expanding like an un-clipped hedge, creating Divisions (originally known as Committees of Professional Psychologists) as well as increasing the number of specialist interest Sections – this was indeed an exciting time of optimism and growth. Some of the larger and more well-established Sections even began to develop their own sub-groups, considering training, or categories of membership, sometimes in parallel with what was going on centrally. At times, this strayed into the ethical domain, though once again the status of all these groups is very unclear, and in general the documents they produced seem to have been advisory, or produced as guidance, or good practice, or in some way peer advice.

The Granting of a Royal Charter

As part of the drive to delineate an area that might be called psychology, and to enhance the legitimacy and expertise of its members the British Psychological Society was successful in gaining chartered status and was granted a Royal Charter in 1965.

The stated objects of the Society were now "to promote the advancement and diffusion of a knowledge of psychology pure and applied and especially to promote the efficiency and usefulness of Members of the Society by setting up a high standard of professional education and knowledge." The first aim appeared to be establishing a library and some laboratories whilst the second aim was "to maintain a Code of Ethics and Conduct for the Guidance of Members and to compel the observance of strict rules of professional conduct as a condition of membership." At last the impetus that the Society needed to act in this area – one would have thought.

In the early 1970s, in an attempt to accommodate and try to harness the growth and disparate interests of the Society, a governance restructure created a Scientific Affairs Board (later Research Board) and Professional Affairs Board (later Professional Practice Board) which it was hoped would centralise policy, training and guidance in their own areas.

This was not entirely successful; the various subsystems (as the Sections and Divisions were collectively known) continued to produce various sorts of advice, often within their own system publications (such as newsletters) that overlapped, and sometimes impacted the field of ethics, often without reference to either of these central "Boards."

To return to the project; the Committee on the Legal Registration of Psychologists had a subcommittee on the practical implications of a draft Code of Professional Behaviour 1972–1973; and in 1973, the main Committee asked all the Divisions to submit draft codes of ethics for their own areas.

Some, like the Division of Educational Psychologists had devised theirs as far back as 1970 (working together with the Association of Educational Psychologists). Others, for example the Division of Occupational Psychology started work on theirs in 1972. One of the first tasks of the new Professional Affairs Board was to try to ratify these codes (by that stage there were ten rather different codes).

The major impetus for the pre-existing Divisional codes was probably because most of the "Divisional" psychologists then employed were employed in government (local or central) service. Thus the majority of clinical, forensic, and educational psychologists, as well as a number of occupational psychologists, were employed in hospitals and clinics, prisons, schools and local authorities or the Ministry of Defence (for example).

In some of these contexts, psychologists became members of unions in order to have more power vis-a-vis the vastly more powerful employers. We would suggest, therefore, that part of the reason for a Divisional interest in specific codes was a broadly political one in that "best practice" could be overtly incorporated into terms and conditions, and protection of role achieved. At that time there was a good deal of concern about grade, pay and *status* of psychologists as compared with the other professionals with which they worked. The incorporation of best practice (or perhaps a "gold standard") would have the consequence that if psychologists wanted to do something that might be managerially or administratively inconvenient (for instance requiring additional supervision or training), they could use their Divisional rules as a bulwark to argue they "had" to have it. This was a tactic that largely worked successfully at that time. For example, the Division of Occupational Psychology after two years of drafts finalised their code of professional conduct in 1974, as did the Clinical Division. These formed part of the "understood" duties, rights and responsibilities of psychologists in those contexts. As well as the protection of the profession (and its professionals) we hope and expect that there may have been other motives, for example protection of the public, but that is another debate that we find little record.

The First Modern Code, 1985

Galloping through the years we now arrive at the mid-1980s. As we will later explain, a new Royal Charter was enacted which enabled some individual psychologists to signal their professional standing as a member of the Division of Clinical Psychology by using the title "chartered clinical psychologist"). In order to do this those psychologists were obliged to join the British Psychological Society and then apply for chartered status. Chartership was required if they wanted to work as a clinical psychologist in the National Health Service. This status provided quality control to the NHS. (Anecdotally, some clinical psychologists who had never been members of the British Psychological Society joined, acquired the status, and then immediately left.)

The British Psychological Society, at this point, had become, in effect, the regulatory body for all those "chartered psychologists". (We need to point out that then, as now, anybody in the United Kingdom can call themselves "a psychologist"; nor is membership of the British Psychological Society, or of the health and care professions Council compulsory, although employment in some sectors, such as the National Health Service is not possible without that registration.) However the BPS even then, having been able to protect the broad title "psychologist", core to initial 1937 debate was viewed by some as a failure (Kwiatkowski, 2003). All of the long-held efforts of the British Psychological Society to become the legal, statutory regulatory body for the practice of psychology in the United Kingdom were severely hampered, as was its influence, because it had not become a full statutory body for psychologists. The ultimate aim had been that all psychologists would be "registered" with the British Psychological Society and (by mechanisms not yet created) the practice of psychology could therefore itself be regulated. However even with the new Charter, and its creation of Charter Status it was recognised that the Society would need to have a coherent set of principles of conduct for its members. Thus, a British Psychological Society wide "code of conduct for psychologists" had been agreed on May 1983 as a necessary preliminary step to the granting of the Charter. This was ratified by a vote of the membership, mulled over by the Steering Committee on registration, and eventually published and enacted in 1985 (Appendix 2).

In our view, this is perhaps the first modern code that was widely recognised and seen as having legitimacy. It was published in the Bulletin of the British

Psychological Society (British Psychological Society, 1985), but again in the same cautious way in the preamble it states "the code does not supplant earlier statements by the Society on matters of ethics and conduct it merely supplements them in a more systematic way". What on earth could this possibly mean except that somehow, through some magical process of osmosis, or of understanding of implicit expectations, or of the history of psychologists *unquestionably* (!) behaving well, that members would somehow know what to do.

It is perhaps important to remember that this was at a time when professions were widely respected, and where potential abuse (for instance of clients or patients) was far less acknowledged and visible than it is today. It "enjoins" members and contributors ("and in the future chartered psychologists") to take into account any other guidelines they might happen across produced by any of the subsystems.

The code was added to over the years in a very confusingly ad hoc manner; some of the sections would seem perfectly reasonable to us now (ethical principles for conducting research with human participants, guidelines for use of animals in research, equal opportunities policy statement, sexual harassment at work and the ethics of dual relationships), others seem very much of their time or even anachronistic (guidelines for penile Plethysmography (PPG) usage).

All these various sets of guidelines were brought together and published in one document. It would perhaps be helpful to see what the page count was at that time; this will become particularly striking when we consider the present (2018) code.

Table 10.1 Word count of current 2018 Ethics Code

Topic	Pages
Code of conduct	4.5
Ethical principles for conducting research with human participants[1]	7
Guidelines for psychologists working with animals[2]	12
Guidelines on advertising the services offered by psychologists	3
Descriptions	7
Regulations for the corporate use of the title 'Chartered Psychologist'	2
Equal opportunities policy statement and policy	3
Sexual harassment at work and the ethics of dual relationships[3]	4
A briefing paper on sexual harassment at work and the ethics of dual relationships	12
Guidelines for penile plethysmography (PPG) usage[4]	1.25
TOTAL	55.75

The document reflects to a large extent the concerns of academic psychologists; for example at that time many psychology departments had an "animal laboratory" perhaps housing invertebrates such as snails or spiders, and, even in some cases rats and other mammals, even occasionally primates. Additionally, at that time there was a growing realisation that sexual harassment, and particularly inappropriate relationships between students and lecturers needed to be addressed. Of course, this continues to be a concern, and as already noted the process of setting up a register of chartered psychologists was an ongoing preoccupation; with sections on "use of the title", or of whether other people might "pass themselves off" as psychologists. In some ways this reads more as a policy document, or perhaps a reflection of anxieties than a practical easy-to-read and easy-to-apply code.

Whilst there were many developments within psychology over the next ten-year period, and whilst membership of the British Psychological Society grew steadily (though not spectacularly), and there continued an inexorable expansion of new Sections and Divisions, the 1985 code essentially remained in place. During that time, the Society once again became a bit more confident; it wanted, as ever, to delineate psychology, to protect members of the public from "charlatans", and to establish itself as a regulatory body. A full description of the machinations and manoeuvres is not really for this paper; suffice to say, that the British Psychological Society then turned its attention to the need for an Ethics Committee and a clearer code of ethics and conduct.

It set up a two-stage investigation and disciplinary process, with its own staff, and sought to regulate the behaviour of chartered psychologists. Anecdotally, it was said that this process (relying in part on the employment of external barristers to support the British Psychological society making a case and so on) cost several million pounds a year. It did not, of course, have any legal power, but the consequences of being "struck off" did have immediate and significant ramifications for psychologists working in the public sector, as well as obvious reputational issues for those outside (in the majority of cases legal action, for instance for assault, did not take place as this would have had priority).

Any attempt to remove chartered status or impose sanctions was resisted. Barristers, often paid for by professional indemnity insurance, were therefore frequently employed on both sides. The process was careful, long and complicated, with various checks and balances and appeal processes built-in. Once proceedings had been finished, commentaries on particular suspensions or disciplinary conditions, naming the psychologists involved, would routinely appear in *The Psychologist*, the in-house publication of the British Psychological Society, which was sent to all its members, as well as in press releases. The number of psychologists struck off was relatively small; and, as one might expect, the majority of complaints were against psychologists involved in a therapeutic relationships (for example clinical psychologists) with their patients. These were often complicated, traumatic, and upsetting cases. It was also the case, (and continues to be so today) that some employers would utilise the complaints system as part of their own internal disciplinary processes.

The New Ethics Committee

In 1998, the British Psychological Society Ethics Committee was established. It was chaired by Sue Gardner, who had been Chair of the Division of Clinical Psychology and who went on to be President of the Society, and deliberately included senior members of the various Divisions (for example one of the authors of this chapter was there by virtue of being past chair of the Division of Occupational psychology), and included a number of prominent external members, for example Baroness Warnock[1] and Prof Peter Rickman,[2] both philosophers and ethicists who it was judged could contribute to the root and branch creation of a new code of ethics. Other external members included the chair of "Witness" (formerly POPAN), the body concerned with assisting the survivors of professional abuse, a representative of the CIPD (the Chartered Institute of Personnel and Development, reflecting links to industry), and a student representative. The committee would also invite specific external experts to come and give "evidence" about their area of expertise in order to inform the committee; such people included those concerned with environmental matters, community psychology, and defence.

A change in the zeitgeist, a diminution of automatic deference, the questioning of professions, and the presence of non-psychologists, as well as a new mind-set in a number of the individuals involved in the Ethics Committee led to a less introspective, defensive, and protectionist view. The realisation that psychologists could do harm, could behave badly, and could act in their own interests rather than those of their clients, patients and colleagues informed the thinking of the committee. Ideas of protecting the public and exercising responsibility came to the fore.

The Genesis of the Modern Code, 2006

The ebb and flow of discussion in the Committee, between it and stakeholder groups, between it and external bodies is a very complex and partly political process. When finally accepted, the revised code had gone through 14 drafts and taken eight years to achieve agreement. This was in large part because it was not (as had been initially expected in some parts of the Society) a mere updating of the 1985 code, but, rather, turned into a debate about what the code was for, what it should contain, and, crucially what ethical and philosophical values should underpin it. External members and commentators such as Eric Droggin and Jon Williams were particularly useful in helping to pare down the code.

It is striking that under each Chair of the Committee (Sue Gardner, Richard Kwiatkowski, Tony Wainwright, Phil Stringer (acting), Kate Bullen, Mohammed Bham and Roger Paxton) the Ethics Committee has been very vigorous in resisting outside interference, particularly from within other subsystems (from 2001 known as Member Networks) in the Society, other Boards (including the Trustees and council) and appointed senior managers. They represent Clinical, Occupational, Clinical, Forensic, Child, Educational and Academic branches, respectively, and are senior members of the profession in their own right, which perhaps explains why they have been able to act in this way.

The new code of 2006 explicitly stated that it was influenced by "the British eclectic tradition" of philosophy. Rather than focus on specific behavioural guidelines (which would change over time) the significant focus was on creating a set of enduring values that all psychologists could agree with. Once the values had been agreed, it was felt, then specific actions and behaviours would "fall out" of those.

This, then, was perhaps the most significant change in ethical emphasis in the history of the British Psychological Society, and endures to the current code of 2018.

The table below, taken from Kwiatkowski's PhD thesis (Kwiatowski, 2009) uses the new headings of the new code to facilitate comparison with the old code.

Table 10.2 Comparing the headings of the new code with those of the old code

Source/Topic		Significance/Importance of change
2006 CODE	1985 CODE	
Introduction	*Introduction and General*	
i Uphold the highest standards of professionalism (p. 4)	*Does not bring discipline into disrepute*	Use of ethics as a positive force promoted; rather than essentially a set of rules to be obeyed
ii Protection of the public (p. 4)	*Complaints of misconduct*	The rationale for the existence of the code of conduct is the protection of the public, rather than avoiding complaints
iii Range of contexts (p. 4)	*Not mentioned*	There is a realisation and acknowledgement of the importance of context in influencing ethical thinking and behaviour
iv Focus on range of Roles that psychologists occupy (p. 5)	*Psychologists' focus is on science and research*	"Colleague, consultant, manager, employer, supervisor" all included; an acknowledgement of the complexity of psychologists' roles
v Basis for ethical consideration, difficult decisions under changing circumstances (p. 5)	*Minimum standards – required to comply*	A very different way of considering a code of *ethics* rather than a code of conduct; assisting with complex and difficult decisions versus a straightforward rulebook
vi Importance of professional relationships (p. 5)	*Not mentioned*	An understanding of the complexity of professional relationships demonstrated
vii Underlying Philosophical position (p. 6)	*Not mentioned*	An understanding demonstrated that a code of ethics and conduct must perforce have some coherent philosophical underpinning
viii Power disadvantage of clients (p. 6)	*Not mentioned*	The importance of power is raised many times, and an acknowledgement that power requires responsibility from the more powerful
ix Decision-making (two pages)	*No equivalent section*	A set of rules needs little decision-making guidance associated with it, since one simply follows the rules, if we acknowledge that the context /situation is more complicated, then decision-making skills are essential
x Ethics pervades professional activity (p. 7)	*Not mentioned*	The code of conduct (1985) is presented as a set of rules rather than acknowledging the centrality of ethics in psychology

(Continued)

Table 10.2 (Cont.)

Source/Topic		Significance/Importance of change
xi Overlap between ethics and psychology (p. 7)	*Not mentioned*	Since both psychology and ethics make statements about human behaviour there is a clear overlap in their interest areas
1. Ethical Principle: Respect (p. 10)		
xvi Statement of values (p. 10)	*Not mentioned*	The code of conduct (1985) does not have explicit value statements, the underlying values or their inference is apparently assumed; the 2006 code explicitly states these values
xiv Rights (p. 10)	*Not mentioned*	The notion of people's rights (not specifically human rights which has a legal meaning) is acknowledged as a key determinant of ethics
xv Self-determination of clients (p. 13)	*Not mentioned*	The code of ethics (2006) has a more humanistic stance towards the rights of clients
2. Ethical Principle: Competence		
xvi Statement of values (p. 14)	*Not mentioned*	The code of conduct (1985) does not have explicit value statements, the underlying values or their inference is apparently assumed
xvii Awareness of ethics (p. 14)	*Not mentioned*	New code states that part of being a competent professional psychologists it is being aware and applying this ethical code
xviii Ethical decision-making (p. 14)	*Not mentioned*	Rather than a detached role for psychologists the centrality of decision-making in professional life is emphasised in the 2006 code
xix Remain abreast of scientific ethical and legal innovations	*Not mentioned*	Code of conduct (1985) focuses on psychology, the new code (2006) broadens that to broader scientific, ethical and legal changes that impact on professional practice
xx Be sensitive to developments in broader social political organizational contexts	*Not mentioned*	The code of ethics (2006) emphasises the embeddedness of psychological interventions, in social, political and organisational contexts
3. Ethical Principle: Responsibility		
xxi Statement of values (p. 17)	*Not mentioned*	The code of conduct (1985) does not have explicit value statements, the underlying values or their inference is apparently assumed

(Continued)

Table 10.2 (Cont.)

Source/Topic			Significance/Importance of change
xxii	Avoidance of harm (p. 17)	*Discussed in supplementary document on research*	However the code of conduct itself (1985) is silent on this fundamental aspect of many professional codes
xxiii	Weighing of interests of clients (p. 17)	*Not mentioned*	The importance of professional judgment is emphasised (2006)
4. Ethical Principle: Integrity			
xxiv	Statement of values	*Not mentioned*	The code of conduct (1985) does not have explicit value statements, the underlying values or their inference is assumed
xxv	Of avoiding exploitation and conflicts of interest (p. 21)	*Discussed in supplementary document on harassment*	The code of ethics (2006) presents a much more complex and sophisticated understanding of conflict of interests than the earlier code and supplementary documents which seemed to view it mostly in terms of sexual harassment
xxvi	Multiple relationships (p. 21)	*Discussed in supplementary document on harassment*	As above: the new code (2006) understands and acknowledges a range of different relationships that need to be taken into account
xxvii	Maintaining personal boundaries (p. 21)	*Not mentioned*	The new code (2006) demonstrates a more sophisticated understanding of the importance of maintaining personal boundaries, not just in a sexual arena
Conclusion			
xxviii	Professional judgment (p. 23)	*Scientific basis of psychology emphasised*	The importance of professional judgment is once again emphasised in the 2006 code, as against a much more "detached scientist" model in 1985
xxix	Importance of reflection (p. 23)	*Not mentioned*	In accordance with its philosophy of "guide not punish" the 2006 code emphasises thinking (p. 6) and reflection

Historically, it may be of interest to know how this position was arrived at. The previous code was carefully scrutinised, and many international and national codes were consulted, including United Nations documents, such as the Universal Declaration of Human Rights, the Helsinki and Singapore protocols, international psychological codes, and codes of ethics of adjacent professional bodies, such as psychotherapy and medicine. These included the APA code. This was felt to be too complex and legalistic and was not followed; the Canadian code of ethics was far more influential in the committee's deliberations. This was partly because the emphasis was shifting from a set of rules to a set of values and principles. Once these had been agreed and established, a whole range of appropriate and legitimate, but hard to predict or prescribe, behaviours were then expected to be generated.

However, most importantly, whilst having to adhere to this professional code it was recognised that it would be impossible to legislate for every possible situation. (In part for this reason explicit reference to specific legislation was avoided). Further, the Ethics Committee moved more and more towards the idea that underpinning professional behaviour was professional judgement. Having therefore acknowledged the agency and autonomy of thinking that is a necessary aspect of being a professional, the Committee was of the firm opinion, as it said in the introduction to the code that "*thinking is not optional*". This meant that the code was a set of expectations and a guide to behaviour but that the individual psychologist concerned would, under all circumstances, have to make an active decision as to what to do, be guided by the values, and be able to justify it within the parameters of the code.

This is why, after much deliberation the word "should" rather than "must" was decided upon. As Peter Rickman memorably commented, an action can be illegal but still ethical. Further (and please see below) the Committee became increasingly aware that the Health Professions Council (now the Health and Care Professions Council) and not the British Psychological Society was going to have the legal powers to regulate psychologists' behaviours; their code (see below) was necessarily generic across a range of health-related professions, and therefore in coming to an opinion about fitness to practice (for instance after a complaint) it was felt that they might very well consult the British Psychological Society's code of ethics and conduct for specific advice. The basis of this advice, namely of the importance of underlying values and principles, and the importance of exercising active professional judgement, and taking responsibility for those decisions, was felt to be crucial.

The Health and Care Professions Council, 2006–2009

As has already been noted, the British Psychological Society's aim was to be the regulatory body for psychologists in the UK. However, at that time the number of regulators was actively being reduced by successive governments, which were astonished by the rise of different, often parallel regulators in adjacent professions. Not only that, but regulators of groups of regulators had also appeared. The government favoured a consolidation of a large number of different health-related regulators within the Health Professions Council.

During this time, the British Psychological Society made what could be argued to be a tactical error. Without the explicit formal approval of the wider membership, preliminary negotiations with the Health Professions Council (HPC) began. This, of course better, suited parts of the profession but not others; for example, some clinical psychologists could see advantages in being regulated by a body that already regulated many of their colleagues, and whose mechanisms paralleled many of those already existing in the NHS. However other Divisions, such as occupational psychology, few of whom had anything whatsoever to do with healthcare, were troubled by this "cosying up" to a health regulator, who, they felt, had a "National Health Service" mind-set and assumed that services were being delivered to "patients" rather than espousing other models of professional interaction (as championed, for example by the Division of Counselling Psychology). Again, this is not the place for an in-depth account of this time; the upshot was that when significant parts of the Society mobilised to stop this course of action, and withdraw from HPC negotiations it was too late.

The HPC pressed ahead with its idea of regulating psychologists. Having decided formally (by vote) not to be involved, the British Psychological Society withdrew from formal negotiations or consultations; however the HPC continued to involve individual psychologists in its deliberations, and its attempts to understand how the new profession of psychology could be included within its broader guidelines, and what specific additional requirements might be necessary. The disadvantage of the HPC asking for opinions from the general body of psychologists, was that this was a self-selecting group of psychologists who were by no means representative of the British Psychological Society or of the profession as a whole, if indeed a consensus was possible. Therefore, when the government decided that psychologists should be regulated by the HPC, the model that was applied was felt by some psychologists to be unsatisfactory. In particular, a number of occupational psychologists, chose not to register with the Health Professions Council, even though at that stage, a grandparenting system applied so that if you had chartered status you could be written across into the new register fairly easily.

The 2009 version of the relatively new 2006 code was changed (and one of the authors was involved in this change) in order to make it clear that the British Psychological Society from that moment on had no power in the formal and now legal regulation of psychological practice. It is fair to say that since that time the British Psychological Society, bereft of one of its key sources of power, has not been as influential as perhaps it might have been, if, say, it had managed to achieve the status of one of the Royal Societies or a Regulatory Body. But that is a debate for another paper.

Other Developments

Whilst we have here been focusing on the development of the code of ethics and conduct, the Ethics Committee undertook a lot of other work that was consequent on developing the code itself. For example, two codes of "research with human participants" (first proposed in 1978) were produced during this time. Interestingly the subcommittees tasked with putting these together were in each case chaired by an academic psychologist (Max Velmans and John Oates) whereas the Ethics Committee itself was chaired by a professional practitioner psychologist (the first author was the only member of both committees). Both these codes followed the value system of the overall code, except that they also included the notion of societal value.

One of the major external influences of the Code was that via this route (i.e., by creating a robust and detail research code) it was significant in the development of the Academy of Social Sciences code of ethics, which sought to pull together disparate social science codes into one overarching (but necessarily more general) code.

Other initiatives were undertaken; for example one of the authors remembers the excitement caused by the presence of "media psychologists" at the Ethics Committee where it was decided that the involvement of psychologists in the television media (such as reality shows including Big Brother) were a topic of legitimate interest for the Society. This committee has proved to be extremely influential (under the chairing of John Oates) and regularly works with Ofcom, other regulators, and numerous production companies seeking to protect participants and providing psychological insights into possible consequences (for instance of invasion of privacy).

Another initiative involved the creation of a document explaining how "ethical competence" could be taught across all levels of psychology. Support was also provided to the development of a "community psychology" section within the British Psychological Society. Other bodies regularly sought input from the ethics committee, often in the form of comments on their own revised codes, these ranged from psychological societies (e.g. The Hong Kong Psychology Society) to medical groups (e.g. The Royal College of Psychiatry).

The Ethics Committee took on other roles – for example after it began to seem, with the demise of the BPS Standing Committee for Equal Opportunities (which existed in various guises between 1983 and 2008), that this aspect of psychology might be neglected, one of the authors (in negotiation with Sue Gardiner, then President of the British Psychological Society) included responsibility for what was then termed "equal opportunities" within the remit of the Ethics committee. One of the ways in which this was kept alive was an annual prize for outstanding contributions in this area. A new 2019 Presidential taskforce in Equality, Diversity and Inclusion is perhaps the successor to this Standing Committee; nevertheless it is intriguing that the Ethics Committee felt confident enough to continue to champion this, when it appeared at that time to have inexplicably to have faded in importance within the Society.

In a bit of a "knee-jerk reaction" to its loss of power regarding the regulation of psychologists, the British Psychological Society secretariat rapidly, and without consultation, produced some Membership Conduct rules. The Ethics Committee spent several years pointing out that these rules were potentially illegal, inconsistent, and illogical. Eventually, the British Psychological Society's Board of Trustees agreed that these rules should be modified. At the time of this writing it is clear that, just as in the case of the code of ethics, the British Psychological Society will have to return to first principles in order that these "rules" can claim to have any legitimacy.

Of course, it is impossible to summarise the huge number of initiatives that the Ethics Committee undertook. Most recently, with the development of professional practice guidelines, the decision was made to further pare down the code of ethics and conduct.

An Even More Pared down Code, 2006 to 2018

From its development based on a set of values or principles, it was expected that the code of ethics would be essentially that. However, since additional guidance was not readily available across all specialities at the time of its first publication in 2006 that version contains specific bits of practical advice, simply because they were not available anywhere else. (We do note that several Divisions did have their own guidelines but these were, as in the 1970s, produced separately and there were some gaps).

Within the British Psychological Society the Professional Practice Board (successor of the Professional Affairs Board) now decided that specific advice was required, some of it generic, across professional areas regarding how professional psychologists should behave. This fitted well with the philosophy adopted by the Ethics Committee and endorsed by the Board of Trustees. Once this generic practice-based document was produced (and it is an ongoing project and needs regular updating and refinement) it became apparent that the code of ethics itself could be changed.

Therefore the 2018 Code of Ethics (Appendix 3) is, in the authors' opinion, the logical culmination of the thinking changes that were made in the mid-2000s. It is pared down to essentials (and if the direction of travel continues may end up purely values based). In fact, the examples provided and the explanatory paragraphs (possibly unnecessary) were included largely because some parts of the Society were anxious about a code that just contained the values statements. The key parts of the code (which we reproduce in Appendix 3) is only just over 600 words long.

The model as reproduced in the introduction to the code suggests that the following format applies.

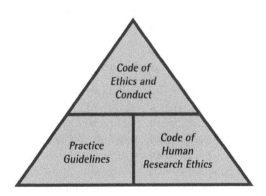

Figure 10.1 Code of Ethics and Conduct Feb 2018 British Psychological Society © BPS 2018

To allow the reader a flavour of the position of the code we include (below) the introduction and the key principles.

Introduction

1.3 The Code contains the professional standards that members of the Society should uphold. The aim of the Code is to provide a framework for guiding the decision-making for all psychologists.

The framework allows sufficient flexibility for a variety of approaches, contexts and methods and reflects the ethical standards that apply to all. Psychologists need to familiarise themselves with any legal frameworks, regulatory requirements and other guidance relevant to the particular context in which they work including any specific guidance in the *Code of Human Research Ethics* and *Practice Guidelines.*

2 Structure of the Code

2.1 This Code is based on four ethical Principles, which constitute the main domains of responsibility, within which ethical issues are considered. These have been agreed after many years of consultation within and outside the profession. The manner in which they apply and the contexts that they apply in will inevitably change over time.

They are:

i   Respect;
ii Competence;
iii Responsibility;
iv Integrity.

2.2 Each Principle is described in a statement of values, reflecting the fundamental beliefs that guide ethical reasoning, decision making and behaviour. Under each principle we list issues and considerations that Psychologists should be aware of in applying the Principles in their work. Broad "headline" categories are included and a list additional resources that expand on the application of these values in the Psychologist's field of work are provided at the end of this document.

Conclusion

The British Psychological Society does not legally regulate the professional practice of psychology in the UK. That is now the role of the Health and Care Professions Council. However, we believe that the BPS continues to have significant sway, through specification of training, its membership and as a learned society. It may have failed in its 100-year project to regulate psychology, but as a consequence, perhaps, its code has evolved in interesting ways, that are different from many other codes, and yet appear to be influencing many other psychological societies' globally, and impacting adjacent social sciences.

Although the current code of ethics shares some principles with other psychological codes, it has become smaller and more pared down; and has moved towards a values-based position where the code provides access to a set of shared beliefs rather than a set of rules. It has moved from prescriptive to encompassing shared high-level values which enable psychologists to understand the core philosophy and behaviours of being a psychologist. We would argue that these principles, whilst a product, naturally of a specific time and place, can have, currently, universal psychological application. This has moved beyond the implicit mores of a self-selecting privileged group to something more available and more explicit. Behaviours are specified in subsidiary codes that "fall out" of the code of ethics and conduct. For such a conservative body this is actually a radical position with individual and collective implications.

The code influences the 25,000 chartered psychologists in the UK and abroad as well as 100,000 psychology students at Universities (at any time) in the UK, as well as several times that number doing school "A" levels in the subject. It also impacts adjacent professions and it has influenced research councils and research ethics committees across the UK. The British Psychological Society has reciprocal arrangements with Societies all over the world. It is striking that when a new Psychological organisation emerges the need for a code of ethics is taken as read. And, inevitably the BPS code is read before the new code is constructed.

We believe that although it has taken a long time to get here that the BPS Code of Ethics encapsulate the values that underpin what it means to be a psychologist. While the code may change, we confidently predict that the values of respect, competence, responsibility and integrity will endure.

A Final Caution

As a long-standing member of the Ethics Committee (first author, over 20 years, including as Chair) and the British Psychological Society's current archivist (second author), we are acutely aware of the subjective nature of this attempt to briefly examine the history and development of ethics within the British Psychological Society. We have to emphasise that this is a partial version of what we think has happened over the years within the British Psychological Society. Our account is partial and selective; particularly because the first author knew many of the people involved in earlier codes and worked on many of the others. There is some speculation here, but we are clear when we are guessing and when we have good evidence; we trust we do not do a disservice to any of our colleagues living or dead when we tentatively ascribe motives and thoughts to them; in our defence we have to say that this seems to us the most likely story, yet it is necessarily going to be subjective. We are aware of the work of the IUPS, of the European meta code, of the important and influential comparison of US and UK codes by Drogin and Williams, but have not chosen to reference them in what has already become a very long chapter. Similarly, we have not commented on various Division level initiatives, for example the excellent Clinical Psychology Forum Ethics Columns which have been appearing since 2009, amongst many others; often instigated by members of the BPS Ethics committee and significant others. We hope this short chapter will be useful to readers, but can in no way be held to be an official or complete version.

Appendix 1

Standards of Professional Conduct of the British Psychological Society 1955. Appendix to the Annual Report of 1954–1955. ©*BPS*

Members are asked to note that

This document is confidential to Members.

It is to be regarded as a tentative draft which will be revised with reference to criticisms received. These should be addressed to Professor F V Smith, Department of Psychology, The University of Durham.

The final form will probably be much smaller than the present list of possible items.

A suggestion from the Charter Committee which is approved by the Council is that the content might be subject of discussion at local Branch meetings.

It is an obligation for Members to discourage the practice of psychology by unqualified persons and to assist the public in identifying psychologists qualified to give professional services.

Members will endeavour at all times to respect ethical codes and professional standards of members of other recognised profession with whom they may be associated.

Criticism of the professional conduct of a Member of the British Psychological Society should never be made publically, but through the Council of the Society.

Subject to the law of the land, information acquired by a member about an individual or an organisation in the course of professional activities (which include the teaching of psychology) must be regarded as confidential. Normally such information should only be communicated with the consent of the person concerned, and in no circumstances should it be communicated to other persons or organisations unless the individual or organisation has been obliged by an authority, which the Member accepts, to submit to examination.

Work which is published or orally reported by Members should include specific acknowledgement to any personal or written contributions of which use has been made.

Members should not claim, either directly or by implication, professional qualifications other than those actually attained. The individual Member is responsible for correcting those who misrepresent his qualification.

In interpreting the subject of psychology to the public, and in dealing with its applications, there is an obligation for Members to avoid unwarranted claims. Public statements by Members should be characterised by caution and scientific exactitude.

The use of psychological techniques primarily for entertainment or in any way inconsistent with the best interests of the person or persons to whom they are applied should be avoided.

When using the results of psychological techniques in published work or for any teaching purposes, adequate precautions should be taken to ensure that the anonymity of the person to whom they have been applied is respected.

A Member should refuse to apply psychological techniques in circumstances which could involve harm to the person or persons involved or to the professional standing of psychologists.

[sic] Cases in which there is evidence of a difficulty, the investigation or treatment of which lies beyond the competence of the psychologist, should always be referred to the appropriate specialist. In such cases, the welfare of the person concerned is the psychologist's responsibility until it is assumed by the professional person to whom the case is referred, or the relationship with the psychologist is terminated by mutual agreement or by a clear understanding with the persons who may be deemed to be responsible for the welfare of the case.

Members should endeavour to ensure that psychological techniques are administered only by suitably trained persons. Students or imperfectly qualified persons should be adequately and continuously supervised by a psychologist in the administration of psychological techniques and in the use of their results.

The teacher of Psychology should in general respect the right of the student to maintain a reasonable degree of privacy.

Students with Personal Qualities that are likely to be a disability in later professional work should in general be discouraged from entering fields of Psychology where personal relationships are important.

Members advising students wishing to enter honours and post-graduate courses in psychology with the intention of becoming professional psychologists should ensure that the students are information of the prospects of employment and are familiar with the pre-requisites for entry to professional posts.

Appendix 2

1983 Code of Conduct published 1985[3]

Bulletin of The British Psychological Society (1985), 38, 41–43 Printed in Great Britain ©1985 The British Psychological Society ©**BPS**

The British Psychological Society

The following Code of Conduct has been adopted by the Society following a postal ballot in which all Members were given the opportunity to vote. The code does not supplant earlier statements by the Society on matters of ethics and conduct, it merely supplements them in a more systematic way. Members and Contributors of the Society and, in the future, Chartered Psychologists, are enjoined also to take account of any further guidelines which may be issued by the Society and its subsystems relating to the specific fields of psychological practice or research in which they are engaged.

1 General

In all their work psychologists shall value integrity, impartiality and respect for persons and evidence and shall seek to establish the highest ethical standards in their work. Because of their concern for valid evidence, they shall ensure that research is carried out in keeping with the highest standards of scientific integrity. Taking account of their obligations under the law, they shall hold the interest and welfare of those in receipt of their services to be paramount at all times and ensure that the interests of participants in research are safeguarded.

2 Competence

Psychologists shall endeavour to maintain and develop their professional competence, to recognize and work within its limits, and to identify and ameliorate factors which restrict it.

Specifically they shall:

2.1. refrain from laying claim, directly or indirectly, to psychological qualifications or affiliations they do not possess, from claiming competence in any particular area of psychology in which they have not established their competence, and from claiming characteristics or capabilities for themselves which they do not possess;

2.2. recognize the boundaries of their own competence and not attempt to practise any form of psychology for which they do not have an appropriate preparation or, where applicable, specialist qualification;

2.3. take all reasonable steps to ensure that their qualifications, capabilities or views are not misrepresented by others, and to correct any such misrepresentations;

2.4. if requested to provide psychological services, and where the services they judge to be appropriate are outside their personal competence, give every reasonable assistance towards obtaining those services from others who are appropriately qualified to provide them;

2.5. take all reasonable steps to ensure that those working under their direct supervision comply with each of the foregoing, in particular that they recognize the limits of their competence and do not attempt to practise beyond them.

3 Obtaining consent

Psychologists shall normally carry out investigations or interventions only with the valid consent of participants, having taken all reasonable steps to ensure that they have adequately understood the nature of the investigation or intervention and its anticipated consequences.

Specifically they shall:

3.1. always consult experienced professional colleagues when considering withholding information about an investigatory procedure, and withhold information only when it is necessary in the interests of the objectivity of the investigatory procedure or of future professional practice;

3.2. where it is necessary not to give full information in advance to those participating in an investigation, provide such full information retrospectively about the aims, rationale and outcomes of the procedure as far as it is consistent with a concern for the welfare of the participants;

3.3. refrain from making exaggerated and unjustifiable claims for the effectiveness of their methods, from advertising services in a way likely to encourage unrealistic expectations about the effectiveness of the services offered, or from misleading those to whom services are offered about the nature and likely consequences of any interventions to be undertaken;

3.4. normally obtain the consent of those to whom interventions are offered, taking all reasonable steps to ensure that the consent obtained is valid, except when the intervention is made compulsorily in accordance with the provisions and safeguards of the relevant legislation;

3.5. recognize and uphold the rights of those whose capacity to give valid consent to interventions may be diminished including the young, the mentally handicapped, the elderly, those in the care of an institution or detained under the provisions of the law;

3.6. where interventions are offered to those in no position to give valid consent, after consulting with experienced professional colleagues, establish who has legal authority to give consent and seek consent from that person or those persons;

3.7. recognize and uphold the rights of recipients of services to withdraw consent to interventions or other professional procedures after they have commenced.

4 Confidentiality

Psychologists shall take all reasonable steps to preserve the confidentiality of information acquired through their professional practice or research and to protect the privacy of individuals or organizations about whom information is collected or held. In general, and subject to the requirements of law, they shall take care to prevent the identity of individuals, organizations or participants in research being revealed, deliberately or inadvertently, without their expressed permission.

Specifically they shall:

4.1. endeavour to communicate information obtained through research or practice in ways which do not permit the identification of individuals or organizations;

4.2. convey personally identifiable information obtained in the course of professional work to others, only with the expressed permission of those who would be identified, (subject always to the best interests of recipients of services or participants in research and subject to the requirements of law) except that when working in a team or with collaborators, they shall endeavour to make clear to recipients of services or participants in research, the extent to which personally identifiable information may be shared between colleagues;

4.3. in exceptional circumstances, where there is sufficient evidence to raise serious concern about the safety or interests of recipients of services, or about others who may be threatened by the recipient's behaviour, take such steps as are judged necessary to inform appropriate third parties without prior consent after first consulting an experienced and disinterested colleague, unless the delay caused by seeking this advice would involve a significant risk of life or health;

4.4. take all reasonable steps to ensure that records over which they have control remain personally identifiable only as long as is necessary in the interests of those to whom they refer (or, exceptionally, to the general development and provision of psychological services), and to render anonymous any records under their control that no longer need to be personally identifiable for the above purposes;

4.5. only make audio, video, or photographic recordings of recipients of services or participants in research (with the exception of recordings of public behaviour) with the expressed agreement of those being recorded both to the recording being made and to the subsequent conditions of access to it;

4.6. take all reasonable steps to safeguard the security of any records they make, including those held on computer, and, where they have limited control over access to records they make, exercise discretion over the information entered on the records;

4.7. take all reasonable steps to ensure that colleagues, staff and trainees with whom they work understand and respect the need for confidentiality regarding any information obtained.

5 Personal conduct

Psychologists shall conduct themselves in their professional activities in a way that does not damage the interest of the recipients of their services or participants in their research and does not undermine public confidence in their ability to carry out their professional duties.

Specifically they shall:

5.1. refrain from practice when their physical or psychological condition, as a result of for example alcohol, drugs, illness or personal stress, is such that abilities or professional judgement are seriously impaired;

5.2. not exploit the special relationship of trust and confidence that can exist in professional practice to further the gratification of their personal desires;

5.3. refrain from improper conduct in their work as psychologists that would be likely to be detrimental to the interests of recipients of their services or participants in their research;

5.4. neither attempt to secure or to accept from those receiving their service any significant financial or material benefit beyond that which has been contractually agreed, nor to secure directly from them any such benefit for services which are already rewarded by salary;

5.5. take steps to maintain adequate standards of safety in the use of all procedures and equipment used in professional practice or research;

5.6. not allow their professional responsibilities or standards of practice to be diminished by considerations of religion, sex, race, age, nationality, party politics, social standing, class or other extraneous factors;

5.7. where they suspect misconduct by a professional colleague which cannot be resolved or remedied after discussion with the colleague concerned, take steps to bring that misconduct to the attention of those charged with the responsibility to investigate it, doing so without malice and with no breaches of confidentiality other than those necessary to the proper investigatory processes.

Appendix 3

Key part of the 2018 Code of Ethics and Conduct ©BPS 2018

Ethical principles

3.1 Respect

Respect for the dignity of persons and peoples is one of the most fundamental and universal ethical principles across geographical and cultural boundaries, and across professional disciplines. It provides the philosophical foundation for many of the other ethical Principles.

Respect for dignity recognises the inherent worth of all human beings, regardless of perceived or real differences in social status, ethnic origin, gender, capacities, or any other such group-based characteristics. This inherent worth means that all human beings are worthy of equal moral consideration.

Statement of values: Psychologists value the dignity and worth of all persons, with sensitivity to the dynamics of perceived authority or influence over persons and peoples and with particular regard to people's rights.

In applying these values, Psychologists should consider:

   i Privacy and confidentiality;
  ii Respect;
 iii Communities and shared values within them;
  iv Impacts on the broader environment – living or otherwise;
   v Issues of power;
  vi Consent;
 vii Self-determination;
viii The importance of compassionate care, including empathy, sympathy, generosity, openness, distress, tolerance, commitment and courage.

3.2 Competence

Psychologists, whether academic, practitioner or in training, may offer a range of services that usually require specialist knowledge, training, skill and experience. Competence refers to their ability to provide those specific services to a requisite professional standard.

A psychologist should not provide professional services that are outside their areas of knowledge, skill, training and experience.

Statement of values: Psychologists value the continuing development and maintenance of high standards of competence in their professional work and the importance of working within the recognised limits of their knowledge, skill, training, education and experience.

In applying these values, Psychologists should consider:

   i Possession or otherwise of appropriate skills and care needed to serve persons and peoples;
  ii The limits of their competence and the potential need to refer on to another professional;
 iii Advances in the evidence base;
  iv The need to maintain technical and practical skills;
   v Matters of professional ethics and decision-making;
  vi Any limitations to their competence to practise taking mitigating actions as necessary;
 vii Caution in making knowledge claims.

3.3 Responsibility

Because of their acknowledged expertise, Psychologists enjoy professional autonomy; responsibility is an essential element of autonomy. Psychologists must accept appropriate responsibility for what is within their power, control or management.

Awareness of responsibility ensures that the trust of others is not abused, the power of influence is properly managed and that duty towards others is always paramount.

Statement of values: Psychologists value their responsibilities to persons and peoples, to the general public, and to the profession and science of Psychology, including the avoidance of harm and the prevention of misuse or abuse of their contribution to society.

In applying these values, psychologists should consider:

i   Professional accountability;
ii Responsible use of their knowledge and skills;
iii Respect for the welfare of human, non-humans and the living world;
iv Potentially competing duties.

3.4 Integrity

Acting with integrity includes being honest, truthful, accurate and consistent in one's actions, words, decisions, methods and outcomes. It requires setting self-interest to one side and being objective and open to challenge in one's behaviour in a professional context.

Statement of values: Psychologists value honesty, probity, accuracy, clarity and fairness in their interactions with all persons and peoples, and seek to promote integrity in all facets of their scientific and professional endeavours.

In applying these values, Psychologists should consider:

i   Honesty, openness and candour;
ii Accurate unbiased representation;
iii Fairness;
iv Avoidance of exploitation and conflicts of interest (including self-interest);
v   Maintaining personal and professional boundaries;
vi Addressing misconduct.

Conclusion

4.1 This Code cannot and does not aim to provide the answer to every ethical decision a Psychologist may face. The Code provides the parameters within which professional judgements should be made. However, it is important to remember to reflect and apply a process to resolve ethical challenges.

Notes

1   https://thepsychologist.bps.org.uk/volume-32/june-2019/baroness-mary-warnock-1924–2019
2   https://philosophynow.org/issues/102/Peter_Rickman_1918-2014
3   1983 Code of Conduct published 1985. *Bulletin of The British Psychological Society* (1985), 38, 41–43. Printed in Great Britain ©1985 The British Psychological Society ©BPS.

References

British Psychological Society, 1950. A code of professional ethics governing the disclosure by qualified psychologists of psychological information about individuals. *Quarterly Bulletin of the British Psychological Society*, 1(8), 317–323.

British Psychological Society, 1954. *Annual Report*. British Psychological Society.

British Psychological Society, 1985. A code of ethics for the British Psychological Society. *Bulletin of the British Psychological Society*, 38, pp. 41–43.

Bunn, G. C., 2001a. Charlie and the Chocolate Factory. *The Psychologist*, 11(November), 576–579.

Bunn, G. C., 2001b. Introduction. In G. C. Bunn, A. D. Lovie, & G. D. Richards, eds. *Psychology in Britain: Historical essays and personal reflections*. Leicester: BPS Books.

Edgell, B., 1947. The British Psychological Society. *British Journal of Psychology*, 37(13), p. 130.

Jackson, C., 2019. A history of psychology in the United Kingdom. Meeting of minds – the road to professional practice. *British Journal of Psychology*.

Kwiatkowski, R., 2003. We are not adjectives, we are psychologists. *The Psychologist*, 16(9), 456.

Kwiatkowski, R., 2009. Cranfield Ceres. Retrieved from https://dspace.lib.cranfield.ac.uk/handle/1826/6975

Kwiatkowski, R. et al, 2006. What have we forgotten and why? *Journal of Occupational and Organisational Psychology*, 79(2), 183–201.

Lovie, A. D., 2001. Three steps to heaven: How the British Psychological Society attained its place in the sun. In G. C. Bunn, A. D. Lovie, & G. D. Richards, eds. *Psychology in Britain: Historical essays and personal reflections*. Leicester: BPS Books.

Myers, C. S., 1911/1922. *A text book of experimental psychology*. Cambridge University Press.

NIIP Jubilee Issue, 1970. *Occupational Psychology*, 44 (Jubilee Issue).

Shimmin, S., 1994. The war years. In *Fifty years of occupational psychology in Britain*. Leicester: British Psychological Society.

11

THE DEVELOPMENT OF THE EUROPEAN FEDERATION OF PSYCHOLOGISTS' ASSOCIATIONS' META-CODE OF ETHICS

Geoff Lindsay[1]

Introduction

The focus of this chapter differs from that of the majority of chapters in this book. Rather than discuss the ethical code of a particular country, I describe the nature, development and use of a transnational code: The European Federation of Psychologists Associations' (EFPA) Meta-Code of Ethics. This EPFA Meta-Code is, as far as I'm aware, original. It was developed by a transnational European organisation, EFPA, previously the European Federation of Professional Psychologists' Associations (EFPPA). This was set up to be a Federation of the main society or association of psychologists in each country within Europe, which was a member of the EFPPA.

At its origin, EFPPA had a more specific focus on professional applied psychology, hence its name. At an early stage of its development in the 1980s, the need to have a common code of ethics across all member associations was recognised. A Task Force for Ethics was set up at the General Assembly in Rome, 1988. Since then, the EFPPA changed its constitution to become a federation of associations of all psychologists, not only professional psychologists and became the European Federation of Psychologists' Associations (EFPPA). This important change therefore potentially brought all psychologist members of national associations of psychologists within its remit.

In this chapter, I shall describe the development of the EFPA Meta-Code of ethics against this backdrop of the differing nature of the organisation. In summary, rather than a code that guides, and in some cases may be used to govern, the ethical thinking and behaviour of individual psychologists, the Meta-Code was designed to guide the nature and content of the individual association codes themselves. I review reasons for this difference from national codes of ethics for psychologists, and the pathway to develop the Meta-Code itself. The influence of the Metacode on EFPA member associations and also on individual psychologists will be reviewed. During this process I shall also consider the main issues addressed by accompanying chapters with respect to national codes but from the perspective of this transnational Meta-Code of ethics.

The Development of the EFPA Meta-Code of Ethics

Birth

The original organisation (EFPPA) was founded in 1981 by 12 national psychological societies/associations (see Freeman, 2011; Lunt, 1996, Tikkanen, 2007 for the early development of EFPPA and then EFPA). During the 1980s, the organisation expanded with new member associations and developed its policy objectives. Over this period, Europe was also changing with gradual enlargements of the European Union (EU). With the original focus during the EFPPA period on professional psychology, a major EU issue concerned the movement of psychologists between countries, which was the fundamental tenet of the EU: 'Freedom of movement'.

Within this context, EFPA saw the importance of addressing the initial training of professional applied psychologists the need for a common code of ethics. The aim of these initiatives was to ensure high standards of psychologists' practice not only in their home country but also within other European countries to which they might transfer in order to practise. In this sense, the development of a common code of ethics would, it was hoped, complement the achievement of commonality of standards of professional practice. The 1988 General Assembly of EFPPA in Rome gave its approval to set up a task force on ethics. The remit was to set up a 'common European ethical code for professional psychologists' (Lindsay, 2011, p. 122).

First Meeting: Challenges

The first Task Force convenor, Geir Nielsen (Norway), had been appointed in March 1989 and seven national associations of psychologists each sent a representative to the first meeting. The other six came from the German Federal Republic, Hungary, Netherlands, Spain, Switzerland, and myself representing the British Psychological Society in the UK. Our remit was to:

> explore the possibility of, and to work towards the realisation of, common European ethical codes for professional psychologists. The Ethical Principles of Scandinavian Psychologists will, as an example of codes that are well developed and international serve as an important

point of reference for the Task Force. A report and possible proposals shall be presented at the next General Assembly.

(Lindsay, 2011, p 122)

The first meeting of the Task Force on Ethics was held in 1990 when we met in Copenhagen, Denmark, 12–13 January. This comprised all except the representative from Germany. Over this first weekend session I was appointed Secretary and the main language was determined to be English, which all members spoke. Our main tasks during this meeting were to consider the remit set by the General Assembly and to plan how we would carry out our responsibility to produce 'common codes'. But first, and indeed over the whole period of the work, we had to develop understanding of each other's context. The common background was that we were each senior members of national psychological associations, and had interest and expertise in ethics. Second, representing countries in the EU, we were aware of the general policies and practices that were driving the aim of the EFPPA General Assembly. However, it became very clear during the first meeting, that it was essential to take account of the range and variety of the different contexts in which each association operated. There were different cultural, historical, socioeconomic, linguistic, and other domains in which each national association operated. For example, the nature of homogeneity and heterogeneity of population groups differed substantially between countries, as did trajectories of change in immigration and mobility patterns.

More specific to psychology itself, there were also many differences. For example, some countries such as UK and Netherlands had a single dominant member association for psychologists. Others such as France had many different such organisations. Hence whereas the British Psychological Society (BPS), being the member UK association for EFPPA, was not controversial, this was not the case in all countries. For example, at an earlier EFPPA meeting where I had represented the BPS to develop a new journal, *European Psychologist*, there were two members from France who had both arrived claiming legitimacy in representing their country.

Second, the nature of national association members of EFPPA varied in terms of whether they fulfilled a purely scientific or learned society role, or whether they were also engaged in practice of supporting members, which in the UK would be undertaken by a trade union. The BPS for example, has a Royal Charter as a learned society which prevents any such trade union action. These, and other factors, were recognised at the very start of the Task Force's work. They were also peculiar to our role in creating a transnational code.

The main business of the first meeting with respect to the potential code itself, focused on three fundamental questions.

1. Is there a basis for a common European code?

We examined the codes of several countries, including the US (American Psychological Association: APA), Canada (Canadian Psychological Association: CPA) and UK (BPS). We were pleased to find a good deal of commonality of *content* but great dissimilarity in terms of *structure*. We took this as a positive basis.

Similar content across these example codes together with individuals' knowledge of their national codes regarding content would be a good basis from which to work.

2. Is it useful to have such a code?

This question is easy to miss, assuming that having an ethical code must be a 'good thing,' but it is an important fundamental query that must be asked. When the APA was discussing the possibility of developing its first code of ethics in the 1940s and early 1950s, one contributor to a group of papers in the *American Psychologist* argued against having any code of ethics for APA members. Hall (1952) made the following argument: "I think it plays into the hands of crooks on the one hand and because it makes those who are covered by the code feel smug and sanctimonious on the other hand."

However, we argued that a common code would be useful for the situation across Europe for the reasons stated above; for example, the implications of free movement and also *common training* would be helpful in the development of standardised expectations and requirements, and hence to provide guidance for practice for comparable standards of psychologists' practice.

3. How should we work towards a Common Code?

We decided that a single common code of ethics for individual psychologists, to be applied in each country through its national association, was not practical: at least in the short term, and was probably not practical at all. The four reasons for our thinking relate to the discussion above. First, national associations varied in their rationale and nature of membership: science-based, practice-based or both; comprehensive, generic membership or focus on sub-groups, even within this categorisation, for example a focus on health/clinical practice but not on other professional domains such as educational psychology.

The second challenge related to the existing code of ethics of each EFPPA member association. We identified that these differed in terms of content and structure, style and degree of specificity. Third, not all national associations had a code of ethics for its members. Some were in the process of development and associations preferred to complete that task first: this would delay the creation of a common code. Fourth, there were constitutional challenges. These were autonomous associations, which we expected to change to having a common code. They would need to arrange for the common code to be approved through their internal decision-making system. This might be by a committee or, as in the case of the BPS, a vote of the total membership. Suppose an association did not like a particular clause and decided against its inclusion? This would prevent a common code being feasible. Given the variation in existing codes of which we were aware, and the differences between cultural norms across countries in Europe, this was identified as a real challenge in developing a common code.

The Way Forward: Meta-Code of Ethics

This first meeting in 1990 agreed, as a way forward, to broaden the evidence and conceptual bases on which we would undertake our work. We collected other codes for psychologists for analysis. We also made the major and fundamental decision that we should not aim for a common code for psychologists within EFPPA member associations. Rather, we decided to develop a *Meta-Code*, which would guide and govern the nature of national codes of ethics. This would not be a code for individual psychologists, therefore, as was the case with existing national codes. Rather, we decided to develop a framework for the national codes in terms of its principles and content. That is, the Meta-Code would identify common core issues that would be applicable to all member associations, and hence ultimately to the individual psychologists in Europe, through each association's own code.

This approach would enable national associations to take account of national, cultural and local factors which might be important to include in that specific country but not necessarily in other countries. For example, at that time, there was a major difference in whether professional psychologists typically worked for the state: for example, in the UK at that time, almost all clinical psychologists would be employed by the National Health Service and nearly all educational psychologists were employed by local authorities. A second important issue concerned billing, and the nature of relationship between a psychologist and client with respect to payment of services. In many countries in Europe and also the US there was a recognised need to govern the financial relationship with respect to payment for services. However, this was essentially irrelevant where the psychologist provided a service to a client that was free at the point of delivery, as in the UK.

We were prescient in deciding to have the major aim of future-proofing the ultimate Meta-Code. We wanted to prepare for future intra- as well as international variations and also trajectories of change over time. As I will show below, this has proven to be an important decision, for example, with the gradual privatisation of psychological practice in countries, such as the UK. This has not been straightforward, and politicians may deny that privatisation is actually happening or is an aim for their policies. The reality, however, is that the employment status of many professional psychologists has been, and/or is changing from a clear link to the state (national or local) with respect to payments, for example schools or indirect clients. In short, the decision to develop a Meta-Code was an important and fundamental move based on an analysis of both the then current cross-national situation and our judgement of potential future trends.

The Process

Having identified the way forward, there was then a hiatus and we did not meet again as a task force until 27–28 February 1993. Instead of the two meetings a year the convenor had proposed, he instead produced in June 1991 a 'tentative draft Meta-Code' for the Task Force based on elements in the existing Scandinavian code and drawing on elements of the APA, BPS, Canadian, Austrian, German, Hungarian, and Spanish Psychological Associations. This consultation paper was submitted to the group remotely for comments. This process produced only three responses so Casper Koene (Netherlands) and I met with Geir Nielson in Amsterdam (31 October to 1 November, 1992), together with the staff member of the Netherlands Institute of Psychology Yoke Bravenboer, to review the responses.

The new 1992 APA code (American Psychological Association, 1992) had recently been published by this time and we also considered this. We rejected adapting the APA code to form the basis of the Meta-Code as their standards had two high a level of specificity: a clear problem given our requirement for flexibility, as discussed above. The APA code, therefore, we agreed would be used only where it was helpful to the development of the new Meta-Code as was the case of the other codes to which we had given attention. We did, however, agree that the APA *General Principles* formed a useful model and structure.

This productive meeting was fundamental in forming a clear, agreed approach and a sound basis for the process of developing the Meta-Code itself. We then developed a framework for the Meta-Code. We tried an original three-dimensional model of basic values, professional relationships and stage of relationship between the psychologist and the client. However, this was found to be impractical with empty cells and a lack of useful generalisability to different types of practices.

The draft general framework we developed was then considered by the next (that is, second) full meeting of the Task Force (February 27–28, 1993) in Amsterdam, when Casper Koen was appointed convenor in replacement of Pier Nielson who had resigned. We confirmed again that we would meet twice yearly. In one sense this appears an extended period of creation and indeed could be frustrating: surely, we could do more work at a distance? Consider document drafts? Today in this era of the pandemic because of Covid-19, society has had to make major changes to 'normal' practice. As I write, my university has basically been closed from March 2020 and planning the re-opening in late September for the start of the new academic year. My research centre is closed and we all conduct our work at home, which includes series of remote meetings and research supervisions. Therefore, planning, supporting, advising, creating new research and other work have fundamentally changed. However, at that time, in the early 1990s, the use of remote conferences, for example, was very limited and generally not very practical on a long-term basis.

In addition, we found the concentration of effort into a weekend from Friday night arrival to Sunday afternoon departure a positively intense period: not only to do the basic work on the Code but also to develop our understanding of the nuances and subtleties of different cultures. These and other factors related to the contextual basis for the Meta-Code content and implementation. These weekends therefore, while separated by about six months, were essential for both 'real work' and social interaction. The challenges mentioned above of grasping many nuances of the same issue as processed by a colleague from a different country and culture were much more easily dealt with face to face in a group and over a concentrated weekend time-period.

In between meetings of the Task Force, I produced minutes, new drafts and, together with other Task Force members, produced various working documents. Looking back, the strategy for 'work time' as a group comprised just five long weekends before we presented the Meta-Code of Ethics to what had now become the EFPA general assembly, July 1995 in Athens.

Challenges Overcome

The first challenge at the Paris meeting 1993, for the whole Task Force, was to agree on the general directions proposed by the small informal group. At first, we also had to consider the relationship of the Meta-Code with the *Carta Etica*. This was a relatively recent document developed by South European countries – its worth was recognised but it was agreed that it should remain as a separate document, for use by the associations that had developed it. It was however, added for information as an appendix to the first published Meta-Code.

Second, we had a fuller discussion of use of the new 1992 APA Code of Ethics. The interesting issue that arose here was a strong reconfirmation of the principled view that whereas borrowing the APA Code could be useful in a practical sense, this was not appropriate. In addition to the limitations outlined above, the Task Force was strongly of the view that the Meta-Code should be clearly a new *European* code, not one that was substantially borrowed from elsewhere. Although this might be seen, and to a degree was, a result of Euro-centrism, there were sound reasons regarding variations across countries, culture and time (including the future) as discussed above, that were important. The group also recognised the benefits of the CPA's code and its substantial inclusion of training and development material (Canadian Psychological Association, 2003). Furthermore, the Task Force agreed on the usefulness of the structure used by both the APA and CPA codes on a set of *principles* and separate specifications/standards, which elaborated the behaviours related to each principle.

Third, having confirmed the general structure: how many principles and what should they be? At that time the CPA had four and the 1992 APA Code had six. There was concern in the Task Force about 'Social Responsibility,' This, it was argued, went beyond the practice of psychology per se into the realm of general social judgements: "They (psychologists) are encouraged to contribute a portion of their professional time for little or no personal advantage" (Lindsay, 2011, p. 124). The result was an agreement that there should be four principles in the EFPA Meta-Code: Respect for a person's rights and dignity, Competence, Responsibility, and Integrity; preceded by a Preamble.

At the following three meetings (Amsterdam and Ljubljana in 1994, and Zurich in March 1995), we developed the content and finalised the Meta-Code. We developed, with much discussion, the *Specifications* that were associated with each *Principle*. We also decided not to have Principles in a hierarchy. Rather, we argued for the importance of recognising the *inter-dependence* of principles. Indeed, research had demonstrated that ethical dilemmas were often the result of conflicts between following one principle rather than another (Lindsay & Clarkson, 1999: Lindsay & Colley, 1995; Pope & Vetter, 1992; see also Bersoff, 2003 pp. 165–171 for a useful discussion of the case of Tarasoff v Regents of the University of California).

Cross-cutting Themes

Client

At that time, there had been a good deal of discussion and research about the relationships between psychologists and their clients. The 1992 APA code, with its detailed standards of behaviour, stated in its Therapy section that sexual intimacies with clients were forbidden. But what of past clients? This version of the APA Code stated that:

> Psychologies do not engage in sexual intimacies with a former therapy patient or client for at least 2 years after cessation or termination of professional services.
>
> *(Ethical Standard 4.07a: Lindsay, 2011 p124).*

This seemed to the Task Force to be very problematic: to define ethical behaviour here in terms of an arbitrary time period. Furthermore, Standard 4.07b provided a fuller statement that there was an obligation on the psychologist not to engage in this behaviour at all. This seemed to be both ambiguous and unhelpful in a code.

Therefore we set out four cross-cutting requirements in the Meta-Code:

Professional psychologists' ethical codes must take the following into account:

- Psychologists' professional behaviour must be considered within a professional role, categorised by the professional relationship.
- Inequalities of knowledge and power always influence psychologists' professional relationships with clients and colleagues.
- The larger the inequality in the professional relationship and the greater dependence of clients, the heavier is the responsibility of the professional psychologist.
- The responsibilities of psychologists must be considered within the context of the stage of the professional relationship.

Inter-dependence of the Four Principles

We recognised that there will be strong inter-dependencies between the four ethical principles and their specifications. This means that in order to resolve an ethical question or dilemma, psychologists will require reflection and often dialogue with clients and colleagues, weighing up different ethical principles. Making decisions and taking actions are necessary even if there are still conflicting issues.

Culture

Increasingly, individual countries are becoming more 'multi-cultural' in the sense of their population becoming more diverse with migration patterns and immigration from other countries and cultures. This is a long-standing characteristic of some countries, for example England, where well over 250 home languages other than English are spoken in London schools (http://projectbritain.com/regions/la nguages.htm accessed 10.09.20). Within Europe, there is also a history over many centuries of population movement and also political demographic changes as a result of wars, empires being formed and lost, and marriages between royal families. The US also has had different major immigrations at different times but these have focused in terms of scale on the past two to three centuries.

Against this diverse background, where there are different degrees of diversity between countries, we also wanted to recognise diversities between cultures of different countries, and even within countries. In short, cultural variation was seen as highly complex but a major reality to be taken into account. As noted above, the Meta-Code's design included this factor and experience has demonstrated that this has been very successful. Recognition of this inter-nation cultural variation was also fundamental to the development of the later *Universal Declaration of Ethical Principles for Psychologists* led by Janel Gauthier and colleagues (International Union of Psychological Science, International Association of Applied Psychology, 2008).

Language

Language is an important element of culture and has varying degrees of complexity within different countries across the world. Nations may have a single dominant official language, a number of official languages, or a wide range and number of different languages which are not official in the legal sense. The original EFPPA had three official languages for its business at its inception and early years (English, French and German). However, this was recognised to be unwieldy and English was confirmed as the sole official language (Freeman, 2011). As a Task Force, we had two challenges. The main challenge was to produce a document that would be amenable to translation into all European official languages such that there was no ambiguity, which could lead to different interpretations. The second, more immediate challenge for the Task Force was to ensure that we members could discuss matters effectively. Given that the output was to be a Meta-Code written in English, we put great emphasis on ensuring that each concept was understood and each phrase and sentence was agreed to be translatable into other languages – as well as making sense conceptually. Of course, the Task Force did not include speakers in many of the other European languages but the evidence from other member associations, for example at our ten-year Review (see below), confirmed that we had been successful.

Which Psychologists?

The Task Force started its work under a remit from EFPPA, a body for *professional applied psychologists*. During the period of our work, however, EFPPA became EFPA as noted above, that is an organisation of national associations for *all* psychologists. This change had little impact on our work as from the very start we focused on principles and on specifications that were to be developed to ensure relevance to the local (national) situation. Again, the structure of the Meta-Code proved very helpful in enabling this, and the Meta-Code was appropriate for both scientific as well as professional practice and hence for the new EFPA.

The Meta-Code of Ethics

The Meta-Code was approved by the EFPA General Assembly 1995. The Task Force's work was finished and the General Assembly set up its replacement, a Standing Committee on Ethics (SCE). The SCE was largely based on the Task Force membership but with extended representation. We were committed to a review process to check the usefulness of the Meta-Code and, as noted above, this was undertaken over the ten-year period 1995–2005. We knew that some Codes of Ethics, for example that of the APA, had been changed more than once over time, and in some cases – and the APA is again a good example – there were major changes in format, structure and content. Was our Meta-Code, designed to be principle-led but also flexible in its *specifications*, successful? An initial survey of member associations followed by 2 invited international symposia of member associations in Prague (March 2003, October 2004) supplemented by contributions by members of the SCE to symposia at biennial European Congress of Psychology meetings and open Meetings of Ethics held in Lisbon (1998, 2006) enabled an in-depth consideration of the Meta-Code's resilience.

We found that only a small number of changes to the Meta-Code were necessary. These included:

1) adding the use of *Mediation*, a process used in many fields in addition to disciplinary procedures;
2) firming up the issue of self-determination and autonomy;
3) adding a new specification to oblige caution when using newly developed methods whose evidence of effectiveness and appropriateness was in the process of being created through research; and
4) addressing psychologists' actions when a person's consent had not or could not be given (see Lindsay, 2011, p. 126–7).

Success of the Meta-Code

The measure of the Meta-Code's success is the very limited change to the 1995 original. The community of EFPA member associations have found the Meta-Code fit for purpose. Second, the Meta-Code has been used as intended, that is to provide a template to enable national EFPA member associations to produce their own national Code of Ethics that was compliant with the Meta-Code, but also reflected local and national circumstances. By the EFPA General Assembly in Oslo (2009), the number of national associations with ethical codes that were judged to be compliant with the Meta-Code had risen to 11 (Lindsay 2009a, 2009b); and the number of compliant national associations has continued to increase.

Third, although the Meta-Code was designed for associations, we also found that it was considered very useful by individual psychologists in countries where there was no existing code of ethics. As a result, our input into international meetings and congresses proved useful at both the individual and association level. We also engaged in specific capacity building, e.g. in South East Europe, together with colleagues engaged in the Universal Declaration (Gauthier) and the outreach work of the APA (Behnke) – see Gauthier, Lindsay, Korkut and Behnke (2009). In addition, to support training and professional development, four longstanding members of the SCE produced a book *Ethics for European Psychologists* specifically for European psychologists (Lindsay, Koene, Ovreeide, & Lang, 2008). I later joined with colleagues from the US, Argentina and Turkey to edit the *Oxford Handbook of International Psychological Ethics* (Leach, Stevens, Lindsay, Ferrero, & Korkut, 2012).

Further developments since 2005 include the change from a Standing Committee on Ethics to a Board of Ethics in 2011. We had also developed a series of guidance documents during the 1995–2005 period and these have been expanded by the Board of Ethics more recently, in particular the development of the EFPA Model Code in 2015. Here, the Meta-Code formed the basis of a template to aid member associations to produce their own national code (www.ethics/efpa/ guidelines accessed 13.08.20).

Conclusion

To modify the Conclusions of my paper on the development of the EFPA Meta-Code (Lindsay, 2012, p. 130), on which this chapter has substantially been based, I complete this chapter with the following updated thoughts.

I am proud to have served on the EFPPA/EFPA Task Force on Ethics, and later the Standing Committee on Ethics, from 1990–2009 initially as its Secretary and then during the final 10 years as Convenor. The work of the EFPPA/ EFPA Task Force on Ethics (1990–1995) and the Standing Committee on Ethics (1995–2005) produced initially an innovative transnational Meta-Code of Ethics (1995) which has stood the test of time. Our review in the period leading up to its ten years of use indicated that only a small number of minor amendments were necessary. That second edition in 2005 is still in use and has been the basis for the development of national codes across Europe.

The Meta-Code has supported the development of ethical practices throughout Europe. This was supplemented and extended by the work undertaken by the Task Force and SCE through wider activities to develop ethical thinking and provide support for psychologists' associations, and indeed individual psychologists over this 20-year period. The experience of working on this important task with this group of wise and committed psychologists was both highly effective and successful. I feel privileged to have benefitted personally from the experiences through these collaborative endeavours. I thank my colleagues for their collegiality, hard work and commitment.

The importance of ethics has never been so great, not only in psychology but also in wider society. In the latter, our role is that of a citizen in our respective socio-political contexts. Within psychology, we have direct opportunities – and responsibilities – to educate, support and maintain high ethical standards. This book makes an important wide-ranging contribution to this endeavour. I hope this history of the development of this unique initiative to create a transnational European Code of Ethics will be helpful to psychologist colleagues across the world.

Appendix

The EFPA Meta-Code (2005) Structure

The EFPA Meta-Code (2005) can be accessed on the website (www.ethics.efpa.eu/metaa nd-model-code/meta-code).

An outline of its structure and content follows:

1   Preamble
2   Ethical principles

    2.1 Respect for a person's rights and dignity
    2.2 Competence
    2.3 Responsibility
    2.4 Integrity

3   Content of Ethical Codes of Member Associations

    a   Clients
    b   What professional psychologists codes must take into account:

        • Professional role
        • Inequalities of knowledge and power
        • The magnitude of the inequality and dependence of clients on the responsibility of the psychologist
        • The context of the stage of the professional relationship

    c   Inter-dependence of the four principles

The specifications:

3.1 Respect for a person's right and dignity

3.1.1 General respect
3.1.2 Privacy and confidentiality
3.1.3 Informed consent and freedom of consent
3.1.4 Self determination

3.2 Competence

3.2.1 Ethical awareness
3.2.2 Limits of competence
3.2.3 Limits of procedures
3.2.4 Continuing developments
3.2.5 Incapability

3.3 Responsibility

3.3.1 General responsibility
3.3.2 Promotion of high standards
3.3.3 Avoidance of harm
3.3.4 Continuity of care
3.3.5 Extended responsibility
3.3.6 Resolving dilemmas

3.4.1 Integrity

3.4.1 Recognition of professional limitations
3.4.2 Honesty and accuracy
3.4.3 Straightforwardness and openness
3.4.4 Conflicts of interest and exploitation
3.4.5 Actions of colleagues

Example of style of specifications

Instead of being written descriptions of what a psychologist should do (or not do), all specifications are written with the audience being the national association and the action referring to the writing of the association's code, e.g., in the section "Privacy and Confidentiality"

    i) restriction of seeking and giving out information to only that required for the professional purpose.

This text may be used to produce one or more specifications in the association's code.

Note

1 This chapter is based on my earlier paper on the development of the EFPA Meta-Code: Lindsay, G. (2011). Transnational ethical guidance and the development of the EFPA Meta-Code of ethics. *European Psychologist, 16* (*2*), 121–131. doi:10.1027/1016–9040/a000090.

References

American Psychological Association (2002). Ethical principles of psychologists and code of conduct. Washington, DC: Author. www.apa.org/ethics/code/code-1992#:~:text=This%20Ethics%20Code%20provides%20a,most%20situations%20encountered%20by%20psychologists

Bersoff, D. N. (2003). *Ethical conflicts in psychology* (3rd ed.). Washington, DC: American Psychological Association.

Canadian Psychological Association (2003). *Canadian code of conduct for psychologists* (3rd ed.). Ottawa, Ontario: Author.

Gauthier, J., Lindsay, G., Korkut, Y., & Behnke, S. (2009). *How to use ethical principles for creating or reviewing a code of ethics.* South Eastern Europe Regional Conference of Psychology. Sofia, Bulgaria, 30 October–1 November.

Freeman, R. P. J. (2011). The history and organisation of the European Federation of Psychologists' Associations – Reflections on the first 30 years. *European Psychologist,* 16(2), 90–99.

Hall, C. S. (1952) Crooks, codes, and cant. *American Psychologist,* 7(8), 430–431.

International Union of Psychological Science, International Association of Applied Psychology (2008) Universal declaration of ethical principles for psychologists. www.researchgate.

net/publication/228985261_The_universal_declaration_of_ethical_principles_for_psycholo gists_Third_draft

Leach, M. M., Stevens, M. J., Lindsay, G., Ferrero, A., & Korkut, Y. (Eds.) (2012). *The Oxford handbook of international psychological ethics*. New York: Oxford University Press. doi:10.1037/a0031573

Lindsay, G. (1998). Ethical codes and ethical dilemmas. In V. Claudio (ed.) *Psicologia e Etica: Actas do Coloquio Europeu de Psicologia e Etica, Lisboa, Marco, 1996.* pp 3–9. Lisboa: Instituto Superior de Psicologoca Aplicada.

Lindsay, G. (2006). Developing ethical practice: A European perspective. In V. Claudio et al. *Il coloquio Europeu de psicologicia e etica* (pp. 49–68). Lisbon, Portugal: ISPA.

Lindsay, G. (2009). *Report of the Standing Committee of Ethics to the General Assembly in Oslo.* Brussels, Belgium: European Federation of Psychologists' Associations.

Lindsay, G. (2009). *Ethical dilemmas of psychologists: How are these affected at times of national security? In V. Claudio et al. (eds) III coloquio Europeu de psicologica e etica* (pp 213–220). Lisbon, Portugal: Instituto Superior de Psicologica Aplicada.

Lindsay, G. (2011). Transnational ethical guidance and the development of the EFPA Meta-Code of ethics. *European Psychologist. 16(2)*, 121–131. doi:10.1027/1016–9040/a000090

Lindsay, G. & Colley, A. (1995). Ethical dilemmas of members of the Society. *The Psychologist: Bulletin of the British Psychological Society*, 8, 214–217.

Lindsay, G. & Clarkson, P. (1999). Ethical dilemmas of psychotherapists. *The Psychologist: Bulletin of the British Psychological Society*, 12(4), 182–185.

Lindsay, G., Koene, C., Ovreeide, H., & Lang, F. (2008). *Ethics for European psychologists*. Gottingen, Germany and Cambridge, MA: Hogrefe.

Lunt, I. (1996). The history and organisation of the European Federation of Professional Psychologists' Associations (EFPPA). *European Psychologist*, 1, 60–64.

Pope, K. S. & Vetter, V. A. (1992). Ethical dilemmas encountered by members of the American Psychological Association. *American Psychologist*, 47, 397–411.

Tikkanen, T, (2007). 25 years of EFPA: From exchanging information to making policy. *European Psychologist*, 12, 156–160.

PART 5

South and Central American Countries: Chile, Colombia, Guatemala, Venezuela

12

PROFESSIONAL CODE OF ETHICS

College of Psychologists of Chile

Sergio Lucero Conus

"Ethics is a task, a process, a path: it is the thoughtful way of life inasmuch as it leads to the good life, as the Greeks would say, or the least harmful possible life. It is the only true wisdom."

André Comte-Sponville

Brief introduction

This essay underlines the importance of professional ethics and ethical codes in the development of this discipline and profession in our country. Since its inception, efforts to design the training of psychologists sought to bestow upon it the stamp of both rigor and academic excellence, which in themselves have ethical connotations.

In the same way, it is evident that within the association efforts have focused on the development of tools – both guidelines and the codes of conduct themselves – to assure among members the ethical exercise of their profession.

These efforts were greatly disrupted by the civic–military dictatorship, which lasted 16 years (1973–1989). During this time, Chile witnessed the "university boom," the appearance of a great number of new universities and schools of psychology, as well as the elimination of obligatory membership in professional associations, the neglect of ethical standards, and the suppression of professional associations' "legal right to supervise members" performance, and to assure conformity with ethical norms and high professional standards.

In Chile, both social ethics and personal and professional practice were severely debilitated.

History of the Development of the Code of Professional Ethics of the College of Psychologists of Chile

Historical background

The ethical issue was important for Chilean psychologists since the establishment of the first Special Course in Psychology at the Faculty of Philosophy and Education of the University of Chile in the years 1947/48. From the selection phase to enter, and throughout the training process, the ethical aspect had an important presence. This was a connotation of what the psychological work of professionals involved with the most delicate and intimate aspects of people, since the training was focused on clinical practice.

This first course was probably a pioneer in Latin America. In 1950, the Department of Psychology was created in the Faculty of Philosophy and Education, with the aim of training psychologists as a university profession. The Department depended on the Pedagogical Institute. On October 1, 1952, the title of Psychologist was created by the Faculty of Philosophy and Education, and endorsed by Decree 3012 of September 24, 1954 (Lucero, 1995).

The first graduates of the Department of Psychology of the University of Chile, Faculty of Philosophy and Education, created the Association of Psychologists of Chile showing the interest of psychologists to group together and visualize their consolidation and professional development as a collective process. A sense of professional group and belonging had already been generated in the training process, which did not make the mandatory association requirement necessary (Espinoza & Moreno, 2007). Even though initially there was no written code of ethics, the exchange about the ethical dimension of the profession had a repeated presence.

On November 1, 1976, as a College of Psychologists, ethical standards were issued, which would be considered our first code of ethics. The Chilean College of Psychologists was created by Law No. 17,033 on December 9, 1968, with legal status under public law, therefore with broad legal powers to safeguard the ethical behavior of psychologists.

The civic–military dictatorship, by Decree Law 3,621 of February 3, 1981, reduced all professional colleges to the status of union associations, losing their category of institutions with legal status under public law, therefore, fully limiting their powers legally regarding the regulation and ethical control of Chilean professionals and abolishing the compulsory tuition for the exercise of professions. In the case of psychologists, this decree was proclaimed twelve days after the promulgation of our first code of ethics, in January 1981, immediately limiting the exercise and implementation of the newly established ethical standards for professional psychologists, and limiting them only to associates. In so doing, it therefore weakened their actions in the protection of the profession, professionals, and users of our services.

The Professional Ethics Commission created in April 1996, initially as the Ethics Committee, proposed the development of a new Code of Professional Ethics and a Manual of Procedural Procedure was a priority aspect of its objectives. This is how the code currently in force was promulgated in November 1999, and the

Procedural Manual in 2000, later being amended as "Regulation of Procedure in Ethical Trials," which likewise remains in force until today (Lucero, 1995).

Construction Process of the Code of Professional Ethics

- Analysis of the old code keeping in mind the need for updating, and going beyond a code of ethics.
- Appoint a Technical Commission for the elaboration and proposal of a new Code of Professional Ethics.

Stages of the process:

- Study of the 1981 Code of Ethics that incorporated an important article on Human Rights approved in the Tokyo Convention (Lucero, 1995) and the Ethical Norms approved in 1976, which were an almost verbatim translation of the Ethical Norms of the American Psychological Association (APA) (Alvear et al., 2008).
- Review of the codes of ethics of other professions in Chile: Bar Association, Medical College, College of Engineers, etc. Bibliography study referring to professional ethics and codes of ethics.
- Study of codes of ethics of schools or associations of psychologists from other countries: Code of the American Psychological Association (APA), of the Official College of Psychologists of Spain,
- Discussion-reflection on the choice of what type of code was more appropriate to our reality: Regulatory, Educational, Aspiration or Expectations? How general? How comprehensive? (Gyarmati, 1992). It was decided that the central focus of each type of Code had a presence in the structure of ours, a draft code of ethics that was more comprehensive than just the normative aspect of deontological codes.
- Delivery of weekly progress of the studies of the Technical Commission to the plenary of the Ethics Commission for exchange, discussion and improvement. It was a rigorous and lengthy process.
- Call in 1999 for the "First Professional Ethics Work Sessions" addressed to the community of psychologists, which was held with the assistance of more than 40 psychologists from the Clinical, Labor-Organizational, Community, Legal-Criminological specialties, Academic Psychologists, Psychologists without specialization and Student Community.

Its objectives were to present, motivate and make known to professionals and students of psychology, the advances in the development of a new code of professional ethics.

Following the expository part, group meetings of the six attending specialties were held within the scope of the same days, to meet and collect their specific proposals and proposals for the new code. The work of each group was coordinated by members of the Ethics Commission.

193

Subsequent to the conference, representatives of the specialties of the profession were called to continue the work begun at the event, with three group meetings planned by specialty, to complete the analysis and diagnosis of specific ethical issues and their subsequent proposals. At this stage, the academics were not present, instead the Child-youth specialty that had not been able to attend the conferences was added with their contribution taking into account their clinical and educational areas.

Once the draft code had been prepared, copies of the text were sent to all psychology programs and courses at the country's universities, explicitly requesting study and feedback. The response was less than expected. There was also mass distribution of copies of the project to the community of psychologists, at the national congress prior to its approval, requesting reading and proposals with few responses.

Finally, a re-study of the project was initiated by the Technical Commission, and respectively by the plenary of the Commission, taking into account the contributions received. This resulted in the promulgation and publication of the new Code of Professional Ethics of the College of Psychologists of Chile in 1999.

The Code of Ethics of the College of Psychologists is available on the website of the College of Psychologists of Chile (AG) for consultation of psychologists and the general public. In fact, requests for information about ethical issues or complaints to the professional Ethics Commission of the College about alleged transgressions of the code by registered psychologists are based on prior consultation of the code. The same is true of the public or private institutions they consult. The reiteration is valid, in the sense that the Commission only has jurisprudence on collegiate professionals. Regarding non-collegiate psychologists, the Ethics Commission has the option of informing the accused that a complaint has been filed against them and offering them the possibility of a peer trial, if they voluntarily accept the jurisdiction of the Ethics Commission.

Objectives of the Study of Codes of Ethics from Other Countries

The experience and eventual differences in the ethical outlook of other countries were collected and with that contribution, optimizing the elaboration of our own code. The codes of ethics of some Latin American, European and North American countries, mainly Brazil, Spain, and the United States, were studied. The Code of Ethics of the American Psychological Association (APA) was the instrument that contributed the most for the design of our code. Otherwise, it was evident that it had also served as a model for other codes studied. The APA code is further supported by task forces, many studies, periodic reviews, and specific ethical guidelines, such as ethical guidelines for forensic psychologists. Obviously, in the reformulation of our code it will be important to keep this working model in mind since it does not seem functional that a code of ethics can contain the entire universe of guidelines, conduct guidelines and rules for the different specialties of the profession.

From the study of the codes and the corresponding literature, a draft code was developed that considered aspects of different types of codes: Regulatory, Educational, Aspirational or Expectations, as explained above. The structure of our code includes:

- General Ethical Principles in which the characteristics of the Aspirations or Expectations codes are incorporated, which express the ideals of the profession that are difficult to reduce to standards.
- General Ethical Standards in which the focus of the Educational Codes is represented, which aim to provide guidelines, general guidelines for professional conduct, for confronting dilemmas, sensitizing and educating in aspects related to ethical responsibilities, and professional relationships in different areas.
- Specific Ethical Norms in which the objectives of the Regulatory (deontological) codes that attempt to establish clear rules or criteria regarding what constitutes transgression for a professional group are present.

Regarding the degree of generality or exhaustiveness option, an attempt was made to reach a balance: an instrument neither so general that it is inapplicable to concrete transgressions, nor so exhaustive that it does not give space to the subtleties that are characteristic of ethical performance or to the reasonable margins of interpretation that a court must handle (Lucero, 1995).

Influence of Culture, the History of the Country and in particular the History of the Profession in Chile for the Drafting of the Professional Ethics Code of the College of Psychologists of Chile, Currently in Force

The history of psychology in Chile begins in the 19th century in coherence with the country's sociocultural and scientific development. The University of Chile, the main institution of the state in public higher education, was created by Law of the Republic on November 19, 1842, just 32 years after the Declaration of Independence of our country. It had been preceded in colonial times by the University of Santo Tomás (1622) and the Royal University of San Felipe (1647) arranged by King Felipe V of Spain.

The first known works in the history of psychology date from 1893, *The Origin of Sensations* by Professor Schneider, and *Applied Psychology* by Professor Villalobos. Between 1905 and 1907, Professor Rómulo Peña, formed by the doctor and psychologist Wilhelm Wundt in Germany, created with his students the first laboratory for Experimental Psychology in the city of Copiapó, Northern Chile. In 1908 Dr. Guillermo Mann, bringing experiences and instruments from European countries and the United States, created a complete Laboratory of Experimental Psychology at the Faculty of Philosophy and Education of the University of Chile and wrote *Experimental Psychology as a Guide to Forensic Practice, Introductory Lessons to Experimental Psychology,* and others. Mann wrote: "the profession of instruments for psychological research can be none other than to fix in an exact and measurable way the physical conditions related to the psychological processes that we are trying to study." He was faithful to Wundt's purpose of attaining the status of science for psychology. The second director of this laboratory was Dr. Luis Tirapegui, a graduate of Columbia University. He assumed office in 1923. He promoted the Behavioral Clinics and adapted the Binet-Terman Scale for Chile. A few years later, the second university-level Experimental Psychology laboratory was founded, now at the Catholic University of Chile, Faculty of Philosophy. Both laboratories had as their main objective at the beginning, support for the training of educators.

In October 1941, the Laboratory of Experimental Psychology gave rise to the Institute of Psychology of the University of Chile, which sets out in its objectives

> To promote psychobiological research. To study all problems of a psychobiological nature of children and adults that require the services of the institute. To develop the applications of psychology to psychopedagogical, social, legal and medical problems, from the national point of view.

In 1944, the Archives of Psychology began to be published to publicize the investigations carried out at the institute, which have to do mainly with adaptation of tests and studies of the psychosocial reality of the abandoned and delinquent child. At that time, Psychology Services were created in some public sector institutions, such as the National Health Service, the Institute of Criminology, and the House for the Rehabilitation of Minors.

In this rich cultural and scientific context, the study of psychology begins early, linked to the studies of philosophy and education, at the Faculty of Philosophy and Education of the University of Chile. The psychology degree began as a Special Course in Psychology at said university in 1947.

In 1950 the Department of Psychology was created at the Pedagogical Institute of the Faculty of Philosophy and Education with the aim of training psychologists as a university profession. In 1952, the professional career category was consolidated. The first director of the psychology degree was Professor Egidio Orellana, with studies in the United States.

The first qualified psychologists created the Association of Psychologists of Chile, to which they began to associate as a natural step to graduate. Membership of the Association was considered a rank of professional prestige.

In 1954 and 1955, the Hungarian professor Bela Szekely was invited to give extension courses at the Pedagogical Institute of the Catholic University and in 1957, the School of Psychology of that university was created. Its first director was Father Hernán Larraín, a psychologist with a degree from the University of Munich.

In 1959, the Psychology degree at the University of Chile became independent from the Pedagogical Institute, as a Department of Psychology.

The consolidation of these two professional schools had a huge influence on the training of psychologists, on the social validation of the career and on constituting organizational and curricular models for the new schools of psychology. They have the character of foundational universities.

In terms of research, in 1972 a publication appeared, edited by the Department of Psychology, called *Notebooks of Psychology*, with research clearly relevant to the social context, such as "Comparison of the Evolution of Moral Concepts between Proletarian and Bourgeois Schoolchildren." The magazine only managed to publish this first number.

The Department of Psychology of the University of Chile became an examining body for the first psychology courses that were created in the new universities that emerged, Universidad de La Frontera in Temuco (1981), Universidad Gabriela Mistral (1981), Universidad Central (1982), Diego Portales University (1982), University of Concepción (1985). Likewise, it contributed to obtaining their autonomy. These universities are in the category of "old universities," as they have several generations of graduates and together with others of later creation, such as the University of Santiago, they have a good development and prestige, as well as social and peer recognition.

Post-degree training was initially obtained through professional teamwork, or with already specialized colleagues. Later on, post-graduate training happened through scholarships and studies abroad, until the first training centers or institutes in the country emerged in 1978. The foundational universities were concentrated on undergraduate studies until 1992, when they started their first post-degree courses.

After some years of united operation as an association, we psychologists were aware of the need to create an instance of greater legal scope and therefore with greater capacity and powers to guarantee professional status, regulate the correct exercise of the profession, facilitate its development and improvement. This is why psychologists took on the task of creating the Order College, which gained legal existence through Decree Law No. 11,033 published on December 9, 1968 in the Official Gazette of the Republic. The College thus became the united and legal body that represents psychologists, whose main objectives − established in the decree − can be summarized as:

- Promote and ensure the rationalization, development, protection, improvement, progress and prerogatives of the profession of psychologist and regulate the correct exercise of the profession. Stimulate scientific research of psychological interest and hold national and international conferences.
- Collaborate with educational organizations in vocational training and seek professional exchange with other countries.
- Stimulate professional development and promote the dissemination of the profession by all means available to it.

From these objectives, it is possible to derive united, legal, organizational, social, professional, scientific and ethical functions, the latter the most important dimension of professional associations, from our point of view (Lucero, 1995).

In 1973, the civic-military dictatorship commanded by Augusto Pinochet unloaded the violence against people, institutions and society as a whole, closed university faculties, especially those that could have a social influence or connotation, among them the Department of Psychology of the University of Chile.

Teachers were expelled and some were imprisoned as political prisoners in detention centers or concentration camps. There are colleagues who suffered torture. The year after the military coup, the department was re-opened with a director appointed by the dictatorship, who arbitrarily appointed teachers. A labor climate of tension in relations and permanent persecution was generated, a situation that would continue throughout the dictatorial period. The ethical issue and the validation of professional merits were in very vulnerable terrain.

In 1981, the professional associations, as previously mentioned, lost their legal powers to represent all the professionals of each university career, to protect the proper practice, to exercise regulation and ethical control. It was even impossible to investigate and report the illegal exercise of the profession because there were no official lists of qualified professionals in the country. The extent of authority of the professional associations was limited to professionals who, by personal choice, remained or joined the associations. The College of Psychologists managed to subsist, and gradually it was recovering positions based on its moral authority vis-à-vis its associates and even, achieving a progressive recognition of public and private institutions regarding their representativeness of the association.

The Association was frequently consulted regarding peer affiliation, participation in conferences, scientific events and receives requests for technical reports on issues or problems of public interest. However, with the disappearance of compulsory tuition as a condition for professional practice, the number of associates became limited. The Chilean College of Psychologists, AG (Gremial Association), had just over 6,000 members and a percentage close to or less than twenty percent with an active association, and that is the only part of the population of psychologists that it could protect proper practice, and exercise regulation and ethical control.

In democracy, from 1990 until now, there have been several bills to return to the Professional Associations some of their previous powers. In some legislative periods, they were urgent. However, these projects lost priority and were postponed from one legislative period to another, until today. This is related to the impediments left by the 1980 Political Constitution created by the dictatorship to support the neo-liberal socioeconomic model, in addition to the model's own set of interests. The College of Psychologists has been active in actions of professional ethical safeguarding, as well as in all aspects related to professional development. The College participated in the constitution in July 1994 of the National Network of Academic Units of Psychology, defined as a "peer-to-peer instance" whose "central objective is to promote mutual exchange and collaboration relationships, especially on issues related to selection modalities of students (admission), plans and training programs, establishment of common criteria in relation to professional practices and theses" (Lucero, 1995). The importance of interaction with new schools and collaboration towards their own unification efforts and development processes was a focus here. Likewise, our College has actively participated, until today in the Federation of Professional Colleges, in reflection and actions to regain the powers of professional colleges through proposals to the corresponding bills.

At the ethical level, the College of Psychologists actively participated in the Latin American meetings of the Mercosur Commission of Ethics for Psychologists and the elaboration of the Framework Ethical Protocol for Psychologists, which was signed by all the member countries, and promulgated in Santiago de Chile in our V National Congress and V Integrative Meeting of Mercosur Psychologists, held on November 7 and 8, 1997.

The radical establishment of the neo-liberal, consumerist, free-market socio-economic model –which generated the enormous inequalities and feelings of injustice that ended up causing the social explosion of October 2019 in our country – ended with free higher education. At the same time, the neoliberal policy regarding education left the door open for the creation of numerous universities, many of them of very heterogeneous quality and with predominantly mercantilist zeal. In an investigation carried out in 2007 by academics from the Universidad de Santiago de Chile and Universidad San Sebastián (Winkler et al., 2007), it was established that there were:

- 63 university institutions, of which 25 belong to the Council of Rectors (all autonomous).
- 38 are private (31 autonomous, one in examination and six in accreditation).
- Of the 63 institutions that are distributed in 198 branches throughout the country, 69.2% correspond to branches belonging to private institutions and 30.8% to public institutions.

In this context, a large number of psychology courses or programs were created in consideration of the prestige that the profession had acquired and the ease of economic implementation. It was the "boom" time for schools of psychology.

From the website of the Ministry of Education that provides documented information of more than 35 years, it was established that "Until 1983 there were two degrees in psychology, both in Santiago, at the University of Chile and at the Catholic University of Chile." "Between 1996 and 2000 the number of university schools that teach psychology increased by 25.8, this increase being more evident for private institutions." In "the year 2005, there are a total of 40 houses of study with a degree in psychology in the country," "offering a total of 109 (130 to January 2007) psychology programs," 79% during daytime hours. Further, "As of June 2005, only the psychology courses of 8 university establishments (20%) satisfy the quality criteria of higher education established by the National Accreditation Commission (CNAP, currently CNA-Chile)." Probably as of today, this percentage has increased by the development and natural effort of the universities, which have already titled several generations of psychologists.

Currently, there are more than 50,000 psychologists with degrees, frequently with enormous difficulties in finding work, or underemployed, earning very low incomes and/or engaged in other activities. Young professionals or recent graduates are often pressured to work in more than one specialty without having enough support from specialization studies, which may create ethical vulnerabilities that are not conducive to submitting to a professional code of ethics.

The psychosocial, cultural and economic context is defining a way of life in society, building and modifying the system of relationships between people and therefore its ethical structure. In our country, the neoliberal socioeconomic system was producing a change in values. Today we are a society with a very marked individualism, consequent rivalry, distrust and greater signs of violence, overcoming values of solidarity and collective sense. The latter has shown a certain awakening, first in the social protests of October, and then in the face of the effects of the pandemic that has shown the poverty and precariousness of the livelihoods of an important part of our society. It has promoted solidarity and different actions/forms of support such as empowerment of common areas for subsistence in the most unprotected sectors. In any case, the transgenerational effects of the dictatorship and the characteristics of postmodernism have caused changes in social ethics and consequently in personal and professional ethics. In the different areas of society, an ethical relativism was generated in our country, which has progressively shown a derivation towards an increasingly present ethical breach, which can be seen in institutions and people, and of course is reflected in the exercise of professions.

Sygmunt Bauman states in his book *Postmodern Ethics* (2004), "that unlike what happened in modern times, at this time people are no longer willing to make an effort to achieve moral values, nor defend moral values" (p. 3). In his book *Vida de Consumo* (2007), it connotes "Human solidarity is the first loss of which the consumer society can boast" (Lucero, 2008). On the other hand, Humberto Maturana, prominent Chilean biologist, philosopher and writer, in an interview carried out by C. Aldunate, entitled "The Ethics of Mutual Respect," in 1994, stated: "In the space of competition, the best is the one that has the ability to eliminate the other" (Lucero, 2008).

The consequences of the psychosocial trauma generated by the dictatorship are severe in the different areas of coexistence. They remain until today and of course are manifested in the ethical aspect. According to Ignacio Martín Baró (1998), in his *Liberation Psychology* the central characteristics that denounce a psychosocial trauma, in a society that has gone through the historical trance of a dictatorship, are: "violence," "social polarization," "lie institutional," to which I add "distrust," characteristics all present in our society.

Studies by Volkan and other authors have adopted the concept of psychosocial trauma and incorporated that of "transgenerational transmission of trauma," which affects at least three generations (Lucero, 2008). It is evident that the effects of the dictatorship remain in Chilean society and even they reactivate with tributes to those convicted of crimes against humanity, and a lack of respect or recognition of detainees and relatives of detainees who disappeared, which has effects of re-traumatization, not only for the relatives, but for the entire sensitive society. Thus, the ethical problems of our society are not only explained as characteristics of the postmodern age. The experience of other countries, such as Spain for example, confirms how traumatic situations can affect several generations.

In 2003, Adela Cortina explained that, in the face of modernity, the ethics of the professions necessarily require registering in a citizen ethic, capable of engaging in the public tasks of society as a whole, through the action of all its associated plans, in that it is necessary to articulate the unified concerns, and the actors and social actors involved, in this case psychologists and users of their services. Her accurate reflections contrast with the difficulty of participation and real integration that people and even institutions have in a society that we could characterize as a "relative" democracy.

If we think of professional associations, which in almost 40 years have not been able to recover their rights or legal powers, and that the codes of ethics that are the reason for this work have such limited applicability, it is evident that the ethical issue in Chilean professions has remained in a precarious or vulnerable place, perhaps only safeguarded by the country's tradition of institutionality.

Meaning of the Professional Code of Ethics for the Members of the College of Psychologists and for Society in General

The meaning of the code of ethics for psychologists is closely associated with the importance of professional ethics in the training process. Both topics have been the subject of research works that although carried out in 2007 and 2008, are still valid references in the present. Regarding the issue of the meaning or importance of the code of ethics for psychologists, research carried out by academics from the Diego Portales and Universidad de Santiago de Chile Universities in 2008 will be taken as a reference, as part of a project by the National Fund for Science and Technology (FONDECYT). It consisted specifically of

> the application of a questionnaire designed to find out the opinion of Chilean psychologists about the Code of Professional Ethics of the College of Psychologists of Chile and their propensity to adhere to its standards. [...] The sample was obtained by means of a non-probabilistic sampling, by self-selection arrangement, made up of 170 psychologists with degrees from more than 20 different universities, mainly young psychologists who work in a wide range of professional fields.
>
> *(Alvear et al., 2008)*

This work provides significant information in its conclusions:

- The psychologists who value the Code of Professional Ethics of the College of Psychologists of Chile the most and at the same time show more adherence to its regulations are those who practice in the clinical field, are affiliated with the College and are older, among those surveyed.
- The results show that the highest percentages of consultation of the Code of Ethics are given by professionals who, by age and year of degree, "could be thought to have accessed the Code of Ethics mainly during their training as psychologists, as part of the process that involves approaching the professional field and the identity of the role."

- "From the results obtained, it can be assumed that the subjects in the sample put other strategies and resources before them to address ethically sensitive situations" such as their own criteria, and that they would also be "not very inclined to adhere to established norms or criteria deontologically."
- In fact, "more than half of the respondents declared themselves contrary to the codes of professional ethics."
- The researchers think that what was stated in the previous points "is attributable to the postmodern context, where the subjective gaze and the generation of particular codes are privileged," as well as "rejection of norms and obligations, and the plurality of ethics" (Sanabria, 2001)
- "The link with the College of Psychologists operates mostly in virtual space."
- The researchers conclude by stating that: "the results of this research show the urgency of updating the Chilean code. At the same time, the task of developing specific guidelines and guidelines that respond to the diversity of professional work that our discipline has experienced remains pending."

The text of the research also mentions "some results of an exploratory type study" carried out in 2004 by the Association of Legal Psychology on the occasion of the First National Meeting of Forensic and Legal Psychology, "which aims to contribute to a preliminary review of the code of ethics, which considers the psychosocial, cultural and economic transformations experienced in recent years in our country." Despite the fact that "the majority of those surveyed affirm that they know the Code of Ethics and have read all the articles ... 82.4% answered that it would not be useful for confronting, solving problems and ethical dilemmas related to the legal practice and forensic."

The latter fully coincides with the last point of the conclusions of this study. The current code, despite the explicit intention of avoiding a bias towards the clinical field, is in fact more useful or beneficial for that professional field. The need to amplify its use through studies and systems of norms and specific guidelines for the different professional fields will make it more functional, attractive and useful for the profession in general, to the extent that it would help to solve ethical dilemmas and problems or doubts specific to the different specialties.

Regarding the presence that professional ethics has in the process of training psychologists in Chile, the benchmark is another research work carried out jointly by academics from the University of Santiago and an academic from the Santo Tomás University, Chile (Winkler et al., 2007). The research was mainly based on information from the websites of the Ministry of Education (MINEDUC), the Higher Council for Education and the Council of Rectors of Chilean Universities (CRUCH). The curricula and professional profiles declared by the different schools or departments of psychology were investigated. In the title of the study that refers specifically to ethical training and the presence–absence of ethics courses, it is verified that

of the 36 Schools of Psychology that provide the curriculum on their website (equivalent to 90%), 22 of them contain ethics courses, which corresponds to 55% of the programs. [...] The moment of inclusion of ethics courses in the curricular grid can be considered an indicator of the orientation that is intended to be delivered to the subject. It is reasonable to think that at the beginning of the career and with students who have little instruction in psychology, the subject has a rather introductory and general orientation, while the emphasis will be more applied and professional at the end of the training.

Regarding the way to include ethical training, the option at stake is to do it through a transversal delivery or a subject. When the Ethics Commission had the opportunity to do so, it stated that the aforementioned were not antagonistic options but could have the character of complementary. The desirable option was the transversal delivery through the various subjects and activities of the training, and the incorporation of an Ethics subject that would allow the elaboration and systematization of what was delivered transversally. In studies cited by Morales and Avendaño (1992 and 1996) it is made explicit "when analyzing the curricula of 24 psychology schools in the country," they observed "that training in ethics has a minimum percentage of training time."

The categories that the authors of the study set out to investigate regarding training were: "implicit ethics vs. explicit ethics" in the study of the professional profiles declared by the schools of psychology. Understood by explicit ethics is when the term ethics (50%) is included in the set of values and principles to be delivered in training. Implicit presence is considered when the profile description "alludes to values in relation to others, such as social sensitivity, respect for diversity, tolerance, consideration of the dignity of the human being," as well as respect for human rights (40%). In addition to these two categories, the professional profile of 16 psychology schools did not mention the term ethics or values associated with the concept. Objectives related to professional and scientific development were highlighted, as well as training to perform in the different areas of professional practice and research (10%). In any case, "for the largest proportion of psychology schools, the ethical-value aspects are relevant enough to incorporate them in the description of the professional profile." However, the researchers concluded that "the outlook is high risk" in the ethical field due to the legal situation and lack of unity in the professional associations. More specifically in our case, the Association of Psychologists with their loss of legal powers in ethical control, and limitation to the restricted scope of associate psychologists has been pointed out several times throughout this document.

The research on which we are relying emphasizes two other important aspects. The first is the inclusion in a new code of a "section on Vocational Training," which implies reflection and agreement on the inclusion of the "minimum requirements" in ethical training, linking it to subsequent professional practice. Secondly, also very important is "the inclusion of the gender dimension ... that would imply an enrichment of training, with the consequent effects both in the complexity of theorizing in the discipline, and in the experience of the psychology student themselves."

Rest & Narváez (1994) in their "model of moral development," point out "the professional training of psychologists and psychologists must address, both cross-sectionally in the curricular mesh and in the specific courses on ethics, the development of ethical sensitivity, ethical reasoning, of ethical motivation and of ethical character" (Winkler et al., 2007).

Martínez, Buxarrais, & Bara (2002) emphasized the importance of ethical training in the university over applied ethics referring to professional practice, suggesting that

> The pedagogical treatment of ethics in the university environment is not just a matter of a modification of the plan of studies or the incorporation of a new subject. It is, above all, a change of perspective in relation to what it represents today to achieve a good level of university training, and what should mean the commitment to the public of a university that aims to train good citizens.
>
> *(Winkler et al., 2007)*

Final Comments

In closing, I believe it is important to note that the five original universities, called "old universities," recovered relatively quickly. In the 20 years since the "university boom," some of the new institutions have closed, while others have solidified. It is important to add that from their beginnings some of these institutions, both in Santiago and regions, have maintained high academic and ethical standards, and at present enjoy prestige and widespread recognition.

Furthermore, since 2006 Chile has a quality control system created by the National Accreditation Commission (CAN), an institution charged with evaluating and guaranteeing excellence in universities, professional institutes, and technical formation centers, in addition to the degrees and degree programs they offer. Accreditation is part of a voluntary program in which independent higher education institutions participate and is granted for one to seven years, as determined by an ongoing evaluation process. Accreditation must be renewed when its duration expires. At present most of these universities and degree programs are accredited, but only one of them, for a seven-year period.

Regarding professional ethics, however, much remains to be done before solid, universal and uniform standards of academic performance can be assured. These standards are closely tied to the issue of social ethics. Surprisingly, the social uprising of October 2019 (also called the "Chilean awakening") and the dramatic repercussions of the Covid-19 pandemic, especially among the most impoverished sectors of the population, have sparked gestures of solidarity and a greater collective consciousness in Chilean society. This also has strong ethical implications.

A constitutional process, agreed upon during the months of the social uprising, could lead to a new Chilean constitution, and lay the basis for a more just and ethical society.

References

Alvear, K., Pasmanik, D., Winkler, M. I., and Olivares, B. (2008). Codes in post modernity? Opinions of psychologists about the Code of Professional Ethics of the College of Psychologists of Chile (A.G.). *Ter Psicol*, 26 (2), 215–228.

Baró, I. M. (1998). *Liberation psychology*. Trotta.

Code of Professional Ethics (1999). College of Psychologists of Chile.

Colegio de Psicólogos de Chile (2018) *Codigo de ética profesional*. http://ponce.inter.edu/cai/bv/codigo_de_etica.pdf

Espinoza, L. S. and Moreno, D. P. (2007, November). Psicología en la Universidad de Chile: Una propuesta de estudio para comprender la historia de la psicología chilena. *Cuad. neuropsicol.*, 1(3).

Gyarmati, G. (1992). Códigos de Ética Profesional ¿Quién vigila a quién? *University Journal P. Universidad Católica de Chile*, 37.

Lucero, S. (1995). *Ética y psicología en Chile. Breve historia sindical de la temática*. Inter-American Congress of Psychology SIP, Puerto Rico.

Lucero, S. (2008). *Psicodrama, género y trauma. Transmisión transgeneracional*. V International Conference on Traumatic Stress, December 2008.

Sanabria, J. (2001). Ethics and postmodernity. Retrieved from www.grupologosula.org/dikaiosyne/art/dik059.pdf

Winkler, M. I., Pasmanik, D., Alvear, K., and Reyes, M. I. (2007). When the psychological well-being is at stake: The ethical dimension in the professional training of psychologists and psychologists in Chile. *Terapia Psicológica*, 25 (1), 5–24.

13

THE COLOMBIAN PSYCHOLOGICAL CODE OF ETHICS AND BIOETHICS

A Historical Perspective

Paulo Daniel Acero Rodríguez and Rubén Ardila

The current Code of Ethics and Bioethics regarding the practice of psychology in Colombia has had crucial relevance for the development of psychology in the country. It is necessary to conceptualize it in order to better comprehend the development of psychology as a science and profession in Colombia.

The Context

With this premise in mind, it is important to mention the creation of one of the first psychology training programs in Latin America at the Universidad Nacional de Colombia (National University of Colombia) on November 20, 1947 when the Instituto de Psicología Aplicada (Institute of Applied Psychology) was created under the leadership of Mercedes Rodrigo (1891–1982).

In 1954, only seven years later the Federación Colombiana de Psicología (Colombian Federation of Psychology) was founded through the initiative of students from the Faculty of Psychology at the National University of Colombia, which attained legal recognition in 1958 (Flórez 2003).

As background information to the present Code of Ethics and Bioethics of the Colombian Association of Psychologists (Colpsic), it is worth noting that the Codes that were proposed in the previous decades had sections and conclusions that were integrated into the current Code.

The development of several Ethical Codes across time and the Colombian professional psychological organizations in which they were created will be presented below.

Colombian Federation of Psychology

As was previously noted, the first association of psychologists that was formed in Colombia was the Colombian Federation of Psychology. It was founded in 1954 at the National University of Colombia as the *Federación Universitaria de Psicología* (University Federation of Psychology) and in 1955 it became the Colombian Federation of Psychology, which obtained its legal status in 1958. Its objective was to serve as the voice for the emerging profession of psychology, to shed light on the training of these professionals, to provide a legal framework for the practice of psychology and to offer ethical orientation. This Federation was the official association of Colombian psychologists until the beginnings of the 1980s.

Since the establishment of the Federation, several well-known psychologists in the country began to think about the development of professional psychology and the regulation of its practice. One of them was Rubén Ardila. He was initially a student member of the Federation's Board of Directors, then held the position of Treasurer and later President during the periods 1970–1972 and 1972–1974. The Colombian Federation of Psychology proposed a Code of Ethics during its IX Assembly on August 14 and 15, 1965. This initial Code, which also included an analysis of the duties and training of psychologists in the country, was updated and modified on February 1, 1974. It was during his presidency that Professor Ardila projected a five-year plan, which included the legal regulation of the profession and the creation and approval of the Code of Ethics. It was completed in 1974 and was the basis of Law 58 of 1983.

In the 1965 Code of Ethics, the following basic principles were included: responsibilities with society and the profession, professional secrecy, requirements for the practice of psychology and others (Colombian Federation of Psychology, 1974, pp. 274–278). This Code of Ethics is one of the first in Latin America. The 1974 version was more detailed, updated and was a pioneering document in the continent. It included several sections such as the following ones: the psychologist's ethical framework, professional secrecy, professional practice and the teaching of psychology.

In the first section, regarding the ethical framework of the psychologist it is stated that:

> The psychologist in the practice of his or her profession is within a society that has explicit and implicit ethical norms towards which he or she shows deep respect and appreciation, and recognizes that any violation, made by him or her, of the morality and the existing norms in the community can involve their clients, disciples or colleagues in serious problems and personal conflicts, and can undermine his or her own name and the reputation of his or her profession.
>
> *(Colombian Federation of Psychology, 1974, p. 274).*

The document "Duties, responsibilities and the ethical code of the psychologist" (1974) was proposed to the Federation´s Assembly and was unanimously approved by the Board of Directors. Its members were Rubén Ardila (President), Manuel

Morales (Vice-President), Gonzalo Amador (ad hoc Secretary), Jaime Giraldo (Treasurer), José Antonio Sánchez (Professional Vocal), Regina Otero (Student Vocal) and Mateo V. Mankeliunas (Fiscal Auditor).

The Federation was the main association of psychologists in Colombia between approximately 1958 and 1980.

Colombian Society of Psychology

The organization that was in charge of professional psychology in the country after 1980 was the Colombian Society of Psychology (CSP). It was founded in 1978 and received its legal recognition on January 15, 1979. It had multiple activities such as the organization of the Colombian Congresses of Psychology the first of which took place in 1982. This Society had a leading role in the legal recognition of professional psychology in Colombia with Law 58 of 1983 which "recognizes Psychology as a profession and regulates its exercise in the country." Additionally, ethical standards were included within this law particularly Article 12 which refers to "General Duties of the Psychologist."

Law 58 of 1983 regulated the profession until 2006, when Law 1090 presented by the Colombian Association of Psychologists (Colegio Colombiano de Psicólogos, Colpsic) was approved by the national government and replaced the previous Law 58 of 1983.

It is worth highlighting that although the codes prior to Law 1090 of 2006 presented standards and regulations for psychologists, these codes did not include professional or legal consequences if the standards or regulations were not followed. Furthermore, in Law 1090 of 2006 a structured authority was established for the first time with the objective of evaluating the alleged cases of malpractice. This authority was named Psychology Ethical and Deontological Courts.

Going back to the activities accomplished by the Colombian Society of Psychology between 1979 and 2006 we find the enactment of an Ethical Code in 2000. It states at the introduction that

> We have consulted for the preparation of this Code of Ethics with the International Union of Psychological Science (IUPsyS), the American Psychological Association (APA), the Interamerican Society of Psychology (SIP), the European Federation of Psychologists Associations (EFPA), the Official Association of Psychologists of Spain (COP), the Mexican Society of Psychology, various codes of other Latin American countries, ethical codes of other professions in Colombia, the laws currently in force in the country, the current 1991 Political Constitution of Colombia, etc.
>
> *(Colombian Society of Psychology, 2001, pp, 7–8)*

Colombian Codes of Ethics in Psychology

As previously mentioned, the first Code of Ethics was proposed by the Colombian Federation of Psychology in 1965. A new revised Code was proposed in

1974 also by the Colombian Federation of Psychology. In the first law that regulated the profession of psychologist in Colombia (Law 58 of 1983), ethical regulations were included particularly in Article 12.

The Colombian Society of Psychology (CSP) presented a restructured Code of Ethics in 2000.

The Colombian Association of Psychologists (Colpsic) proposed and implemented the current Code of Ethics and Bioethics (2006).

Code of Ethics, SCP (2000)

In Law 58 of 1983, a *Consejo Profesional Nacional de Psicología* (National Professional Council of Psychology) was created as an auxiliary body of the National Government for the control and monitoring of the practice of this discipline with the duties of collaborating with the Government in the monitoring of strict compliance with this Law and its regulatory decrees, issue its own regulations, submit to the Ministry of Education comments on the approval of new programs of study and the creation of Educational Centers related to this profession, prepare and keep the registry of professionals updated, inform the competent authorities about the breaking of the Law as well as the norms on professional ethics, for the enforcement of the corresponding penalties, to encourage psychological research in a direct way or in collaboration with the authorized entities or with the psychological associations legally approved, and to foster the associations of psychologists as well as monitor their operations.

The following general duties were established in the Law, among them: to deeply respect the explicit and implicit ethical norms of the society in which they practice their profession, to behave consistently with their professional ethics, and to preserve at all costs the dignity and decorum of the profession.

It is expressly stated that: people who illegally practice psychology without having fulfilled the requirements in this Law, that carry out any actions that are exclusively for the profession, will have penalties established for the illegal practice of the profession.

The elaboration of the Psychologist's Code of Ethics proposed by the Colombian Society of Psychology (SCP) was a collective effort. Deans of psychology programs, the leadership of the main psychological associations, ethics professors, practicing professionals, psychologists with doctorate degrees, etc. participated in this process. The initial document was prepared by an *ad hoc* committee and submitted to all psychology Faculties and psychological professional associations in the country and to psychologists from different regions around the country. It was also discussed in academic events such as symposia and Congresses. Many people sent suggestions and important contributions which were mostly incorporated into the final version of the Code. Given the above, it could be said that this version was a Psychologist's Code of Ethics achieved by consensus through the Colombian psychological community.

At the ground of this Code of the year 2000, promoted by the Colombian Society of Psychology, it is stated that

> The Psychologist's Code of Ethics aims to provide general principles that help psychologists make informed decisions in most situations they confront. Their objective is the protection and well-being of individuals and groups the psychologist works with, and to guide and protect them in their professional practice. It is the personal responsibility of each and every psychologist to achieve the highest standards of professional conduct, within the current state of knowledge. To achieve these objectives, the professionals must develop a commitment throughout their life to act ethically, encourage ethical behavior in students, colleagues and the public with whom they work with, and maintain an open attitude towards change and new knowledge.
>
> Psychologists are committed to respect and follow the principles established by the Universal Declaration of Human Rights. They seek for their professional activities to be characterized by responsibility, competence, integrity and impartiality. Psychologists respect individual, cultural and gender-based differences, sexual orientation, socioeconomic status, ethnicity, ideology and should not be involved with any discriminatory practices.
>
> *(Colombian Society of Psychology, 2001, pp. 9–10)*

The Code of Ethics presents specific measures on the following aspects: professional competences, integrity, scientific and professional responsibility, social responsibility, respect for others, professional secrecy, preventing harm to others, interference in professional activity, therapeutic relationship, evaluation and diagnosis, scientific research, applying professional knowledge and social context, relationships with colleagues and other professionals, relationships with society and the state, and disciplinary regime.

Law 1090 of 2006

The reform of the Colombian Political Constitution in 1991 allowed institutionalization and provided a stable framework for legally recognized professions to organize themselves in associations and obtain public delegations accordingly, in article 26. Given this, initiatives arose to create a professional association of psychologists that approaches this legal framework.

In this context, a group of psychologists from several universities which were members of *Asociación Colombiana de Facultades de Psicología – Ascofapsi* (the Colombian Association of Psychology Faculties) set out to work on a new Law for the recognition of psychology as a profession. This would modify Law 58 from 1983. Ascofapsi assembly held in the city of Pasto in 1999, placed forward the idea of creating a professional association. From that moment, the *Asociación Colombiana Profesional de Psicología – Acolpsic* (Colombian Professional Association of Psychology) was created.

At the same time, the *Colegio Oficial de Psicólogos – Copsic* (Official Association of Psychologists) was functioning. This was an initiative of the Colombian Society of Psychology (CSP).

For the advancement of the profession, the dialogue between these two organizations (Acolopsi and Copsic) facilitated the overcoming of their difficulties. The leadership promoted the best possible relationship between the two organizations as they pursued similar purposes. They both started to work towards the same objectives, which would generate an important benefit to the psychologists in the country.

An important event that showed these common goals between both organizations was the making of a bill. Representatives of different organizations related to the profession of psychology participated, including Acolpsic and Copsic, with the perspective of merging them to create only one association that represented psychology professionals and could receive public delegations.

Recognizing the importance and benefit of this union an integration proposal was presented. Copsic joined Acolpsic, giving rise to the current Colegio Colombiano de Psicólogos, Colpsic (Colombian Association of Psychologists – Colpsic), an entity that would thus preserve the trajectory and history of each of these organizations. It had the fundamental objective of developing professional organized psychology in Colombia.

With this merger, one of the new Colpsic's main responsibilities was the elaboration and the promotion of the necessary process to implement a new Law to regulate the psychology profession. Members of the Colpsic Board of Directors attended and participated actively in different political meetings to discuss and defend it. In the various debates in the Senate of the Republic, several changes and deletions of articles were made to Law 1090. Even today, some of the articles that were suppressed in that moment are still considered significant to the profession.

With this Law, the National Congress of the Republic granted public delegations to the Association, namely the issuing of the Professional Card or license, the registration of professionals at the Ministry of Health in the *Registro Único de Talento Humano en Salud* (Single Registry of Human Talent in Health) and to constitute the Deontological Courts. These facts allowed the consolidation and strengthening of the organization.

Current Code of Ethics and Bioethics

Law 1090 of 2006, which regulates the professional practice of Psychology gave origin to the Code of Ethics and Bioethics, as well as other measures. It is structured as follows:

- Title I in which the definition of psychology is presented, understood as "a science based on research and a profession that studies the development of cognitive, emotional and social processes of the human being, from the perspective of the complexity paradigm, with the purpose of promoting the development of talent and human competences in different domains and social contexts such as: education, health, work setting, justice, environmental protection, well-being and the quality of life." This title states that "regardless of the area in which he or she works in both public and private practice, he or she belongs mainly in the field of health, due to this the psychologist is also considered a health professional."

- Title II that presents "General Measures" which highlights that "Psychologists that practice their profession in Colombia will follow these principles: Responsibility, Competence, Moral and Legal Standards, Public Announcements, Confidentiality, User well-being, Professional relationships, Evaluation of Techniques, Research with human participants and, the use and care of animals."

- Title III is focused on determining what activities are considered in Colombia as professional ones of the psychologist and their sphere of action. It is specified that the practice of psychology implies "any teaching activity, the application and indication of psychological knowledge and its specific techniques" in various scenarios, always with a solid ground in scientific and social validity criteria.

- Title IV integrates the legal requirements for the practice of the profession of psychology and clearly outlines what is to be understood as illegally practicing the profession, which expressly states that people who practice this way and are not psychologists, will not be judged by the Deontological and Bioethical Courts of psychology but by a regular law.

- Title V lists the Rights, Duties, Obligations and Prohibitions of psychology professionals.

- Title VI specifies the public delegations assigned to the Colombian Association of Psychologists Colpsic by the National Congress, namely issuing the Professional Card or License, registering psychologists in the National Registry of Human Health Talent, a tool of the Ministry of Health and, finally, establishing the National Deontological and Bioethical Court of the professional practice of psychology.

- Title VII specifically has the Code of Ethics and Bioethics for the professional practice of psychology, which includes Articles 13 to 56, divided into seven chapters containing the eight general ethical principles for its professional practical (beneficence, no maleficence, autonomy, justice, truthfulness, solidarity, loyalty and fidelity); the listing of psychologist's duties with users, psychologists' duties with persons who make use of their professional services; duties to colleagues and other professionals; duties with institutions, society and the state; indications on the use of psycho-technical material and on ethical aspects in the framework of scientific research, intellectual property and publications. From Articles 57 to 91, the Law has a chapter on the organizational structure of the Courts and how the deontological process must be executed, regarding possible legal recourses, annulments, the statues of limitations within disciplinary action and complementary legislation on the disciplinary process. Finally, in Article 92, the Law establishes November 20 as "National Psychologist's Day" and in Article 93, all the previous codes are nullified, especially Law 58 of 1983, and explicitly states that this new Law will be applied from the moment it is published.

There are a total of 93 articles that make up this Law 1090 of 2006 that started to operate on September 6, 2006.

National Deontological and Bioethical Court

In agreement with Law 1090, the Colombian Association of Psychologists (Colpsic) established the National Deontological and Bioethical Court in 2007 and, progressively between 2008 and 2011, established the six regional Courts through which coverage is provided to oversee the practice of psychology throughout the country. Each of the Courts has the support of secretarial lawyers and, with an average of seven Magistrate psychologists who execute an *ad honorem* service.

The Courts have an Executive Director that gives support with the administrative and logistic aspects, and with the financial funding of the Colombian Association of Psychologists, as is established by the Law.

In addition to fulfilling the public delegation (administrative – process of sanctions) given by the Law, the Magistrates of the Courts continuously make efforts to outreach psychological services to the general public, users and among the students of various psychology programs in the country. This is done in order to communicate regulations in the practice of psychology in the country as well as learned experiences that are documented as a result of their work in addressing complaints against professionals.

As part of these learned experiences, the Courts have issued Agreements on aspects that regulate the disciplinary deontological process on the development of the legal process and on how the Magistrates should be appointed, the requirements to practice and all the aspects regarding their duties. For example, in the Legal Agreement number 15 of 2019, it is indicated:

> According to our legal system, only behavior that violates either the duties established by the Constitution or the Law for the professional practice of the psychologist, or the users rights to make use of their services or of any other person who consider that they may be affected by the action or omission of the professional practice of a psychologist. In accordance with the above, this Manual, highlighting the ethical content of such norms, is structured on the basis of ethical principles where its violation, under certain perspectives, can be considered a fault. Thus, it constitutes an ethical misconduct of all duly typified behavior and, even if it is not typified,[1] by a deliberative process is shown to transgress the guiding principles of an ethical nature that should guide the professional's performance.

After the principles are stated, there are clustered behaviors that imply their violation, some directly in the Law and others by the Doctrines approved by the Deontological Courts of Psychology. All these behaviors are shown as an example and can be interpreted as guides to understand similar situations; however, this does not mean that ethical misconducts are limited to these behaviors, there may be other practices not considered in this manual that also violate the ethical principles that should oversee professional practice in psychology. It is the duty of the Psychologist/Magistrate to identify and judge these faults within the framework indicated by the Law and the manual.

Through analyzing behavior, it can be determined if whether or not the behavior indicates a lack of ethics, the Magistrate must start at the guiding ethical principles, and then make the analysis that allows him or her to determine if the behavior that was carried out implies a violation of the law. It is important to clarify that, if the behavior is defined as being against the law, the mere situation is not enough to determine it as such nor to affirm its responsibility upon the investigated person, on the contrary, it should be analyzed, based on the evidence collected in the investigation, even if the behavior caused or didn´t cause harm, or if a guiding principle of the profession was known or unknown. Consequently, when the behavior is punishable within the deliberative process, the Magistrate must make an argumentative reasoning that allows him or her to determine which principle has been violated. This same type of judgment should be carried out when the studied behavior is not in the Manual, but the Magistrate considers it violates a guiding principle.

Lastly, it may be the case that the same behavior violates several principles. For example, a psychologist can commit two ethical faults by disclosing a sexual deviation that he or she learned through the user, while having an implication on professional secrecy and on autonomy. Likewise, the same action can violate the rights of several people. Both types of cases must be judged together and would impact the severity of the sanction.

Additionally, the Courts have published guidelines that focus on aspects within the Code of Ethics and Bioethics that have been identified as the most sensitive in practice, based on user complaints. In this sense, three documents named "Doctrines" have been issued. Although they are not mandatory in the Code, they can be considered reference points for making ethical decisions in practice. Regarding the above, the Doctrine itself has specified:

The Doctrine, thus seen, is the set of ideas or arguments that the Deontological and Bioethical Courts of psychology have about what informed consent is and constitutes a proposal for psychologists,

214

regardless of the psychology field where they develop their praxis. The doctrine does not imply for psychologists a binding or mandatory normative guideline because, as will be seen further ahead, each case a psychologist has is particular and is based on singularity that may or may not apply the precepts of the doctrine.

The Doctrines are established in expert opinions that are not binding, which means, they are not mandatory, but are consultation referents. The doctrine is a judgment reference for the legislator and for the judge, because the outlook and the criteria of experts on a certain subject, shape public opinion both at a particular level, decision- makers, and citizens in general (Lastra, 2005).

Subsequently, the Doctrine is not a set of premises with normative status from which neither psychologists in their praxis nor Magistrates in their deliberations can be separated. Both psychologists in their professional practice and Magistrates in their verdicts may move away from the Doctrine if it is necessary for the case or, in contrast, it should be applied as established; a balanced analysis between legal and ethical aspects should be pursued, the reduction of ethical responsibility though the law is being followed should be avoided, given the exceptional circumstances that the particular case brings. The doctrine has the purpose to make an informed decision beyond solely adapting the psychologist´s behavior to a norm within the law 1090 of 2006, because the type of responsibility that the Magistrate establishes has a subjective nature.

These three Doctrines are focused on the following topics: the first one on how to register and handle information in the different fields of the professional practice of psychology (Doctrine No. 1), the second one on the professional secret (Doctrine No. 2) and the third one on informed consent for the practice of psychology in Colombia.

Impact of the Colombian Code of Ethics and Bioethics in the Region

From the Colombian experience, we have been able to impact regional professional psychology in Ecuador, Mexico and Peru through the exchange of experiences, consultancy on the application of our Code and on the structure and the operation of our Courts. This impact has occurred through face-to-face and virtual meetings, as well as through a web page created together with the Colombian Association of Psychology Faculties (Ascofapsi) and The Rosario University in Bogotá through which reflective documents are shared on ethics in psychology and even an online ethics course is offered free of charge. The web page www.eticapsicologica.org has inquiries from countries across the continent, as can be seen in the following table of statistics as of December 2019.

Table 13.1 Statistics on visits to the webpage eticapsicologica.org in 2019

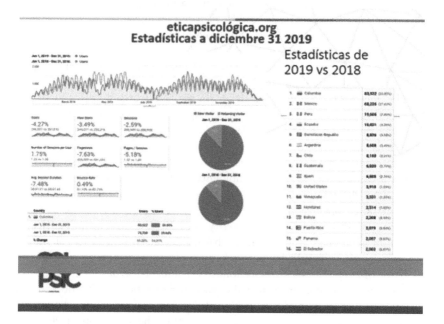

Source: Author

In this way, we hope that the history of the process that gave rise to the current Code of Ethics and Bioethics of Psychology in Colombia has been chronologically organized, contextualized and is comprehensible to the international psychological community.

Additionally, it is important to highlight that, in order to accomplish the current Code of Ethics, there were various factors that had to be overcome. For example, it was a challenge to reach agreements within a professional organization in which, at various moments in history following specific psychological approaches outweighed the vision of psychology as a complex but integrative discipline. There was also an opposition of some people who considered that it was an extremely positivist act to have a code with the force of law, especially when considering that ethical practices go beyond legislation. However, Colombia has historically been characterized as a country of many laws and one can consider that the fact that the Deontological Code is embedded within a Law summons professional in psychology and it is consistent with the characteristics of the country since its birth as an independent nation.

The current Code of Ethics has remained in the history of psychology in Colombia as evidence of the capacity of psychologists to place particular visions aside to prioritize collective interests, which is the result of the current Colombian Association of Psychologists as an entity that groups professionals who practice psychology in the country.

Finally, and related to cultural influences within the Code, the following could be pointed out:

- The sense and philosophy of the Code are aligned with the international context of psychology. The Colombian Code of Ethics, in the Law 1090 of 2006, reflects the relevance of the international psychological community for the work of Colombian psychologists, but at the same time it constitutes a document from which the psychological communities of other Latin American countries can do benchmarking to ethically guide their professional practice.
- Regarding specific aspects of the Colombian culture, the values that are shared as a culture include solidarity, honesty, respect for differences, equity, among others.

In other words, our Code is also fostered by the context of the international psychological community and includes values that are central to Colombian culture, as we have previously indicated.

Last but not least, we appreciate the support of María Luisa Ramírez, Director of the International Affairs Office of Colpsic for the translation of this document.

Note

1 Given the impossibility of the legislator to have a detailed list of behaviors that subsume the possible infractions that a professional of psychology may incur, through the term of "typicity in open disciplinary type," the Deontological and Bioethical Courts of Psychology may utilize a normative complement, including all the legal measures that establishes duties, mandates and prohibitions that are applicable. Thus, the typicity in the infractions is determined by the systematic reading of the norm that establishes the function, the order or the prohibition and in a generic way prescribes that the non-fulfillment of functions, orders or prohibitions constitutes an infraction.

References

Federación Colombiana de Psicología [Colombian Federation of Psychology] (1974). Funciones, responsabilidades y código ético del psicólogo. *Revista Latinoamericana de Psicología*, 6, 265–278.

Flórez, L. (2003). *El legado de Rubén Ardila. Psicología: De la biología a la cultura*. Bogotá: Universidad Nacional de Colombia.

Sociedad Colombiana de Psicología [Colombian Society of Psychology] (2001). *Código ético del psicólogo*. Bogotá: Editorial ABC.

14

A HISTORY OF THE DEVELOPMENT OF THE CODE OF ETHICS OF GUATEMALA

Ana María Jurado

Having a code of ethics was a felt need for psychologists in Guatemala, (Jury & Juarez, 2000). Guatemala is one of the countries with the longest tradition of professionalizing psychologists. The psychology career was born in the Faculty of Humanities of the University of San Carlos, the only public university in the country, in 1948, although since 1946 they had been teaching psychology at that faculty. At the beginning of the Psychology degree, there was only a degree in Psychology and Teaching of Secondary Education in Psychology (Aguilar & Recinos, 1996). The first psychologist graduated from this University in 1952. Henceforth the number of psychology professionals was increasing, especially since private universities opened this career from the sixties. Currently, of the 14 universities in the country, 11 offer the degree and the College of Psychologists has more than 10,000 registered professionals. Despite this long history until the 1990s, psychology professionals were not unionized, and this made it difficult to develop a code of ethics because there was no institutional support to support it. The process of creating the code was long and for the purpose of describing its history, the following events are presented as background.

In the year 2000, Jury and Juarez carried out the preliminary study "Need felt by Guatemalan psychologists to have a code of ethics" in which they concluded that psychologists felt a need to have this code. They also found that 57% of psychologists surveyed did not know a code of ethics and 76% had faced ethical dilemmas in the exercise of the profession.

In February 2000, the College of Humanities of Guatemala and the Court of Honor of said school wrote the document Draft Code of Ethics of the Humanist Professional. This document was not disseminated and it is unknown if it was approved.

218

In November 2000, a group of students of psychology, led by Josefina Antillón Milla at the Universidad del Valle de Guatemala, held a Professional Deontology Seminar, from which the document Code of Ethics for the Guatemalan psychologist was developed. This was neither implemented by nor disseminated to the professional community (College of Psychologists of Guatemala, 2011).

During the IV National Congress of Psychology, in 2004, the Interdisciplinary Forum was held where the need for a Code of Ethics and strategies for its creation were discussed. This forum once again reflected the interest in having a code. In October of that same year, the 1st Regional Congress of the Inter-American Psychological Society – SIP – was held in Guatemala and the conclusions of the previous Forum were presented in the Ethics panel of the Congress.

In the years 2005 and 2006, an inter-institutional group was formed for the study of ethics with the purpose of constructing the Code. The group was made up of professionals from the different universities in the country. The progress of this study group was presented at the XXX Inter-American Congress of Psychology in Mexico, 2007.

Two events contributed significantly to the progress of the construction of the Code of Ethics. The first was the creation of the College of Psychologists of Guatemala on June 25, 2007, after several years of struggle by a group of professionals led by the Ms. Guisela Cárcamo Duarte. Second, in November 2008, the first Court of Honor of the College was chosen, which took office on January 16, 2009, whose priority was the Preparation of the Code of Ethics, a task that began immediately. Finally, through these two events, there was the institutional framework that made possible the legitimization of an instrument that would inspire the behavior of psychologists and psychologists in Guatemala.

The Court of Honor of the College of Psychologists of Guatemala began the process of preparing the Code of Ethics in February 2009, with the development of an initial work plan that was modified according to the needs that arose. These defined the objectives of the work. The review of several codes began, among these, the codes of ethics of Chile, Colombia, Mexico, Dominican Republic, Costa Rica, El Salvador, Canada, New Zealand and the United States of America. During this process, communication was established with Dr. Andrea Ferrero of the University of San Luis, San Luis, Republic of Argentina for the purposes of obtaining guidance and advice. It was then that Dr. Ferrero shared with us the document Universal Declaration of Ethical Principles for psychologists and psychologists (DU), and she thought about adopting it as the basis for the elaboration of the Guatemala code.

In June 2009, the XXXII Inter-American Congress of Psychology organized by the Inter-American Psychological Society, was held in Guatemala. A meeting was held with Dr. Janel Gauthier and Dr. Andrea Ferrero, who offered their advice for the project. It was decided to adopt the principles of the DU, based on the structure of the codes of ethics of Canada and New Zealand. From this meeting, a work plan was elaborated and carefully followed. It began with the review of the Universal Declaration and related documents.

We worked based on a preliminary version of the article "The Universal Declaration of Ethical Principles for Psychologists: A Model with Cultural Sensitivity for the Creation and Review of a Code of Ethics" from Dr. Jean Pettifor. Each of the questions raised was addressed in order to clarify the circumstances that allow for the development of a culturally sensitive code of ethics.

The Court of Honor worked, in groups of two members, on each of the four principles of the DU, and each group presented the work done to the whole Court, in order to discuss the principles, their associated values, the norms, and their applicability and relevance for Guatemala. The presentation and analysis was carried out from September 2009 to February 2010. Within this phase and with the objective of presenting the DU and knowing the ethical dilemmas of psychologists and psychologists in Guatemala, a survey was prepared. This was sent, along with the text of the DU, by email and in print to all members at that time. The survey in question had two objectives:

1   to know the ethical dilemmas faced by psychologists and collegiate psychologists, and
2   to receive and understand their comments about the DU.

In January 2010, following Dr. Ferrero's suggestions, a new work plan that included the following actions was delineated: Preparation of a newsletter to publicize the development of the Code of Ethics and related key issues that would allow a better understanding of the principles and raise awareness of this process. During the process three newsletters were sent by email and in print. In addition, workshops were scheduled and attended in four regions of the country: south central region in the Capital City of Guatemala, northern region in the city of Cobán, western region in the city of Quetzaltenango and northeastern region in the city of Chiquimula. The work in these workshops was carried out according to a plan whose general objective was to publicize the progress of the elaboration of the Code of Ethics, as well as sensitize and obtain feedback from the professionals of the different branches of psychology.

Work guides were developed for these workshops that sought to obtain feedback on the construction of a first draft of the code. Specifically, it was sought to verify the clarity and relevance of the rules and obtain suggestions to improve the version. The results obtained in each of the four workshops were presented in subsequent sessions of the Court of Honor for analysis, consideration and incorporation. The foregoing allowed a review of this first draft and numbering and writing errors were incorporated and corrected. Again, content was discussed and new concerns arose.

Dr. Andrea Ferrero accepted the invitation of the Court of Honor to visit Guatemala during the week of June 21–26, 2010 to directly advise the process, so various activities were carried out with different groups of professionals. First, a professional meeting was held with the Court of Honor, in which an update of the work done up to that point was carried out and the guidelines for the following stages of the process were established. Secondly, two Debate Workshops were held under the direction of Dr. Ferrero. Professionals from various areas of psychology were invited and attended. In addition, Dr. Ferrero gave the lecture: "The impact of the Universal Declaration of Ethical Principles for psychologists and psychologists in the Code of Ethics of Guatemala" in the framework of the 3rd anniversary of the School, aimed at professionals. Finally, a closing session of the work carried out with the consultant was held.

Once the external advisory stage was concluded, the work plan for the Final Phase of the process for preparing the Code was established. This included:

1   review and inclusion of the consultant's observations based on the follow-up document, prepared and presented by her;
2   reformulation of each of the principles, and contextualization based on the suggestions and reflections made during the process;
3   presentation, background, procedure and preparation of the glossary; and
4   sending the document for style review and last revision prior to its presentation before the Assembly of the College of Psychologists of Guatemala.

This assembly approved the code. The code was approved at the extraordinary General Assembly on October 25, 2010, and it was finally printed.

It is important to highlight the fact that, through the process developed, the participation of various groups of the community of psychology professionals was achieved, so the Code became a collective co-construction of the ethical guidelines that will govern the activity of scientific and professional psychologists in Guatemala.

The code was constructed, as we have already stated, based on the four principles of the Universal Declaration of Ethical Principles for Psychologists and Psychologists, which are:

- PRINCIPLE I: Respect for the Dignity of People and Peoples
- PRINCIPLE II: Competent care of the Wellbeing of Others
- PRINCIPLE III: Integrity in Relationships
- PRINCIPLE IV: Professional and Scientific Responsibilities with the Society

Each principle contains inherent values, specific guidelines and the respective rules to each guideline. That is to say that its structure and content are interwoven. To structure the code, we relied on the codes of Canada and New Zealand. The Latin American codes have a different structure that the working group considered punitive and not updated to the needs of our country. The structure chosen was considered innovative and the following was stated in the document:

Therefore, the understanding and incorporation of these principles are essential in professional practice. The psychologist has an obligation to become familiar with the principles, guidelines and norms that this

Code contains. The lack of knowledge or understanding of a rule does not constitute a defense against any complaint or accusation for incurring ethics violations. If your responsibilities conflict with institutional or organizational provisions, you will announce your commitment to the Code of Ethics and take the necessary steps to resolve the conflict in a responsible manner. In the event that you are faced with situations not contemplated in the law or in this code, you should consult with experts on the subject, ethics committees, or act according to your conscience and guiding principle that is to guarantee at all times the well-being of all those individuals, groups or organizations that require their services, within the limits of the practice of Psychology. With the purpose of updating and enriching this Code of Ethics its periodic review is suggested.

(College of Psychologists of Guatemala, 2011, pp. 23–24)

In this way, a document emerged that is characterized by being collaboratively built, inspiring (not punitive), culturally relevant, and according to an advanced model. The Code of Ethics applies to all activities performed by the psychologist as part of their academic, scientific and professional functions. It refers to psychological functions by nature and the services it provides such as clinical practice, diagnosis, research, teaching, supervision of people in training, development and construction of assessment instruments, conduct of assessments, testimony or forensic report, educational advice, evaluation of individuals, systems or organizations, organizational consulting, social, educational, preventive, or therapeutic intervention, administration, advice or statements to the media, whatever they may be, and all those activities proper to the practice of Psychology. They are only applicable in the context of a defined professional, academic, and scientific relationship or role.

As proposed, the code should be reviewed periodically, so the Court of Honor of the College of Psychologists 2017–2018 proposed the revision of the Code. This group of professionals also had the advice of Dr. Andrea Ferrero for the revision and updating of the Code. The methodology included forming groups of outstanding professionals from the professional community to review each of the principles; each group delivered a report and the Court of Honor structured the contributions of the working groups. Basically, aspects that were considered unclear or repetitive were omitted, as well as the comments that were contained in the first edition. These were incorporated into the respective guidelines and articles, as well as aspects related to psychological test management and research tests. Aspects of the use of the internet and technological devices were also incorporated into psychological practice. In the Annexes section, an informed consent model was provided, as this is a little used aspect in professional practice. A complaint form was added to the Court of Honor, as well as an Informed Consent model, and the glossary that was already contained in the first edition was updated.

The Cultural Component

Guatemala is a multilingual, multicultural and multiethnic country, so the construction of the Code of Ethics is based on this declaration that is embodied in the Constitution of the Republic. These three aspects permeate the Code, but they emphasize the guidelines and articles related to respect for cultural diversity. Although it is not explicitly mentioned, we were always aware that Guatemala suffered an internal armed conflict for 36 years, that left important consequences on mental health in the population and that it currently suffers from social problems such as discrimination, poverty, violence, crime. and impunity, factors that plague the general population.

As stated at the beginning, having a Code of Ethics was an imperative, because of the above-mentioned and had not taken the place it should have in the circle of professions in force in the country. Within the Code, the following is said:

> The challenges posed by the rapid technological advance and the changes that societies face worldwide establish the need to review the way in which professionals in general act before the people or groups that request services. In the field of Psychological Sciences, the adherence to ethical norms becomes even more important, given the impact it has on the mental health, life and dignity of the people and groups it serves.
>
> *(College of Psychologists of Guatemala, 2011, p. 13)*

Its main objective is the protection of people or groups against risk situations arising from bad professional practices, a situation that unfortunately occurs in our country. It is necessary, then, to ensure that psychologists can offer optimal care, based on respect for the dignity of people and Guatemalan communities. This code also has a reflective function that should encourage Higher Educational institutions to review and readjust the professional training of psychological sciences, so that, by incorporating ethics, they respond comprehensively to the challenges they pose, meeting the needs of people and groups in different areas of Psychology.

The second edition includes an introduction that expresses the following:

> In Guatemalan society, given its idiosyncrasy, mental health research problems are identified. In this context, from the psychology approach, there is a moral obligation to stimulate, advance, promote and develop the indigenous knowledge that characterizes the diverse social and honorable groups of Guatemala. The responsibility of the professional of psychology regarding the development of science in society requires justifying from an ethical point of view the development of this research and considering the moral impact of these findings. The complexity of Guatemalan society becomes unique in its nature and, therefore, inscrutable to build its own knowledge that accounts for its existence, hence

there is a commitment to guide the acts of psychology professionals with a guide of deontological content.

(College of Psychologists of Guatemala, 2018, pp. 26–27)

Conclusion

Ultimately, given the responsibility implied by the intervention of psychological sciences in the different work areas, an instrument that serves psychology professionals as a source to turn to when faced with dilemmas that pose diverse types of ethical conflicts was essential. Currently, Guatemalan psychologists work in industry, in organizations, in sports, in schools, in public and private medical clinics, serving rural and urban populations surviving the armed conflict, of urban violence, serving children and adolescents victims of psychosocial conflicts, women victims of domestic violence, migrant populations and those from marginal areas, among others.

The Universities of the country are primarily clinical psychologists, but at the same time they have degrees at the bachelor's level and offer academic degrees including: Bachelor of Psychology, Bachelor of Clinical Psychology, Bachelor of Physical Education, Sport and Recreation, Industrial/Organizational Psychology, Educational Psychology, Clinical Psychology and Mental Health, Medical Psychology and Mental Health, Bachelor of Business Psychology, Bachelor of Human Resources, Bachelor of Clinical Psychology, and a degree in family psychology with a specialty in Logotherapy. They also offer masters in Logotherapy and Family and Conjugal Psychotherapy, a degree in Organizational Psychology and Human Talent management, a degree in Clinical Psychology and Social Counseling, Industrial Psychology and Organizational Behavior, a degree in Psychology with a specialization in Educational Psychology, a degree in Psychology with a specialization in Business Psychology, and a degree in Psychology with a specialization in Social Psychology (Cárcamo Duarte & Escobar Martinez, 2015). Professionals graduating from the various universities with a Bachelor's degree in any of the careers mentioned above by law have to enroll in the College of Psychologists of Guatemala and therefore, are subject to the Code of Ethics of the College.

For the professional community this Code represents a great achievement, but unfortunately, there are no programs for implementing the Code, training in it or measuring its impact. This is due to the lack of political will of the presiding authorities in the College. However, it is widely known that undergraduate programs in psychological science careers have professional ethics courses in which the code of ethics is included in the training of future professionals.

By personal observation, it is known that there is a tendency among professionals active in the field to consult the code, consult professionals with more experience in ethical matters, and to cite the document in articles they publish.

To conclude, we highlight that the Code of Ethics of the College of Psychologists of Guatemala is a code based on the Universal Declaration of Ethical Principles for Psychologists and Psychologists (DU). It is inspirational, developed in collaboration with Psychology professionals throughout the country, with cultural relevance, and it includes the most current aspects of professional deontology within the country.

References

Aguilar, G. & Recinos, L. (1996). Historia y estado actual de la psicología en Guatemala. *Revista Latinoamericana de Psicología*, 28(2), 197–232. Retrieved from www.redalyc.org/arti culo.oa?id=80528202

Cárcamo Duarte, A. G. & Escobar Martínez, A. C. (2015). La psicología en Guatemala, un poco de historia y actualidad. *Información Psicológica*, dossier Psicología Iberoamericana, parte II. doi:10.14635/IPSIC.2014.109.9

Colegio de Psicólogos de Guatemala [College of Psychologists of Guatemala] (2011), *Código de Ética*, Author.

Colegio de Psicólogos de Guatemala [College of Psychologists of Guatemala] (2018), *Código de Ética*, Author.

Gauthier, J., Pettifor, J., & Ferrero, A. (2010). The Universal Declaration of Ethical Principles for psychologists: A culture-sensitive model for creating and reviewing a code of ethics. *Ethics & Behavior*, 20(3&4), 1–18.

Jurado, A. M., Cazali, L., Gracioso, M., Seijas, C., Juárez, R., Aguilar, E., Ortiz, K., & Lemus, M. (2007, July). *Proceso de elaboración del código deontológico para Guatemala*. Conversatorio efectuado en el XXXI Congreso Interamericano de Psicología, México.

Jury, A., & Juárez, R. (2000). *Necesidad sentida por los psicólogos guatemaltecos de contar con un código de ética*. Codigo deontologico para el psicologo guatemalteco, Universidad del Valle de Guatemala, Facultad de Ciencias Sociales Departamento de Psicología, Seminario de Deontología Profesional, Guatemala.

Universal Declaration of Ethical Principles for Psychologists (2008). Retrieved from www.iupsys. org/ethics/univdecl2008.html

Universidad del Valle de Guatemala, Facultad de Ciencias Sociales Departamento de Psico- logía, *Codigo deontologico para el psicologo guatemalteco*, Seminario de Deontología Profesional, no editado. Guatemala, (2000).

15

PSYCHOLOGICAL ETHICS IN VENEZUELA

Past, Present and Future

Juan Carlos Canga

Introduction

We often find ourselves talking or reflecting on ethics, its implications and importance, not only in everyday life but also in the expression of the practice of a profession such as psychology. However, many times we do not take enough time to create the necessary conditions around it that allow as to articulate of a series of resources and behaviors in harmony with what we finally agree on as ethical behavior in the discipline. In this sense, when we are fortunate to have a Code of Ethics for Venezuelan psychology as a reference, one of the best things that can happen to us is to have the opportunity to write about it: its history, anecdotes, its strengths, its weaknesses and pending challenges.

This is the precise occasion to relate and describe in a detailed and unprecedented way, as has rarely been done, a part of our history as a discipline as related to our Code of Professional Ethics. We will detail its history, meet the protagonists, and discover details – until now – little known regarding its preparation and approval process. We will also share various aspects of our professional practice as a Venezuelan psychologist. Finally, we will delve into the impact of Information and Communication Technology (ICTs) on our professional practice and the legislation that regulates it, to conclude with a description of the ethical challenges ahead for Venezuelan psychology. Throughout, a rigorous review of the original sources, manuscripts, bulletins, audiovisual records and even interviews with some of the protagonists will create a connection with the new generations of psychologists that allows it to continue.

Brief History of Psychology in Venezuela

According to historians Moreno (2018) and Straka (2018), the interest in Psychology in Venezuela begins at the beginning of the 20th century, when it was studied in the pedagogy courses of the Normal Schools. Rafael Aveledo's book *Psychology Lessons for Teachers*, from 1886, is the first psychology book published by a Venezuelan. In 1911, *Lecciones de Psicología practico* by R. B. Ortega was also published for teachers. The most studied psychologist at that time was J. Dewey.

In the Pedagogical Institute of Caracas, Prieto Figueroa published *Notes for Psychology for Secondary and Moral Education and General Psychology,* in the 1940s. In this same decade, Spanish philosophers and psychiatrists interested in psychology arrived in Venezuela. The philosopher Eugenio Ímaz, from Mexico, founded a chair of psychology within the School of Philosophy of the Central University of Venezuela (UCV). Teachers Guillermo Pérez Enciso and Francisco del Olmo taught psychology classes at the Pedagogical. In 1943, the psychiatrist Ortega Durán founded the Section of Psychometry in the Directorate of School Hygiene of the Ministry of Health.

In 1949, the UCV Institute of Psychology and Psychotechnics was created, under the direction of the Venezuelan psychiatrist Raúl Ramos Calles. This institute is considered the antecedent of the UCV School of Psychology, which was founded in 1956, the first in the country, whose first director was Pérez Enciso. A year later the School of Psychology of the Andrés Bello Catholic University (UCAB) was born, with a study plan conceived by Father Plaza. With these two schools, psychology went from being another department to train teachers, to being a profession.

The continuity of the development of psychological training occurred slowly; after 22 years the third school of psychology arose at the Rafael Urdaneta University (1978), located in the city of Maracaibo. Twenty-one more years elapsed before another school of psychology opened, in the city of Maracay, specifically at the Bicentennial University of Aragua (UBA), in the year 2000.

In the 21st century, there has been a strong push for psychology studies at the undergraduate level in the country. After the UBA school, seven more schools of psychology opened. These included: Arturo Michelena University, Carabobo State (UAM, 2003); Metropolitan University, Miranda State (UNIMET, 2004); Yacambú University, Lara State (UNY, 2005); Lisandro Alvarado Centroccidental University, Lara State (UCLA, 2006–2007); Bolivarian University of Venezuela, Capital District (UBV, 2013); National Experimental University of Táchira, Táchira State (UNET, 2015); and University of the Andes, Mérida State (ULA, 2017).

It is noteworthy that although the greater growth in this career is seen in private universities, in recent years, a rebound has been observed in public sector universities, in which the career of psychology is promoted. Likewise, a distribution of universities can be evidenced in almost the entire country, except in the regions: North-eastern, Insular, Guayana and Los Llanos. The mentioned schools are dedicated to undergraduate training.

The fourth level studies in psychology had a somewhat later beginning, in 1960 with two postgraduate degrees: Clinical Psychology and School Psychology, which had a short duration. In 1965 at the Pedagogical Institute of Caracas (today Universidad Pedagógica Experimental Libertador) a Master's Degree in Guidance was offered, which is still being taught. In 1976, postgraduate studies in Psychology reappeared at the UCV and the Master's Degrees in Group Dynamics were offered (later, this Master's Degree became a Specialization Course), Methodology, Experimental Analysis of Behavior and Social Psychology. In 1981 the Master's Degree in Instructional Psychology was opened, 1986 the Master's Degree in Human Development and recently the Specialization in Clinical Psychology, all with a duration of four semesters and the requirement of a degree work. In 1989 the Doctoral Program of Psychology began at this University, which lasts for four years.

At the beginning of the 70s, the Simón Bolívar University (a public university without undergraduate studies in psychology), developed Postgraduate courses in Psychology, currently offering two Specializations and a Master's Degree. In the 1990s, the Rafael Urdaneta University began offering Master's degrees in the areas of Mental Retardation and Clinical Psychology.

High-level training (postgraduate) has not been an exclusive task of University Institutions. Official bodies such as the Ministry of Health (current Ministry of Popular Power for Health), have promoted the training of psychologists and endorsed specialization courses in Clinical Psychology in the psychiatric services of four hospitals in Caracas. At the level of private organizations, there have been various professional groups that offer training activities (Transactional Analysis, Gestalt, Bioenergetics, Neurolinguistic Programming, among others) that complement the training of psychologists in the country.

The Practice of Professional Psychology in Venezuela

Psychology allows its practice in different economic or productive sectors of the country. This is evident in the presence of these professionals working in the public sector, especially in ministries such as Education, Health, Defense and Justice, among others, in some cases holding high-level positions in them. Institutions of secondary and higher education have been another source of employment, since these professionals have developed activities aimed at teaching or care services.

For its part, the practice of psychology in the private sector has been oriented mainly towards two main aspects: clinical practice and the consulting and training service in the industrial sector. In almost all companies, the position of Human Resource Management, (involving orientation, selection, as well as training of personnel), is performed by psychologists.

Professional Associations and the History of Their Ethics Codes

Currently as a union, Venezuelan psychologists belong to the Federation of Psychologists of Venezuela (FPV), which is comprised of the country's different regional colleges. It has an executive body with legal attributions, represented by a Board of Directors that implements the decisions of the National Assembly, its supreme body. The Federation complies with the regulations indicated in the Law of Exercise of Psychology, its Regulations and its Code of Ethics, which are the legal instruments by which the union has governed since 1978.

Historically, the first formal organization of psychologists was founded on September 21, 1957, called the Venezuelan Association of Psychologists.

It is important to note that the oldest verified antecedent that we have been able to identify dates back to 1957 and is outlined in the "Constitutive Act of the Venezuelan Psychologist Association," where it says: "The members are obliged to ensure compliance with the principles stipulated in the Association's Code of Professional Ethics" (Art. 12).

The foregoing challenged the Association with an imperative to resolve, such as complying with a code of ethics, which did not exist at that time. This situation forced the initiation of an exhaustive review of the bibliographic references available at the time, favoring the following: Principle of Ethics for or Exercise of Psychology (Brazil, 1952); Revue Internationale d'Ethique Professionnelle (Switzerland, 1953) and Revue de Psycologie Appliquée (France, 1954). It was in this last journal, specifically in its April edition, where a translation of the "Ethical Standards of Psychologist" of the American Association of Psychologists (APA) was published.

The document that was finally assumed by the Venezuelan Association of Psychologists as its first reference in the field of ethics bore the name: "The General Principles and Norms for a Code of Ethics for Psychologists." It is important to note that this document was an exact translation of the *Ethical Standards of Psychologist: A Summary of Ethical Principles* and the *Ethical Standards of Psychologists* (from page 279–282, Volume 4 of the *American Psychologist*, 1949). The Venezuelan Association of Psychologists received authorization, through Francisco del Olmo (Secretary General), for its use from Arthur C. Hoffman (Managing Editor of APA), on June 24, 1959. This authorization was to reproduce, translate and distribute to interested psychologists and students, the Spanish version that was prepared by Miriam de Dembo, César De Madariaga and Francisco del Olmo.

Later, the association changed its name and the College of Psychologists of Venezuela emerged, created on November 22, 1961. This date was selected as the celebration of the National Day of the Venezuelan Psychologist. The College chose to adopt the same ethical guidelines as the previous Association, as a normative instrument of psychological practice in the country.

More than 20 years passed until September 11, 1978, when a new association was created, called the Federation of Psychologists of Venezuela (FPV). The creation of the FPV was possible thanks to the approval of a draft Law of Exercise of Psychology of Venezuela, presented at the time in the Congress of the Republic of Venezuela and signed by the president of the time, Mr. Carlos Andrés Pérez. The process of deliberation and consultation of the bill, in the National Congress of the time, took almost ten months of work, until its approval, signature of the execution by the president and publication in the Official Gazette of Venezuela.

This new and innovative Law, exhaustively established in its article 1, the following: "The profession of the Psychologist and its exercise are governed by this Law and its Regulations, the internal regulations and by the Code of Professional Ethics issued by the Federation of Psychologists of Venezuela" (p. 4).

Ethics in Venezuela

Before addressing the development of the Psychology Ethics Code, it is important to understand ethics within the Venezuelan context. In Venezuela, ethics is based upon historical values with deep cultural roots, as well as compliance with laws that allow the harmonious coexistence that is in evidence. At the time of colonization, our country greatly valued the sociocultural need to dominate fiefdoms and exploit others on behalf of the crown, while the country was also under the tutelage of the Catholic Church. In this sense, everything that was against the church and the Spanish crown was considered unethical and contrary to morality.

At the time of independence, the values were oriented towards freedom. Later, during the civil wars, they changed towards the search for equality and social justice. This was clearly in evidence during the revolution led by Ezequiel Zamora, who sought to achieve "free lands for free men," which implied a fair and equitable production for all, not only for a minority.

In the government of Guzmán Blanco, Venezuelan society was influenced by naturalistic thoughts and ideologies, behaviorism and positivism. It allowed the control and organization of the nation based on diverse spaces for education, commerce, industry and agriculture.

At present, the deep political, economic and social crisis that we are experiencing in the country is evident, denominated by some organizations as a "Complex Humanitarian Emergency." All this, in the context of an accentuated moral and ethical crisis that affects the Venezuelan population, where even constitutional principles are compromised.

Ethics becomes an action guide, which allows us to discern between what is correct or not, for a certain field of action. The foregoing led us to strengthen our legal instruments, as a way to strengthen ethical practices in the country. However, if something has been evidenced in the Venezuelan case, it is that having a wide variety of legislative instruments does not guarantee higher levels of ethical behavior.

This whole situation has given rise to behaviors of all kinds that are contrary to ethics, where respect for human rights is even compromised. However, from the analysis of the discourse, it is observed as a group of people who represent different actors of power in various sectors of Venezuelan society, promote moralizing proposals and discourses with a high content of ethical principles. However, these proposals lack, basically, a real link with the practice of ethical behavior, where it is evidenced – through concrete and daily facts – with the proposed ethical principles. This differentiation is of such magnitude that talking about ethics and observing ethical behaviors in these actors has become as difficult as mixing water and oil to obtain a homogeneous and integrated solution.

History of the Current Code of Ethics of Psychology in Venezuela

The ethical precepts in the professional development of the psychologist places them in situations in which they are forced to make decisions sometimes without having all the information they require, without being certain about the circumstances within which they must act correctly, foreseeing what they would be, or the consequences of their actions on people. The exercise of this profession must be guided by criteria, values, principles and high goals that enhance this profession, so professionals in this career are obliged to support their actions on this basis of ethical and deontological provisions.

According to its creators, the code of ethics was developed given the need to protect psychologists, patients and the public in general, encompassing psychology professionals who practice the profession both in public and private institutions. In other words, it was hoped to have a document whose content would include a set of canons through which all can be protected from.

At that time, the Federation realized that psychology professionals, despite having a law that regulated the exercise of the profession, did not have a document in which the ethical criteria that accompanied their performance were reflected. Hence, a working group appointed by the president of the FPV at the time, Erik Becker, was activated, who designated colleagues Ligia Sánchez and later Sigrid Mattar as group coordinators. This commission's central activity was the direct compilation of various information on psychological practice. An example of this was conducting interviews with members of the Scientific Society, psychologists who worked in the Dialysis Unit of the University Clinical Hospital, who provided information of interest for their protection and that of the patients who attended the dialysis service, covering different areas.

Similarly, interviews were carried out with the psychologists who worked at the Children's Hospital, particularly in the intensive care area, who also made an important contribution. This information gathering process also included university professors, particularly those of the psychology career, who contributed information of interest to regulate the actions of the psychologist in the field of teaching, and with whom it was also possible to obtain relevant information on ethics in the field of research.

Information was also collected from the other psychology societies and associations in the world, which already had codes drawn up and, in particular, the Jesuit Father, Luis Azagra, Vice-Rector of the UCAB and Head of the Department of Ethics of the School of Psychology, was requested. By that time, he provided a first draft for consideration. Finally, the psychologist Sigrid Mattar assumed full responsibility for coordinating the preparation of the project with the legal advice of Juan José Bocaranda.

The information gathering also focused on the review of documentary information, including the newspapers at the time. More specifically, this is where complaints could be evidenced, or the exposure of situations in which a psychology professional could be involved or promoted some type of service related to the practice of psychology or any intrusive practice. This allowed for evaluation and consideration of whether it fell within the bounds of the code of ethics.

The process of conducting interviews for the re-compilation of all this information was overseen by Psic. Sigrid Mattar, who was tasked with coordinating this activity. Colleague Matar assumed this arduous activity, which allowed her to learn information related to the fields of health, education and research, among others, directly from professional psychologists.

For the development and revision of the Code of Professional Ethics, other codes of ethics were taken as a reference, such as the ethical code of lawyers and that of doctors, which in some way reflected some aspects relatively common to our profession. During the analysis and evaluation process, the codes of ethics of other countries in the region were reviewed, among which "The General Principles and Norms for a Code of Ethics for Psychologists" stood out, the first ethics code that had been set in place by the Venezuelan Association of Psychologists back in 1959.

Once the information-gathering phase was completed, the content was organized and adapted to the legal framework of the time. The activities included consolidating the information obtained, structuring, legal adaptation and final drafting of the proposal that would shape our Code of Ethics. All this, bearing in mind that its content carried a protectionist sense for the psychologist, patients and the public beyond a sanctioning intention.

Subsequently, the legal evaluation of the document in the hands of the lawyer began. This was done by Juan José Bocaranda Espinoza, who incorporated aspects related to universal law and human rights. The original project consisted of 205 Articles grouped in 14 Chapters. Finally, the code proposal was structured with general provisions, 12 Chapters and 182 Articles.

Next, the discussion phase began at the national level. Several assemblies were convened, with the active participation of the disciplinary courts of the different colleges of psychologists in the country. This allowed them to carry out the evaluation of the document and provide information of interest to it, including the difficulties, limitations and additional aspects, for which it was important to establish some specific ethical standards.

Finally, The Code of Professional Ethics for the Psychologist was sanctioned in the II Ordinary National Assembly of the Federation of Psychologists of Venezuela, held in the city of Barquisimeto, Lara State, on March 28 and 29, 1981. Its approval was unanimous and as the sole point of the assembly, went into effect on March 29, 1981. Before the code was instituted, the regulations had been established by the disciplinary courts. However, it is important to note that these regulations were limited, and therefore their content did not cover all possible areas.

One aspect to be highlighted is the mandate of the assembly to develop in the future the chapters by applied field of psychology: orientation, school, clinical, sports, industrial and organizational and social. This mandate is still pending to date.

The Current Code of Ethics of Psychologists of Venezuela

The Code of Ethics for Psychologists constitutes an instrument through which the set of principles is made available to psychology professionals in which the ethical aspirations of the profession are expressed and the rules that regulate their exercise are defined. This document is intended to benefit those who assist or use the services of those who practice this profession, by establishing the guidelines of what can be expected from a psychologist. The principles established in our code reflect the fundamental postulate that the psychologist must maintain a constant concern about the consequences that their professional performance may have on the lives of their peers, bearing in mind that the responsibility falls on the individual.

The code of ethics of the psychologist in Venezuela comprises 182 Articles that regulate the practice of this profession in the country. It also establishes the sanctions to which practitioners may be subject to for incurring malpractice or contravening the moral custom of society. Next, we will describe the structure of our code:

- Fundamental Principles, Articles 1 to 53
- Chapter I: On Ethical Duties in the Research Area: Articles 54 to 75,
- Chapter II: On Ethical Duties in the Teaching Area (Articles 76 to 84),
- Chapter III: Of the Ethical Duties Relating to Resources and Instruments (Articles 85 to 95),
- Chapter IV: On Ethical Duties Facing Public Authorities (Article 96 to 100)
- Chapter V: Of the Duties of the Psychologist towards the Consultant (Article 101 to 131)
- Chapter VI: Of the Ethical Duties in the Institutional Exercise of Psychology (Article 132 to 141)
- Chapter VII: On the Professional Secretary (Article 142 to 147)
- Chapter VIII: On Professional Fees (Article 148 to 158)
- Chapter IX: Of the Duties of the Psychologist Regarding His Colleagues (Article 159 to 172),
- Chapter X: Of the Duties towards the Guild (Articles 173 to 176)
- Chapter XI: Of the Sanctions and the Causes that determine them (Article 177 to 179),
- Chapter XII: Final Provisions (Article 180 to 182)

Next, we will refer to the most relevant topics that our code addresses. It establishes the obligation of Psychologists to comply with the Code of Ethics, as well as the global scope for all the various organizations of the unions in psychological matters. These Articles include the humanistic sense that the practice of psychology encompasses, as a science framed within a morally adequate practice.

The values that psychologists should have when exercising their profession are established, highlighting the agreement with the humanist sentiment of the doctrines that have defined the fundamental rights of people. It defines the objectivity with which the psychology professional must exercise their services.

Every psychologist must stay at the forefront of the scientific and professional changes demanded by the exercise of the career. It establishes the unrestricted duty of psychologists to preserve the integrity of people, thus guaranteeing the well-being of their patients. It also establishes the impartiality and independence of the practice of psychology, especially when it comes to issuing opinions on patients.

With respect to remuneration, it presents the limitations that psychologists have when it comes to perceiving economic benefits as a result of working in organizations dedicated to psychological practice. It also establishes the principle of non-discrimination on the part of the psychology professional.

The severity of the malpractice, individual, intentional or joint, on the part of the psychology professional is established. It also prohibits the use of esoteric clinical strategies that can serve or be used as tools of psychological practices. More specifically, it establishes the sanctions that psychology professionals would be subjected to if found guilty of committing any irregularity in the professional practice of the career.

The document sets out the necessary conditions to carry out psychological practices for research and experimentation purposes, avoiding any damage to the integrity of the patient. It also indicates the ethical principle with which the psychology professional must operate in the educational area. These articles include the fundamental principles that psychologists must bear in mind towards their consultants, primarily stating the importance of providing a timely and balanced responsible service.

It specifies that the psychology professional is limited to exercising specifically what their professional practice allows them, avoiding excesses that cause difficulties for her patients. It also addresses the management of consultants who have relationships with colleagues in the profession.

It establishes the prohibition of public derision of patients, and promotes the obligation of the psychologist to keep his professional life away from psychological practice, avoiding involving his own experiences in the treatment or consultation of patients. The paramount focus is on the need to maintain and ensure patients' mental health.

Parameters are established for managing the confidentiality of the psychologist with respect to patient information, highlighting the importance of professional privacy, as well as the causes or situations for which the most private information may be disclosed. It also clarifies the ethical relationships that the psychologist must maintain with his colleagues, emphasizing respectful behavior.

Ethics in the Professional Practice of Venezuelan Psychology

The ethical practice of psychology in the country has motivated different initiatives inspired by the Code of Professional Ethics of the Venezuelan psychologist as related to respect for human rights, the right of those affected to receive assistance without any type of discrimination, among others. Among these, it is important to note The Psychological Support Network, created due to the torrential rains that affected the country in 1999; the psychological support programs – free and low-cost – implemented by the Federation of Psychologists of Venezuela to help the Venezuelan population due to social protests, blackouts, and the COVID-19 pandemic; other psychological support initiatives such as Psychologists Without Borders-Venezuela, among other institutions.

In this sense, and in the opinion of Otálora (2012), regarding the ethical behavior of the psychologist in case of emergencies and the political polarization due to the torrential rains of 1999 in Venezuela, he considers that the Code of Professional Ethics of the Venezuelan psychologist, is of fundamental importance, as a guide to action. In his words: "In these lines it is not up to me to solve this dilemma, only to remember that the psychologist has a social responsibility towards the other and a code of ethics that he should not forget," (Otálora, 2012, p. 126). Additionally, among its conclusions, the following is important to highlight: "In emergency and disaster situations, the ethics of governments and their citizens are put to the test," as well as "It is essential to promote solidarity and sensitize university students on ethics and human rights in emergency situations," and "Reflection and the search for meaning are essential when students enter the professional field and, above all, when it comes to humanitarian aid" (Otálora, 2012, p. 127).

Ethics turns out to be a fundamental issue for our discipline and in general for societies. A statement that we can verify when inquiring among colleagues and users of psychological services – in the country – regarding the importance of ethics in professional practice, the answer coincides in an overwhelming way: "It is very important" and even "indispensable." However, when reviewing the psychological practice of colleagues, taking into account the cases reviewed, we were able to identify certain aspects that seem to contradict the aforementioned. By virtue of this, we observe the existence of important gaps between the relevance attributed to ethics and ethical behavior in the professional practice of the Venezuelan psychologist.

The above, although it characterizes Venezuelan professional practice, does not seem to be exclusively our issue. In this sense, Vera-Garcia, Castro-Sacoto & Caicedo-Guale (2019) identified important differences between the level of knowledge of ethical aspects and their inclusion in professional practice. In a sample of psychologists in Ecuador, the authors noted: "It can be evidenced that there is a contradiction in psychologists regarding the knowledge of ethical codes and their application; a large percentage associates them with universal values" (p. 142).

An indicator of the above could be the number of complaints received in the Federation of Psychologists of Venezuela (FPV). In this sense, it is appreciated that this value could be relatively low, in comparison with the indicators of the region and in relation to our universe of union members (approximately 15,000 members). The foregoing could lead us to think that the number of cases finally reported is less than the number of "real cases." Regarding the individual who formalizes their complaint before the disciplinary authorities, we can see that the majority correspond to recipients of psychological services (not psychologists) and a minority to psychology professionals, who, according to the Code of

Professional Ethics, are required to report any malpractice case of which they are aware. An interesting variant of the above is that on some occasions – according to the reports raised – the recipient is motivated to report, after having been in consultation with another psychologist, who guides and motivates him to make the complaint.

Of the complaints received by the Federation of Psychologists of Venezuela, through the established instances, most of the cases correspond to the clinical area. The most frequent reasons for the complaints, according to the Code of Professional Ethics of the Venezuelan psychologist, are those related to faults in the areas of: customer service, use of resources and psychological work instruments, teaching and research.

Another aspect to highlight in relation to reporting malpractice cases is the fact that throughout our republican history and especially at the present time, the Venezuelan population has been losing confidence in the complaint and in its institutions. It is not seen as a way to resolve impasses or punish behavior that violates laws and regulations in general, to compensate the victims or deliver justice in a specific situation. Even, in some cases, it is perceived as a possible cause of future retaliation, towards the complainant(s). Psychology in the country has not escaped from the above; placing ourselves before a complex situation, which requires a multidimensional approach.

Regarding the institutions in charge of receiving and processing the complaints that are finally made, difficulties have arisen with the installation of some disciplinary tribunals at the national level. This is in addition to the difficulties derived from the current situation in the country, as well as the requirement of supervision of any electoral process of the union by the National Electoral Council (CNE), entity of the Electoral Power of the National Executive. The circumstances described above have generated some delays in the renewal of both national and state governing bodies and with them, some operational difficulties of the disciplinary courts have arisen, which ends up affecting their normal functioning.

In general, ethics in Venezuela requires greater focus on teaching, practice, monitoring and control, for which the strengthening of the different institutions related to training and professional practice is required.

Ethical Challenges of Venezuelan Psychology

> The illegal exercise of psychology by people without training and accreditation, the offering of psychotherapy services by various professionals, and the illegal offer of unauthorized psychology degree programs are a permanent source of tension, which demands energetic actions from the union body to protect the beneficiaries of psychology services, the union members and the government.
>
> *(Canga & Yáber, 2015, p. 134)*

The aspects mentioned by Canga & Yáber (2015) continue to be some of the main challenges that Venezuelan psychology faces. Challenges, which require a set of actions where one of the common aspects to all is the ethical component.

Perhaps the most important change that affects the professional practice of the Venezuelan psychologist is the advances in the area of computing and, therefore, Information and Communication Technologies (ICTs). These have occurred since 1981 (year of approval of the Code of Professional Ethics of the Venezuelan psychologist), which makes it unavoidable to update them through the incorporation of ICTs, and their impact on the content of our code of ethics.

Today telepsychology is a reality, with its advantages and disadvantages. The truth is that this new practice escapes – in the Venezuelan case – from the controlling or rigorous gaze of the ethical principles, our codes and norms. In this sense, the FPV, in conjunction with the academy, has been working on a project to update the Code of Professional Ethics of the Venezuelan psychologist. In the opinion of Acuña & Prieto (2020), the incorporation of ICTs requires the revision of the professional identity, which allows adding the digital component. In addition, the characterization of the practice in the new virtual spaces.

In the words of the authors:

> The task of updating the Code of Professional Ethics of the Psychologist of Venezuela incorporating the articles aimed at structuring the virtual psychological task must be assumed based on the phrase of Alfred Korzybski, "Do not confuse the map with the territory," nor the word with what is named, other authors would add. Professional ethics must be inherent to professional work, because being in a virtual space does not vary the action; the flexibility of defined and agreed action patterns endangers the ultimate goal of professional action.
>
> *(Acuña & Prieto, 2020, p. 1)*

However, we consider that the nature of the challenges posed is more far-reaching and even beyond the national scope, to fall on the region at least, taking into account cultural aspects. In these times, the adaptation of national ethical standards or the rigid adoption of regional or international standards is not enough.

The reality of psychological practice through digital environments implies the development and implementation of new ethical standards that allow addressing the various aspects that derive from telepsychology. Most especially, it is those related to the disappearance of geographical spaces, where physical limits are meaningless, since there are no major technical impediments for a psychology professional in a given country to attend to a consultant residing in the same country or in any other country in the world. The opportunity for professional interaction can occur through mobile phone, tablet or computer.

The foregoing places us before a great challenge and ethical requirement, for which we still do not have clear answers, only concerns: Under what conditions or guidelines can we consider telepsychology as an ethically responsible professional practice modality? How to protect Venezuelan clients residing in the country from the misleading offers of psychological services from other countries? How to offer suitable resources so that clients of psychological services – regardless of country – can verify that the credentials presented by the psychologist certify him to provide the telepsychology service offered? In the event of a malpractice complaint against a Venezuelan psychologist in another country or a psychologist of another nationality in another country, what would be the procedure to follow? In the case of being found responsible for violations of the code of ethics, how would the sanction be executed? In the case of a complaint against a Venezuelan psychologist, residing in the country, by a recipient of her psychological services in another country, what would be the procedure and what legal framework would prevail?

The above makes us reflect as to what extent telepsychology, in addition to facilitating psychological care, facilitates the absence of control and the violation of the laws that regulate local psychological practice in different countries with codes or standards in this regard.

Faced with this reality, the first responses are already emerging. The regional Code of Ethics options, although plausible, demand specification due to the diversity of cultural contexts. This would probably make it difficult to reach the necessary consensus in the countries of the South American region, for example. Faced with these difficulties, perhaps a more viable path, already successfully traveled in Europe, would be to think about the possibility of elaborating a Meta-Code of Ethics for the region, which allows having a frame of reference for national codes.

These times require the articulation of joint strategies between associations, federations and colleges of psychologists to strengthen the country's independent psychological practice and especially protect recipients of psychological services. In addition, it will be important to establish mechanisms for the resolution of conflicts or impasses in cases of reporting that involve different countries.

Conclusions

When we refer to ethics in Venezuelan psychology, the first formal reference is identified in 1957, with the creation of the first organization that brought together Venezuelan psychologists, the Association of Venezuelan Psychologists. However, the first approach to a specific code regulating the professional practice of the Venezuelan psychologist occurred in 1959, with the adoption of the Code of Ethics of the American Psychological Association (APA) in force at the time. That situation lasted until 1981, when the Code of Professional Ethics of Venezuelan Psychologist of the recently created Federation of Psychologists of Venezuela was finally approved. Our Code of Ethics does not include elements or guidelines associated with the idiosyncrasy of the Venezuelan. That is, the cultural component is not very marked.

The Code of Professional Ethics of the Venezuelan psychologist consists of 182 Articles grouped into 12 Chapters. At present, although it is still in force, it is in a process of revision and updating, especially due to the impact of ICTs on psychological practice. In another vein, important gaps have been identified between knowledge about ethics and its practice; in addition, of a decrease in the use of the complaint before the disciplinary instances. This requires the institutions responsible for academic training and professional representation; the strengthening of strategies, in such a way that they allow improving professional practice in an environment of knowledge and respect for the ethical principles that govern it.

Regarding the challenges to come, countries have traditionally been responsible for regulating psychological practices. However, with the increasingly frequent use of telepsychology, in part accelerated as a consequence of COVID-19, this traditional field is changing and an increasingly globalized psychological practice is envisioning us, with all its implications; for which we seem to be unprepared. In this sense, it is increasingly necessary to coordinate regional policies that, recognizing the cultural aspect, allow the articulation of strategies and actions between the different actors responsible for regulating psychological practice in each country, to address what seems to become one of the most important challenges in contemporary psychology.

References

Acuña, V. & Prieto, P. (2020). *Review of the Code of Ethics for the professional practice of the Psychologist in Venezuela*. Federation of Psychologists of Venezuela.

Association of Students of Psychology and School of Psychology Central University of Venezuela (1960). Extraordinary National Assembly of Psychologists. *Notebooks of Psychology*, 2(5–6), 6–7.

Becker, E. (1981). Code of Professional Ethics of the Psychologist of Venezuela. In *Directory Federation of Psychologists of Venezuela*, 148–150.

Blanca, M., Castro, J., & Caicedo, L. (2019). The intervention of the psychologist through social networks: A perspective from ethics. *Journal of Didactics and Education*, 10(2), 133–146.

Canga, J. & Yáber, G. (2015). Psychology in Venezuela: Science, discipline, profession and its challenges. *Revista Información Psicológica*, 109, 129–136. doi:10.14635/IPSIC.2015.109.6

Central University of Venezuela. The Compulsory Membership (1965). *Informative bulletin of the College of Psychologists of Venezuela*, 3, 1–7.

College of Psychologists of Venezuela (1962). Constitutive Act. *Venezuelan Journal of Psychology*, 1, 43–47.

Federation of Psychologists of Venezuela (1981). *Code of Professional Ethics of the Psychologist*. II Ordinary National Assembly of the Federation of Psychologists of Venezuela.

Federation of Psychologists of Venezuela (1985). Law of Exercise of Psychology. In *Directory Federation of Psychologists of Venezuela*, 1–4.

Hounds Psychologists [@houndpsicologos]. (2018, November 20). History of academic psychology in Venezuela. Retrieved from www.instagram.com/p/BqbKXM3j6kQ/?igshid=1kckwn5unqy6e

Otálora, C. (2012). The role of the psychologist in emergencies: Ethics in times of political polarization. *Second Epoch Psychology Journal*, 31(2), 115–129.

Venezuelan Association of Psychologists (1957). Constitutive Act. In *Directory Federation of Psychologists of Venezuela*, 7–12.

Vera-Garcia, B. M., Castro-Sacoto, J. A., & Caicedo-Guale, L. C. (2019). The psychologist's intervention through social media: A perspective from ethics. *Didactics and Education*, 10(2), 133–146.

Personal communications

Becker, E., First President of the Federation of Psychologists of Venezuela (September 20, 2020).

Linares, I., Former President of the College of Psychologists of Edo. Carabobo (September 20, 2020).

Matar, S., Editor of the Code of Ethics Project (September 19, 2020).

16

THE UNIVERSAL DECLARATION OF ETHICAL PRINCIPLES FOR PSYCHOLOGISTS

Karen L. Parsonson

Nothing written about international psychology ethics codes would be complete without a discussion of the Universal Declaration of Ethical Principles for Psychologists. This document, adopted by both the International Union of Psychological Science (IUPsyS) and the International Association of Applied Psychology (IAAP) at the International Congress of Psychology in Berlin in July 2008, is highly relevant to psychological ethics codes. In fact, Gauthier, Pettifor and Ferraro (2010) suggested the application of the Universal Declaration as an aid in the development and revisions to international ethics codes on an ongoing basis. For that reason, we will examine the codes presented here in terms of how well they fit with the UDEPP. First, however, a brief history of the document and the principles it presents is important to describe and explain.

There has been enthusiasm internationally towards the development of a Universal Declaration of Ethical Principles for Psychologists (UDEPP) since 2002. The collaborative efforts of a dedicated Ad Hoc Joint Committee from Canada, China, Colombia, Finland, Germany, Iran, New Zealand, Singapore, South Africa, The United States, Yemen, and Zimbabwe resulted in the first draft. In 2005, it was released internationally for feedback and consultation, resulting in a progress report (Gauthier, 2006) and revision in 2007. Globally, psychological organizations and individual psychologists had answered the call, providing their input and feedback that had been incorporated into the revision. Gauthier (2007, 2008) provided a report explaining what had been changed and the reasoning behind those changes. A "Third Draft" represented continuing international feedback that further incorporated language, concepts and definitions that were culturally inclusive.

The research for this Declaration included examinations of ancient historical documents' ethical principles, existing international psychological ethics codes, ethical principles of other international disciplines, the United Nation's Universal Declaration of Human Rights, the Parliament of the World's Religions' Universal Declaration of Global Ethic, focus groups at international meetings globally, as well as symposia held internationally. Very clearly, this document has incorporated wide and varied current international input as well as thoughtfully targeted historical and cross-disciplinary research.

The document itself begins with a preamble and explanations of four ethical principles. It presents four stated objectives for international psychological organizations. The first is "to evaluate the ethical and moral relevance of their codes of ethics." The second is "to use as a template to guide the development or evolution of their codes of ethics." The third is "to encourage global thinking about ethics, while also encouraging action that is sensitive and responsive to local needs and values." The fourth is "to speak with a collective voice on matters of ethical concern" (Gauthier, 2008, p. 1).

With respect to its first objective, the word "relevant," defined as "having social relevance" (www.merriam-webster.com/dictionary/relevant) is particularly salient when it comes to ethics codes. They should reflect the social fabric endemic to each country.

The second objective of using the UDEPP as a template for revisions to current ethics codes and developing new ones reflects the global nature of the development of the UD. Its formulation involved extensive consultation and feedback from outreach to countries all over the globe. As such, it represents a consensus among them.

The third objective appears to be an all-encompassing one, which focuses both on global and local perspective. From the global perspective, even the development of the UD itself engendered global thinking, so that countries worked together towards a framework that was universally representative. From the local perspective, it suggests the importance of not only taking into consideration countries' respective social/historical/political situations but their unique (cultural) values. The encouragement of action attests to the dynamic nature of ethics codes in response to changing conditions.

Finally, "speaking with a collective voice" relates back to the global perspective, of uniting countries worldwide to action on relevant ethical issues. The process of developing the UD, in itself, connecting far-reaching countries with each other would have gone far towards this end. The momentum gained with this document will hopefully continue moving forward into the future, as countries maintain and promote the connections towards a common goal of ethical conduct for psychologists worldwide.

The four ethical principles include Respect for the Dignity of Persons and Peoples, Competent Caring for the Well-Being of Persons and Peoples, Integrity, and Professional and Scientific Responsibilities to Society. The first principle (Respect) is described as the "most fundamentally and universally found ethical principle ethical principle ... it provides the philosophical foundation for many of the other ethical principles put forward by professions" (p. 5).

Further to this universal, global objective and the four ethical principles out-lined, the ethics codes described in this book are examined relative to their pre-sentation of the four ethical principles. While previously (Parsonson & Alquicira, 2019), it had been argued that comparison against another country's ethics code as a "gold standard" was ethnocentric at best, since the UDEPP has been developed with global, culturally sensitive standards based on extensive research and inter-national consultation, this is seen as a non-ethnocentric examination.

The table below demonstrates whether the four principles are outlined in the ethics codes of this representative sample of countries, as well as the EFPA's Meta-Code, the countries of the Mercosur.

Table 16.1 Principles of countries' Ethics Codes as compared to those of the Universal Declaration of Ethical Principles for Psychologists

Country/entity	Respect	Competent care	Integrity	Responsibility to society	# of UDEPP principles
Australia	*	*	*	*	4
Chile	*	*	*	*	4
Colombia	* (2000)	*	* (2000)	*	4
Guatemala	*	*	*	*	4
Hungary	*	*	*	*	4
Indonesia	*	*	*	*	4
New Zealand	*	*	*	*	4
Nigeria	*	*	*	*	4
Singapore	*	*	*	* (2000)	3/4
Slovenia	*	*	*	*	4
UK	*	*	*	*	4
Venezuela	*		*		2
Zambia	*	*	*	*	4
Meta-code	*	*	*	*	4
Mercosur	*	*	*	*	4

The African countries represented (Nigeria and Zambia) delineate the four principles from the UD, as do the two Australasian countries (Australia and New Zealand). Similarly, the European countries (Hungary, Slovenia, and the UK) have all closely followed the UD and its recommendations. Likewise, three of the four South and Central American countries (Chile, Colombia, and Guatemala) have the UD's principles as their centerpiece. While the ethics code of the Fed-eration of Psychologists of Venezuela notes Respect and Integrity among its principles, it does not specifically mention Competent Care or Responsibility to Society. Also of note, the Psychologists' Committee of the Mercosur countries (which includes Chile and Venezuela in our sample) delineate the four principles, with the addition of the principle of Professional and Scientific Commitment.

Of the Asian countries, Indonesia has the first three (Respect, Competent Care and Integrity), but not the fourth (Responsibility to Society) listed among its general principles, but after closer inspection of the explanation of the cultural implications and societal responsibilities explained in the text of Drs. Probowati and Adayanti's chapter, this principle is seen as a "given." The ethics code of the Singapore Psychological Society went through some changes from its first code in 2000 to its most recent in 2019. The first had 19 principles that encompassed the four found in the UD. However, the revised 2019 ethics code focused on three common "themes," more specifically Respect, Integrity, and Beneficence, in which case the UD's principles of Competent Care and Responsibility to Society are not specifically mentioned but the description presented of Beneficence fits quite well with the concept of Competent Care.

The IUPsyS's Universal Declaration appears to represent universal ethical principles for psychologists in many of the countries presented in this sample of ethics codes from around the world. It should also come as no surprise that the four ethical principles found in the UD are identical to those found in the EFPA's Meta-Code of 1995, which was designed as a template for ethics codes in member European countries.

References

Gauthier, J. (2006). Onward toward a universal declaration of ethical principles for psychologists: Draft and progress report. In M. J. Stevens & D. Wedding (Eds.), *Psychology: IUPsyS Global Resource*. Hove, UK: Psychology Press.

Gauthier, J. (2007). The Universal Declaration of Ethical Principles for Psychologists: Second Draft. Retrieved from www.iupsys.org/ethicsdoc.html

Gauthier, J. (2008). The Draft Universal Declaration of Ethical Principles for Psychologists: A revised version. *International Association of Applied Psychology/Newsletter*, 20(2), 45–49.

Gauthier, J., Pettifor, J., & Ferrero, A. (2010). The Universal Declaration of Ethical Principles for Psychologists: A culture-sensitive model for creating and reviewing a code of ethics. *Ethics & Behavior*, 20(3-4), 179–196.

Parsonson, K. L. & Alquicira, L. M. (2019). International Psychology Ethics Codes: Where is the "Culture" in Acculturation?Ethical Human Psychology and Psychiatry, 20 (2): 86–99.

Universal Declaration of Ethical Principles for Psychologists. (2008). Retrieved from www.iupsys. org/ethics/univdecl2008.html

17

AN OVERVIEW OF FINDINGS, NON-ETHNOCENTRIC COMPARISONS, CONCLUSIONS AND IMPLICATIONS

Karen L. Parsonson

Given the detail presented by each country with regard to how Psychology is practiced and its ethics code was developed, there are a multitude of enlightening comparisons to be made. These include the dates of formation of their psychological associations, of their first ethics codes, whether there are revisions to the codes and if so when, other ethics codes consulted in their development, as well as the enforceability and cultural relativity of their ethics codes. These issues will be examined first from an individual, then continental perspective, and finally from an overall point of view.

Participating Countries: Their Psychological Associations, Dates of Formation and First Ethics Codes

Examining the dates of each country's inception of its respective psychological association relative to when its ethics code was fully developed and enacted demonstrates some interesting observations. It is important to note that some countries have had multiple successive psychological associations over time and some currently have multiple psychological associations, with only one governing ethical practice for psychologists within that country. Only the organizations with governing or regulatory authority over their members are presented.

It is evident that there is a wide range in dates of formation of countries' regulating Psychological associations, from the earliest being the British Psychological Society (1901), then the Hungarian Psychological Association (1928) to the most recent in the College of Psychologists of Guatemala (2007) and Zambia (2012/2014).

Table 17.1 Each country, the regulating psychological association(s), the date formed, and date of first ethics code

Country	Regulating psychological association	Date association was formed	Date of first ethics code
Australia	Australian Overseas Branch of the British Psychological Society	1944	1949
	Australian Psychological Society	1966	1968
Chile	Chilean College of Psychologists	1968	1976
Colombia	Colombian Federation of Psychology	1955	1965
	Colombian Society of Psychology	1978	1983/2000
	Colombian College of Psychologists (COLPSIC)	2004	2006
Guatemala	College of Psychologists of Guatemala	2007	2010
Hungary	Hungarian Psychological Association	1928	1975
Indonesia	Indonesian Psychological Association (HIMPSI)	1959	1991
New Zealand	New Zealand Overseas Branch of the British Psychological Society	1947	1986
	New Zealand Psychological Society	1967	
Nigeria	Nigerian Psychological Association	1984	2018
Singapore	Singapore Psychological Society	1979	2000
Slovenia	Slovene Psychologists' Association	1976	1982
UK	British Psychological Society	1901	1954
Venezuela	Venezuelan Association of Psychologists	1957	1981
	College of Psychologists of Venezuela	1961	
	Federation of Psychologists of Venezuela	1978	
Zambia	Psychology Association of Zambia	2012, registered in 2014	2014

Similarly, the dates of the most recent first ethics codes show a wide range of variability, with Nigeria (2018), Zambia (2014) and Guatemala (2010) being the most recent and Australia (1949), the UK (1954), and Colombia (1965) being the oldest.

It is also interesting to note the latency between organizations' inception and their first ethics code. For some countries' organizations, it took quite a number of years before an ethics code was formalized (53 years for the UK's BPS, 42 years for Indonesia's HIMPSI, and 34 years for the Nigerian Psychological Association). For other countries, it was relatively quick (almost immediately for the Psychology Association of Zambia, two years for the Australian Psychological Society, two years for the Colombian College of Psychologists, and three years for the College of Psychologists of Guatemala). For Australia, it had taken five years for the previous association (Australian Overseas Branch of the British Psychological Society) to put one into place. For Colombia, previous psychological associations had similarly taken longer to put their ethics codes into place (Colombian Federation of Psychology, ten years; Colombian Society of Psychology, five years). Perhaps the extensive review process required to develop and revise codes has been stream-lined over time for these countries.

Comparisons in More Detail

We will begin by examining the ethics codes from countries on the same continent. The reasoning behind this is that they have closer geographical proximity and there may be greater cultural similarities due to this. Countries from each continent are examined in alphabetical order, comparing and contrasting the following parameters:

- Initial date of first ethics code, and whether there have been any further revisions
- Any other countries' codes that were used as templates/reference
- Specific items/principles
- Enforceability of ethics code
- Cultural relativity of ethics code (contribution of culture to countries' ethics codes)

Following that, we compare all countries overall, using the same parameters (see Table 17.2 below).

Africa

Two African countries contributed chapters on their countries' ethics codes: Nigeria (Abikoye, Ezenwa & Zamani) and Zambia (Nabukoza, Jere-Folotiya, & Menon).

Nigeria: The Nigerian Psychological Association (NPA) was formed in 1984, producing its first ethics code in 2018. It was primarily modeled after the APA's ethics code, but the BPS code was also examined in its development. There are six principles stated in the NPA's ethics code: Beneficence and Non-maleficence, Fidelity and Responsibility, Integrity, Justice, and Respect for people's rights & dignity. The code also notes Competence among its ethical standards. It is culturally relative, with cultural beliefs and values embedded in its writing. The NPA's ethics code will not have been legally regulated until The Psychology Bill has been approved by the President.

246

Table 17.2 Countries' first ethics codes, codes used in their development, principles, enforceability, revisions, and cultural relativity

Country	Initial	Other codes used	Principles		Enforceable	Revised	Culturally relative
Australia	1949	Minnesota Society for Applied Psychology (1st code), APA, UD, CPA	1	Respect for rights and dignity of people and peoples	Yes	2018 (Working Draft)	Yes
			2	Propriety (beneficence/non-maleficence, competence, professional responsibility to clients, profession and society)		2007 1997 1986 1968 1960	
			3	Integrity			
Chile	1976	Human Rights at Tokyo Convention, APA, College of Psychologists of Brazil, Official College of Psychologists of Spain, Chilean Bar Association, Chilean Medical Association, Chilean Engineers' Association	1	Respect for rights and dignity of people	No	1999 + Constant Revision	Yes
			2	Competence			
			3	Scientific and professional commitment			
			4	Integrity			
			5	Independence			
			6	Social responsibility			
Colombia	1965	UD	1	Responsibility	Yes	2006	Yes
			2	Competence		2000	
			3	Moral and legal standards		1983	
			4	Integrity in relationships		1979	
			5	Impartiality		1974	
			6	Competent care and well-being of people			
			7	Respect			
			8	Confidentiality			

Country	Year	Codes referenced		Principles	Enforceable	Years	
Guatemala	2010	Chile, Colombia, Costa Rica, El Salvador, Mexico, Dominican Republic, CPA, New Zealand, UD	1	Respect for dignity of people and peoples	No	2018	Yes
			2	Competent care of well-being of others			
			3	Integrity in relationships			
			4	Professional and scientific responsibilities to society			
Hungary	1975	French, German, Meta-Code, APA, BPS, Dutch, Scandinavian	1	Respect for human dignity	No	2004	Yes
			2	Fidelity and responsibility		1984	
			3	Integrity			
			4	Competence			
			5	Beneficence			
Indonesia	2001	APA	1	Respect for human dignity	No, working on legal enforcement via Practice Bill	2020	Yes
			2	Integrity and scientific attitude		2010	
			3	Professionalism		2000	
			4	Justice		1991	
			5	Benefits/advantage			
New Zealand	1986	CPA, APA, BPS, APS, Meta-Code, UD	1	Respect for dignity of persons and peoples	Yes	2002	Yes
			2	Responsible caring		Currently under review	
			3	Integrity in relationships			
			4	Social justice and responsibility to society			

(Continued)

Table 17.2 (Cont.)

Country	Initial	Other codes used	Principles	Enforceable	Revised	Culturally relative
Nigeria	2018	APA, BPS	1 Beneficence and non-maleficence 2 Fidelity and responsibility 3 Integrity 4 Justice 5 Respect for people's rights and dignity	Upcoming in Nigerian Council of Psychology Bill	No, under review	Yes
Singapore	2000	APA, APS, Birds and Animals Act (2002), BPS, CPS (2007), Convention on the Rights of Persons with Disabilities (2007), HKPS, Human Biomedical Research Act (2015), PPG, SAC, SPD, BAC	1 Respect 2 Integrity 3 Beneficence	No	2019	Yes
Slovenia	1982	Meta-Code, BPS, APS, CPA	1 Respect for human rights 2 Professional competence 3 Responsibility 4 Integrity	No	2018 2002	Yes
UK	1954	UD, Helsinki and Singapore protocols, APA, CPA	1 Respect 2 Competence 3 Responsibility 4 Integrity	Not Current Version	2018 2006 1985	No

Country	Year	Code	Principles			
Venezuela	1959	Charter of Human Rights, Declaration of Principles of University Professional Colleges	1 Probity 2 Independence 3 Generosity 4 Objectivity 5 Impartiality 6 Fraternity 7 Freedom 8 Justice 9 Equality 10 Respect for human rights	Yes	1981 Currently under review	Yes
Zambia	2014	BPS	1 Respect 2 Competence 3 Responsibility 4 Integrity	No	No	Yes

Note: List of abbreviations
APA: American Psychological Association's Code of Ethics
APS: Australian Psychological Society
BAC: The Ethics Guidelines for Human Biomedical Research, Bioethics Advisory Committee, 2015
BPS: British Psychological Society's Code of Ethics
CPA: Canadian Psychological Association's Code of Ethics
CPS: Chinese Psychological Society Code of Ethics for Counselling and Practice
HKPS: Hong Kong Psychological Society Code of Professional Conduct
PPG: Professional Practice Guidelines: Psycho–educational assessment & placement of students with special educational need, 2018
SAC: Singapore Association for Counselling Code of Ethics, 2018
SPD: Singapore Personal Data Protection Act, 2012
UD: Universal Declaration of Ethical Principles for Psychologists (IUPsyS)

Zambia: The Psychology Association of Zambia (PAZ) was formed in 2012 but not formally registered until 2014. Its first ethics code was in place in 2014. It was modeled after the 2008 BPS code of ethics. There are four principles stated in PAZ' ethics code: Respect, Competence, Responsibility, and Integrity. The ethics code is culturally relative, with cultural beliefs and values embedded in its writing. PAZ's ethics code is not enforceable legally but the authors have described it as very important to the profession and the public perception of the field.

Comparing the two African countries, Nigeria's NPA is older than Zambia's PAZ by almost 20 years. The PAZ ethics code was developed much sooner after the association's inception than that of the NPA. While neither code has been revised at this point, that of the NPA is currently under revision. It is interesting to note that one (Nigeria) followed the APA's ethics code as its model, whereas the other (Zambia) followed the BPS as its model. As the authors have noted, there are historical reasons for this, due to the first department of psychology in Nigeria being established by an American psychologist and many Nigerian psychologists having been trained and worked in the US. Conversely, for Zambia, as the authors have explained, the British historical colonial legacy remains. Following this, the NPA has six ethical principles as compared to PAZ' four, with three principles in common. While the NPA's ethics code is in the process of becoming law, that of the PAZ is not and as such is not legally enforceable at this time. Both countries stress the cultural relativity of their ethics codes.

Asia

Two Asian countries contributed chapters on their countries' ethics codes: Indonesia (Probawati & Adayanti) and Singapore (Toh & Jeevanandam).

Indonesia: Indonesia's first psychological association, ISPSI (Ikatan Sarjana Psikologi) was established in 1959. The current association in Indonesia is HIMPSI (the Indonesian Psychological Association), which was established with its unification with ISPSI in 1979. Before the unification into HIMPSI, the country's first ethics code was in 1991, with the first under HIMPSI in 2001. Revisions to the ethics code were in 2010 and its current revision has been completed as of 2020. The ethics code was modeled after that of the 1992 and 2002 revision of the APA's code. There are five principles within HIMPSI's ethics code: Respect for Human Rights and Dignity, Integrity and Scientific attitude, Professionalism, Justice, and Benefits/Advantage. It is culturally relative, with cultural values and beliefs embedded within it. While the ethics code is not yet legally enforceable, HIMPSI is working on a Psychology Practice Bill/Law to make it so.

Singapore: The Singapore Psychological Society (SPS) was established in 1979, with its first ethics code in 2000. A revision to the ethics code was completed in 2019, with those writing the revision using the APA, APS, BPS, the ethics codes of the Chinese Psychological Society, the Hong Kong Psychological Society, and the Singapore Psychological Society among 13 others for reference purposes. The 2019 revision includes three principles: Respect, Integrity, and Beneficence, as well as a unique ethical decision-making model. It is culturally relative, with cultural values and beliefs embedded within it. It is not legally enforceable, but a new Disciplinary Advisory Committee was established by the Society in 2020.

Comparing the two Asian countries, the psychological association in Indonesia appears to be considerably older than that of Singapore. As such, it has had a version of ethics code in place for longer, but both took some time before their associations produced their first ethics codes. In the meantime, Indonesia's ethics code has gone through revisions (partially due to the amalgamation of organizations) twice with it currently under revision. In contrast, Singapore has a new revision to its first ethics code. Whereas Indonesia used the APA's code as its template, Singapore used multiple codes for reference. HIMPSI's ethics code contains within it five principles, while that of the SPS has three. Two of these principles, they have in common. Whereas the ethics code from Singapore is not legally enforceable, that of Indonesia is currently in the process of promoting a Psychology Practice Bill/Law. Both countries' organizations noted that their ethics codes are culturally relative, with cultural values and beliefs embedded within them.

Australasia

Two Australasian countries contributed chapters on their countries' ethics codes: Australia (Allan) and New Zealand (Fitzgerald).

Australia: Australia's first psychological association, the Australian Overseas Branch of the British Psychological Society was formed in 1944, with its first ethics code in 1949, which was then revised in 1960. In 1966, the Australian Psychological Association (APS) was formed, which resulted in revised ethics codes in 1968, 1986, 1997, and 2007. The ethics code has been in revision since 2018, with a working draft in place. In developing the most recent ethics codes, those from the APA and CPA, as well as the Universal Declaration of Ethical Principles for Psychologists have been referenced. The 2017 ethics code included three principles: Respect for the rights and dignity of people and peoples, Propriety (encompassing beneficence/non-maleficence, competence, professional responsibility to clients, profession and society), and Integrity. The ethics code is legally enforceable and is culturally relative, with cultural values and beliefs embedded within it.

New Zealand: New Zealand's first psychological association was the New Zealand Overseas Branch of the British Psychological Society, established in 1947. In 1967, the New Zealand Psychological Society was formed, with its first ethics code in 1986. This was followed by a revision in

2002, and it is now currently under review. For the development of the 2002 ethics code, the ethics codes of CPA, APA, BPS, APS, and EFPA's Meta-Code were consulted for reference. The ethics code of the NZPS includes four principles: Respect for the Dignity of Persons and Peoples, Responsible Caring, Integrity in Relationships, and Social Justice and Responsibility to Society. In terms of enforcement of the NZPS' ethics code, it has no legal status but is subsumed under the Health Practitioners Competence Assurance Act of 2003. It is culturally relative, with cultural values and beliefs embedded within it.

Comparing the two Australasian countries, both of which had their original psychological associations as affiliates of the British Psychological Society during a relatively similar time-frame, Australia developed its first ethics code much sooner than that of New Zealand. It has also gone through considerably more revisions. Both have referenced the APA and CPA's ethics codes in their codes' development, with New Zealand also including the APS's code and the EFPA's Meta-Code, as well. Whereas the ethics code of the APS has three principles, that of the NZPS has four with great similarity in how their principles are described. The ethics code of the APS is legally enforceable, as does the NZPS' appear to be. Both ethics codes are described as culturally relative, with cultural values and beliefs embedded within.

Europe

Three European countries contributed chapters on their countries' ethics codes: Hungary (Galaczi, Vajger & Olah), Slovenia (Postuvan), and the UK (Kwiatkowski & Jackson).

Hungary: The Hungarian Psychological Association (HPA) was formed in 1928, with its first ethics code in 1975. It has gone through revisions in 1984 and most recently in 2004. Other ethics codes used as reference in its writing included the French, American, German, English, Dutch, and Scandinavian countries ethics codes, as well as EFPA's Meta-Code. The most recent version of HPA's ethics code includes five principles: Respect for human dignity, Fidelity and Responsibility, Integrity, Competence, and Beneficence. The ethics code is not legally enforceable. It is, however, culturally relative, with cultural beliefs and values embedded within it.

Slovenia: The Slovene Psychologists' Association was established in 1976, with its first ethics code in 1982. It has since gone through revisions in 2002 and 2018. The EFPA's Meta-Code, as well as the ethics codes of BPS, APS, and CPA were used in its development. The ethics code is not enforceable by law. It is culturally relative, with cultural beliefs and values embedded within it.

The UK: The British Psychological Society was established in 1901, with its first ethics code in 1954. The code has gone through revisions in 1985, 2006, and most recently in 2018. For the most recent version, the APA and CPA ethics codes, as well as the ethics code of the Psychological Society of Ireland, the Helsinki and Singapore protocols, and the UD were consulted. The current code includes four ethical principles: Respect, Competence, Responsibility, and Integrity. It is not legally enforceable. With respect to its cultural relativity, neither author perceived any particular relativity or contribution of their country's culture to the writing of their ethics code.

Comparing the European countries, the BPS is the oldest organization, followed by the Hungarian Psychological Association, with the most recent one being the Slovene Psychologists' Association. Interestingly, the youngest organization, from Slovenia, developed its ethics code the soonest after the formation of its psychological association, while the rest took considerably longer to put an ethics code into place. All countries' psychological associations have clearly followed the EFPA's Meta-Code in their codes' development. Two of the three countries (Slovenia and the UK) have four principles, while Hungary has a fifth additional one: Beneficence. None of the three countries' ethics codes are legally enforceable. With regard to cultural relativity, both Hungary and Slovenia's ethic codes are culturally relative, but the ethics code of the BPS is not described as such.

The EFPA's Meta-Code was developed as a template for European countries' psychological associations/societies to use in developing their own ethics codes. As such, it is of interest in examining each relative to the Meta-Code, in terms of the revisions made in order to make it uniquely relevant to each country. As we can see in Table 17.1, all three European countries present the same four ethical principles delineated by the EFPA's Meta-Code, as well as the UD.

South and Central America

Four Central and South American countries contributed chapters on their countries' ethics codes: Chile (Lucero), Colombia (Acero Rodriguez & Ardila), Guatemala (Jurado), and Venezuela (Canga).

Chile: The Chilean College of Psychologists was established in 1968, with its first ethics code coming into force in 1976. It was revised in 1999, but is in constant revision. In developing its ethics code, the association referenced multiple ethics codes from other Chilean professional associations, the APA, as well as ethics codes from psychological associations in Brazil and Spain, and Human Rights at the Tokyo Convention. The most recent version of the ethics code includes six principles: Respect for the rights and dignity of people, Competence, Scientific and Professional commitment, Integrity, Independence, and Social Responsibility. In terms of enforceability, the ethics code is not currently legally enforceable. The ethics code is culturally relative, however, with cultural beliefs and values embedded within it.

Colombia: The first psychological association in Colombia was the Colombian Federation of Psychology, which was established in 1955. It developed its first ethics code in 1965, and then revised it in 1974. That association was followed by the Colombian Society of Psychology, with its first ethics code in 1979, followed by revisions in 1983 and 2000. The current psychological association in Colombia is COLPSIC, the Colombian College of Psychologists, whose first and current ethics code was in 2006. In its code's development, COLPSIC referenced IUPsyS's Universal Declaration of Ethical Principles for Psychologists. Previous ethics codes had referenced the APA, the Inter-American Psychological Society, EFPA's Meta-Code, the Official Association of Psychologists of Spain, the Mexican Society of Psychology, codes of other Latin American countries, other professions, as well as laws in force in the country, and the Political Constitution of Colombia of 1991. The current ethics code has eight principles: Responsibility, Competence, Moral & Legal Standards, Integrity in Relationships, Impartiality, Competent Care & Well-being of People, Respect, and Confidentiality. The ethics code is enforceable by law, with a National Deontological & Bioethical Court established in 2007. COLPSIC's ethics code is culturally relative, with cultural beliefs and values embedded within it.

Guatemala: The psychological association is Guatemala is the College of Psychologists of Guatemala, established in 2007. Its first ethics code was in 2010 and the code went through a revision culminating in a new one in 2018. In developing its ethics code, the association referenced the ethics codes of Chile, Colombia, Costa Rica, El Salvador, Mexico, Dominican Republic, as well as the CPA, New Zealand, and the UD. The latter three were the most influential in its development. The association's ethics code includes four principles: Respect for the Dignity of People and Peoples, Competent care of Wellbeing of Others, Integrity in Relationships, and Professional and Scientific Responsibilities to Society. The code is not legally enforceable, but it is culturally relative, with cultural beliefs and values embedded within it.

Venezuela: The first psychological association in Venezuela was the Venezuelan Association of Psychologists, which was formed in 1957, with its first ethics code in 1959. This association was followed by the College of Psychologists of Venezuela in 1961, then the Federation of Psychologists of Venezuela in 1978. The original ethics code of 1959, which was basically a reproduction of the APA's at that time, was revised in 1981. In its development, the Charter of Human Rights and the Declaration of Principles of University Colleges were consulted for reference purposes. The most recent code of ethics contains 10 principles: Probity, Independence, Generosity, Objectivity, Impartiality, Fraternity, Freedom, Justice, Equality, and Respect for Human Rights. The ethics code is not enforceable by law, nor is described as culturally relative or including cultural components.

Comparing the four South and Central American countries, two were part of the six Mercosur countries (Chile and Venezuela) and two were not (Colombia and Guatemala). In comparing Chile and Venezuela, there are clear differences in every regard. While the psychological association in Chile (the Chilean College of Psychologists) came into being in 1968, Venezuela went through three psychological associations (in 1957, 1961, and 1978). Chile's first ethics code was in 1968, with a revision in 1999 while Venezuela's first was in 1959, followed by a revision in 1981. Chile appeared to use many references in the development of its ethics code, while Venezuela used two, both different to those used by Chile. Of the six principles within the Chilean ethics code only one of them (Independence) is in common with the ten principles in the Venezuelan ethics code. Neither countries' ethics codes, however, are legally enforceable. While Chile's is culturally relative, Venezuela's is not.

If we examine the other two codes (that of Colombia and Guatemala) there are more apparent similarities between the Colombian and Venezuelan ethics codes. Colombia, like Venezuela, went through a progression of three psychological associations. However, as compared to the one revision of the Venezuelan ethics code, Colombia went through five more revisions through successive psychological associations. In the development of the Colombian ethics code, the UD was its main reference as compared to two different ones used for the development of Venezuela's ethics code. Of the eight principles that are a part of the current Colombian ethics code, one of the five (Impartiality) is in common with the ten principles found in Venezuela's code. Unlike Venezuela and Chile, Colombia's ethics code is legally enforceable. It is culturally relative like Chile's ethics code, however.

The one outlier (from Central, as opposed to South America) of the four is Guatemala, whose first psychological association was formed in 2007. Its first ethics code was developed quite soon after its association was formed, relative to the other countries. It, too, has gone through revision, making it the newest ethics code of the four countries. Many countries' ethics codes were consulted in the development of its ethics code, whose four principles directly follow those of the Universal Declaration, as do Chile (with two additional principles), and Colombia (with one additional principle). Unlike the other three countries, Guatemala's ethics code is not legally enforceable, but like for Chile and Colombia, its code is culturally sensitive.

Similarities or Differences between Countries on the Same Continent?

As to whether proximity between countries on the same continent is an issue promoting countries' similarities, there are clear differences between the two African countries (Nigeria and Zambia), suggesting unique features of each country that have contributed to not only the profession of psychology, but its psychological associations and ethics codes. For the two Asian countries (Indonesia and Singapore), there are also more differences than similarities. Similarly, for the two Australasian countries (Australia and New Zealand) both originated from their first associations as branches of the British Psychological Society, but there are more differences than similarities from there on. When the European countries' ethics codes are examined and compared (Austria, Hungary, Slovenia, and the UK), there is wide variability, as well, with the largest similarity being that in their most recent version of their ethics at least, they have followed the EFPA's Meta-Code. Finally, for South and Central American countries, there is great variability in their ethics codes, the other codes used to develop them, as well as the history/age of their professional associations, and frequency of revisions to their respective codes.

What all of this suggests is that each country's unique cultural, historical, and socio-political factors have contributed to the development of Psychology in each country. As such, no assumptions can be made, based on proximity or perceived similarities in culture. To do so would be an over-simplification at best and ethnocentric at worst.

Comparing All Countries

The information discussed with respect to countries on the same continent bears further comparison internationally. We have established that proximity (being on the same continent) does not necessarily lead to similarities between countries. The table below provides all of the information for the date of each countries' first ethics code, what other codes were used as templates, the principles cited in each, whether codes are enforceable, whether revisions have been made to their codes, and whether they are seen as culturally relative. In the interests of not only space given the density of information, but also repetition, there is a key below that further defines the respective ethics codes used in developing countries' unique ethics codes.

As we can see, there is wide variation in when countries' first ethics codes were developed and written. From the earliest (Australia in 1949) to the most recent (Nigeria in 2018), it is clear that this is an ongoing process. Similarly, some countries have more recently developed their first ethics codes (Nigeria in 2018), while others have done multiple revisions since their first, such as Australia, Colombia, and the UK. Some are in constant revision (as in Chile), others have done recent revisions (Guatemala, Indonesia, Singapore, Slovenia and the UK) or are in the process of doing revisions (as in Australia and New Zealand). It is quite clear that ethics codes are dynamic, and constantly re-evaluated in light of changes in socio-political climates.

In this sample, there is also wide variation in the codes they used as the templates for developing countries' own codes. The ones most frequently cited were, in order of frequency: the ethics codes of the APA, the BPS, the CPA, the UD, and the EFPA's Meta-Code, tied with the APS ethics code. Clearly, these ethics codes have had a wider impact outside of their own countries. It is worthy of note that all European countries' principles appeared to follow the EFPA's Meta-Code, with a few additional principles included. This attests to the power and influence of the Meta-Code in helping European countries to formulate or revise their respective ethics codes.

The principles, themselves, vary in number and phrasing but there are common themes. As noted in a previous chapter, almost all encompass the UD's ethical principles to the word, as do all in practice when you read the ethical standards of each code. As such, the UD appears to have captured universal ethical principles that define and drive the profession.

Some countries' ethics codes are entrenched in law and enforceable, while others are aspirational depending upon each country's legal landscape, purview, and relative concern with ethical practice of the profession. For countries whose ethics codes are not or not as yet, enforceable legally (Chile, Guatemala, Hungary, Indonesia, Nigeria, Singapore, Slovenia, the UK, Venezuela, and Zambia), many note that they are in the process of attempting to do so, are in the process of doing so, or have the intention to do so.

The one outstanding commonality is that most consider their codes to be culturally relative or culturally sensitive and inclusive. The two exceptions are Venezuela and the UK. As to why these two countries are outliers, in the case of Venezuela, the country's original ethics code of 1959 was essentially that of the APA's ethics code at that time. The revision to the ethics code was made in 1981, in a country that appears to have experienced serious social and political upheaval. That may have gone towards the lack of attention paid to specific cultural factors, in an attempt to develop a code that was not a direct copy of the APA's code. However, the 1981 ethics code is currently under review, which could suggest the inclusion of more culturally relative elements.

When it come to the BPS of the UK, their ethics code has gone through a number of revisions as well, the most recent in 2018. As to why the most recent version is not seen as culturally relevant, as both authors have noted, that may come down to their perspective from viewing it from within the country's culture. Others may perceive it in a very different way.

Nevertheless, in this sample of international ethics codes, the vast majority perceive their ethics codes as culturally relative, attesting to the impact and importance of each country's unique culture on how its ethics code has been developed and written. Although this does not "prove" the well-established contention that Psychology ethics codes are culturally relevant/sensitive, it goes far towards demonstrating it.

Anecdotally, everyone was able to trace the history and development of their ethics code, many having to go back into old archives and revivifying the original committees to ensure the veracity of their information. Interestingly, several had difficulty with writing about the contribution of their country's culture to the writing of their code. As they noted, living within a culture makes it difficult to see outside of it and recognize how it represents their countries' unique values and beliefs. That, in itself, is an interesting point, as often without comparison to another culture, one does not necessarily recognize how their own culture permeates or impacts on what it is that they do or how they live their lives.

Table 17.3 Countries' associations and whether their ethics codes are values-driven, rules-driven, or both

Country/psychological association	Values-driven	Rules-driven	Both values and rules driven
Australia: Australian Psychological Society			*
Chile: Chilean College of Psychologists			*
Colombia: Colombian College of Psychologists		*	
Guatemala: College of Psychologists of Guatemala	*		
Hungary: Hungarian Psychological Association			*
Indonesia: Indonesian Psychological Association	*		
New Zealand: New Zealand Psychological Society	*		
Nigeria: Nigerian Psychological Association			*
Singapore: Singapore Psychological Society			*
Slovenia: Slovene Psychologists' Association			*
UK: British Psychological Society	*		
Venezuela: Federation of Psychologists of Venezuela			*
Zambia: Psychology Association of Zambia	*		

Aspirational and Regulatory Aspects of Ethics Codes: Are There Commonalities?

In reviewing the ethics codes presented here, it is clear that there are variations in whether they are Aspirational, Deontological, or a combination of the two. In other words, are they value-driven, rule-driven, or do they encompass both? In the table below, we see where each ethics code falls on the spectrum.

There is wide variability in whether countries' ethics codes are values-driven (Aspirational) with five countries fitting that approach, rules-driven (Deontological) with one country, or a combination of both seen in seven countries. In terms of countries on the same continent, there is no continuity. Africa's two countries differ in that Zambia's ethics code follows an Aspirational approach while Nigeria's approach is a combination of Aspirational and Deontological. For Asian countries as well, they are different in their approach, with Indonesia's ethics code Aspirational while Singapore's is a combination of the two approaches. Similarly, the Australasian countries differ, with New Zealand's ethics code Aspirational while Australia's is a combination of the two approaches. With regard to

259

European countries, both Hungary and Slovenia's ethics codes take a combination approach, while the UK's BPS follows an Aspirational approach. Finally, with respect to South and Central American countries, there is wide variation in their approach as well. Guatemala's ethics code follows an Aspirational approach, Colombia's a Deontological approach, and both Chile and Venezuela a combination of the two. One thing is clear however: almost every ethics code has an Aspirational component, with the exception of Colombia.

What does this tell us? Clearly, there is great individuality in every regard between countries' ethics codes, with even geographical proximity not a contributing factor in this regard. With respect to this sample, it would appear that the two most popular approaches are the Aspirational approach to ethics codes and the combination of both Aspirational and Deontological. As we have seen with other variables, there are any number of factors and/or combinations of them within each country that have contributed to these differences, including historical, socio-political, and cultural.

There may indeed be other factors involved as well, such as whether ethics codes have been more recently developed or their development was some time ago. However, from inspection of the dates of countries' most recent revisions or current new ethics codes, this does not appear to be a deciding factor. Four of the countries who have followed an Aspirational approach have relatively new ethics codes (Guatemala, Indonesia, the UK, and Zambia), whereas four of the countries following the combination approach have relatively recent ethics codes (Australia, Nigeria, Singapore, and Slovenia). It would be interesting to know whether there may have been changes over revisions in terms of ethics codes' focus from one approach to another.

Conclusions and Implications for the Future

We have seen with this representative sample that every country, regardless of its proximity to others or perceived similarities in culture, has developed its own process for its ethics code's development and revisions, chosen specific other ethics codes for reference, written it with its own unique characteristic beliefs and values in mind, and administers it differently. The growth and progression of Psychology in each country is unique to each, as well, from the formation of its first psychological association to the timing of its first ethics code, through social and political changes and turmoil. Yet in each case, the profession of Psychology has endured, with the dedication of those who treasure its value to make a difference in people's lives.

The authors' descriptions and explanations of their countries' unique cultures, histories, and socio-political landscapes draw attention to the importance of understanding international Psychology ethics codes from the perspective of those from within that context. Everything is about perspective when it comes to true understanding, and theirs cannot be ignored. The detailed explanation of codes' development contributes greatly to explanation of their content and unique approaches.

There are implications for future study and research in the field, practical considerations, as well as collegiality from a global perspective based on the information presented. With respect to the study of international ethics codes, it is clear that there are not only many similarities between countries' ethics codes, but unique differences. The latter cannot and should not be subject to judgment or dismissed as mere artifacts. It is not simply the product (the ethics codes themselves) that bear examination, but the processes each country follows in the code's development and revisions. The unique contribution of culture, history, social and political configuration require exploration in order to best understand and even comment on any country's ethics code by anyone other than a professional from that country.

Practical considerations of greater knowledge about international ethics codes applies not only to the multicultural nature of countries around the world, but the increasing numbers of mental health professionals who relocate or practice cross-border, as well as the teaching of ethics to future mental health practitioners. The increasingly multicultural nature of countries globally requires careful attention to the multitude of cultures mental health practitioners are and will be dealing with in their practice. It behooves not only countries' psychological organizations to take this into consideration in the development and/or revisions to their ethics codes, but also mental health practitioners to understand the ethical perspective each individual client brings along with them. We stress the importance of cultural competence when it comes to clinical practice, but understanding a client's ethical perspective is no less important. For practitioners relocating and/or practicing cross-borders, this should also be an ethical imperative: to be knowledgeable about a country's ethics code in the best interests of those they serve.

In the teaching of ethics to future mental health practitioners, some have called for internationalization of an ethics curriculum in the US (Leach and Gauthier, 2011) and Parsonson (2019) explored the perceived need for it in universities across North America. If we are teaching about an appreciation for diversity and promoting cultural competency, understanding ethics from a cross-cultural perspective is no less important. Nothing should be taken for granted in order to practice ethically with objectivity, and that includes attention to not only clients' ethical perspective, but its impact on the therapeutic process as well. Not only does learning about international ethics codes draw attention to their importance towards cultural competency, it also promotes true ethical acculturation to the field, as opposed to mere memorization of ethics codes in order to avoid ethical missteps.

In terms of collegiality from a global perspective, that the advent of the internet has promoted and advanced it is without question. Yet, there has been international cooperation and collaboration for as long as there has been a profession of Psychology. It is much easier now, however. In the interests of the unquestionable value of non-ethnocentric research, to work with international colleagues in the field is both an advantage and a privilege worthy of exploration. Their openness and willingness to share their knowledge and expertise is invaluable and greatly deserves to be both invited and valued for its unique perspective.

From a personal perspective, it has been a privilege and honor to be able to present the information provided by these insightful and highly respected experts in their field. It is my hope that this will mark a beginning to truly non-ethnocentric understanding and appreciation of countries' contributions to Psychology's ethics from a global perspective.

References

Leach M. M., & Gauthier J. (2011). *Internationalizing the Professional Ethics Curriculum.* In F. Leong, W. Pickren, M. Leach & A. Marsella (eds.) *Internationalizing the Psychology Curriculum in the United States. International and Cultural Psychology.* New York: Springer. https://doi.org/10.1007/978-1-4614-0073-83

Parsonson, K. (2019). Is teaching international ethics codes important for psychology graduate students? *Ethical Human Psychology and Psychiatry,* 21(2), 117–126. https://doi.org/10.1891/ehpp-d-19-00013

INDEX

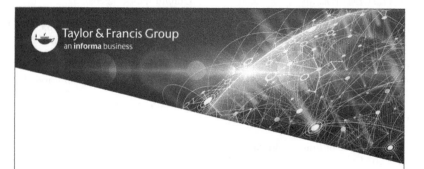